SECRET PARTNERS

SECRET PARTNERS

Big Tom Brown and the Barker Gang

TIM MAHONEY

Minnesota Historical Society Press

www.mhspress.org

The Minnesota Historical Society Press is a member of the Association of American University Presses.

Manufactured in the United States of America

10 9 8 7 6 5 4 3 2 1

♾ The paper used in this publication meets the minimum requirements of the American National Standard for Information Sciences—Permanence for Printed Library Materials, ANSI Z39.48–1984.

International Standard Book Number
ISBN: 978-0-87351-904-5 (paper)
ISBN: 978-0-87351-905-2 (e-book)

Library of Congress Cataloging-in-Publication Data

Mahoney, Timothy R., 1953–
Secret partners : Big Tom Brown and the Barker gang / Tim Mahoney.
pages cm
Includes bibliographical references.
ISBN 978-0-87351-904-5 (pbk. : alk. paper) — ISBN 978-0-87351-905-2 (e-book)
1. Police corruption—Minnesota—Saint Paul. I. Title.
HV7936.C85M34 2013
364.1092—dc23
[B]
2013016071

Photos pages 3, 18, 38 from Minnesota Historical Society collections. All others courtesy *St. Paul Pioneer Press.*

This and other Minnesota Historical Society Press books are available from popular e-book vendors.

CONTENTS

SECRET PARTNERS

HISTORY'S SHADOWS

Among the most dangerous criminals of the public enemies era was a man who has long hidden in history's shadows: Big Tom Brown. In the early 1930s, while police chief of St. Paul, Minnesota, Brown became a secret partner of the infamous Ma Barker gang. He helped plan the gang's kidnappings and profited from their bank robberies, even as they gunned down cops and citizens in his hometown. He teamed up with a corrupt prosecutor to railroad men to prison, he beat confessions out of prisoners, and he was suspected by some of engineering two execution slayings.

Yet justice never caught up to Tom Brown. An overwhelming volume of evidence points to Brown's involvement in illegal activities throughout his tenure as a policeman. But because of decisions made in St. Paul and Washington, Brown was never prosecuted for his crimes and the

Tom Brown, in a photo retouched for use in the *Pioneer Press*, about 1934.

evidence was tested only at a civil service hearing, and not in court. The investigation of Brown never reached whatever allies he had among the city's elite.

The Barker gang's stalwarts, Fred Barker and Alvin Karpis, led a bumbling band of hillbilly burglars until they moved to St. Paul during Brown's tenure as police chief. In the Ozarks, "My life in crime was minor league stuff," admitted Karpis. But under the protection of Tom Brown, and the tutelage of St. Paul's master criminals, his gang evolved into notorious and feared public enemies. Soon Karpis was pulling his "first genuine major league stickup," at a Minneapolis bank.

Barker gangster Volney Davis confessed to the FBI that without the protection of Tom Brown, the gang "would have all been caught in St. Paul." Edna Murray, the "Kissing Bandit," told the FBI that if not for Tom Brown and James Crumley of the St. Paul police, the gang's most infamous crime "could not have been successfully accomplished and certain members of this [Barker] mob would have been in jail a long time ago."

Had the Barker gang never come under Brown's protection, Ma Barker might have died lonesome in the Ozarks, an impoverished, obscure widow. Her son Fred and his pal Karpis would likely have been executed in Missouri before the nation knew who they were. The vicious killer Doc Barker would have remained in prison until he was an old man. At least seven murders and two grievous woundings might never have happened.

But Brown's dark influence spread beyond the Barker gang. If not for the corrupt police force that crystallized during Brown's tenure, the legend of John Dillinger might have ended on an Easter weekend in a snowy St. Paul parking lot. The Lady in Red would have been just another immigrant with visa troubles. No trap would have been set for Dillinger outside the Biograph theater. Newsreel hero Melvin Purvis might have retired as just another FBI functionary. Little Bohemia would be just another rustic Wisconsin resort, and not the site of a leg-endary FBI fiasco.

Many of Tom Brown's fellow gangsters were shot dead, while others were locked up in Leavenworth or Alcatraz. But Brown proved to be the Houdini of gangster-cops. He outsmarted J. Edgar Hoover and the FBI, retiring to collect his police pension and run a tavern in the north country. Despite all the blood on his conscience, all the families whose lives he devastated, and all the dark money he collected, he never spent a night behind bars.

2

"EVERYTHING COULD BE FIXED"

Police corruption in St. Paul didn't start with Tom Brown. The so-called O'Connor System had been the rule for decades before he became chief.

While the modern Twin Cities may be known for civility and culture, at the dawn of the twentieth century they were wild boomtowns. Fortunes were made in railroads, timber, grain, and iron ore. Minneapolis was born at the Falls of St. Anthony, which provided hydropower for mills and factories. Grain and lumber mills arose at the falls, but steamboats could not reach them; the river was too shallow. So the last navigable landing on the Mississippi developed into a separate city. Everything

St. Paul's Seven Corners in the 1930s, looking east along Seventh Street.

and everyone that steamed upriver had to transfer to the rails at St. Paul. As America moved west, the river port of St. Paul prospered.

Americans and foreigners alike bundled up against the frosty climate and came seeking their fortunes. The inevitable gambling dens, saloons, and brothels followed. The city fathers, having no objection to a good time, appointed a police chief known for his tolerance of vice.

He was John J. O'Connor, and he built a corrupt machine that eventually bore his name. O'Connor was police chief for most of the years between 1900 and 1920. His father, an Irish immigrant, was a St. Paul ward heeler. His brother Richard, "the Cardinal," rose to be a top Democrat whose byzantine connections snaked all the way to Tammany Hall.

"The Cardinal" understood that Americans were hypocrites who publicly deplored vices they secretly enjoyed. This notion figured into the economics of St. Paul: "The small town merchant was snowed in all winter," Richard O'Connor wrote, "and in the spring when he came to town to buy his stock of merchandise, he was hungry for a good time, which consisted of drinking good whiskey and playing around with the girls in the sporting houses.

"The competition was so keen that when a jobber got hold of a buyer, he never let him out of his sight, and bought him all the whiskey he could drink and staked him to as many girls as he wanted until the order was signed."

The clever and cynical O'Connor brothers used these and other insights to rule the city and augmented their political earnings by running an illegal horse-race betting syndicate.

A federal Justice Department memo from the 1920s noted that criminals could travel to O'Connor's town, "make their presence known to the chief of police, and stay here with immunity, provided they committed no crimes within the city." Other cities and states would "try in vain to extradite" criminals from St. Paul, the memo added.

That kind of protection had a price. Mobsters from Chicago arrived at the St. Paul train station, ready to trade watches and gold jewelry to police in return for protection, according to a crime reporter of the era. Alternatively, they could check in at a certain speakeasy, pay its proprietor a fee, and enjoy immunity from arrest.

Federal agents discovered that St. Paul's corruption was no secret: "The citizens knew it, the criminals knew, and every police officer in the city knew."

For St. Paul's citizens, the O'Connor System had its benefits. As Richard O'Connor put it, "Never in the history of St. Paul has human life and the property of citizens been so safe, or the virtue of its women so assured." As a bonus, the nightlife was exciting.

Chief O'Connor never denied his methods. If criminals "behaved themselves I let them alone," he said. "Under other administrations there were as many thieves here as when I was chief, and they pillaged and robbed. I chose the lesser of two evils."

Maybe so. But the O'Connor System was about profit, not philosophy. Graft from dice parlors, brothels, and saloons flowed to the police station and city hall.

Cops and politicians were not the only beneficiaries; the profits spread far and wide. Gangsters spent wildly in the speakeasies, casinos, and bordellos. Banks did a booming business not just in bootleg cash but in the proceeds from kidnappings and bank robberies. Stolen negotiable bonds were "held for ransom" or sold to "private detectives" who would return them to the banks at steep discounts. St. Paul retailers dealing in luxury goods such as fancy clothing, jewelry, and automobiles prospered. Often, money would be laundered by small-time hoods and idle youth who went from store to store, buying petty items with big bills, thus turning them into untraceable cash.

Chief O'Connor certainly profited. One newspaper columnist blithely reported that O'Connor donated to charities more money than he earned. Nor did O'Connor neglect spending for his own entertainment. His legitimate salary was $300 a month, but he would bet thousands of dollars on a single horse race.

Over time, the O'Connor System became the true law in St. Paul. Gangsters, eager to keep the good times rolling, would police themselves within city limits. If they wanted to rob a bank, a train, or a payroll truck, they drove to Wisconsin or Iowa or anywhere in Minnesota except St. Paul. During the crime wave of the early 1930s, more than 20 percent of the nation's bank robberies occurred in Minnesota.

But no bank in St. Paul was robbed.

Prohibition only strengthened the O'Connor System. St. Paul served as a trans-shipment point for booze. Bootleggers were always hijacking each other's loads. Railroad cops got into gun battles with liquor thieves. Speakeasies and "soft drink parlors" were raided by cops, who sometimes beat the patrons and proprietors, not so much for breaking the law as for failure to pay off.

Liquor flowed into St. Paul from Winnipeg and other cities in Canada. Young men of the Northwest drifted to the border to make fortunes as smugglers. Cases of booze crossed the border in canoes, sleds, and even backpacks. Loads of liquor were smuggled by night, with repurposed fishing boats bobbing in Lake Superior's dark waves. In Canada, whiskey sold for $2 to $4 a quart, but it was worth five times that amount south of the border. One reporter found that American demand was so strong it was harder to get a drink in Canada than in the States.

Colliers Magazine ranked St. Paul alongside San Francisco as the nation's "wettest" cities. In 1922, St. Paul's chief of police estimated that 75 percent of St. Paulites were making some kind of alcohol at home. As for the professional bootleggers, many people admired them, and why not? They made home deliveries.

St. Paul, a German and Irish city, loved its beer. And beer, too bulky to smuggle, had to be brewed close to home. The city's breweries claimed to make only soft drinks and near-beer, but somehow potent beer found its way to the speakeasies.

In 1930, when Big Tom Brown was appointed police chief, the city had matured to its modern size of 275,000 people. But the boom was over. In the aftershock of the 1929 crash, one family in four had no wage earner. One Depression-era St. Paul mayor noted that "We had forty percent of our people on welfare and 20,000 pieces of property in tax delinquency." Otherwise, the jobless depended on breadlines, soup kitchens, or help from relatives or charities. Unemployment compensation was just an idea being floated by wild-eyed progressives.

People who clung to their jobs often had their wages cut. Minnesota's Twin Cities swelled with jobless railroad workers, miners, grain millers, and lumberjacks. Cops and other public employees endured "payless paydays." Tent cities dotted the frozen, sewer-stinking banks of the Mississippi.

The chief who succeeded O'Connor, Frank Sommer, may have sunk the O'Connor System deeper into the muck of corruption: he was charged with helping plan a payroll robbery and, although later acquitted, was fired on corruption charges.

The O'Connor System evolved until it was drawing criminals to St. Paul from far-off places. In the early 1930s, when Tom Brown was in charge of this system, Doc Barker advised a fellow gangster that he'd "Never seen anything like St. Paul. Everything could be fixed."

3

THE RISE OF BIG TOM

Thomas Archibald Brown was born in 1889 to a coal-mining clan in West Virginia, but he couldn't have worked the mines if he'd wanted to. He grew to be a giant: six foot five and at least 275 pounds. For reasons unknown he found his way to St. Paul in 1910 and took a job as a streetcar conductor. He joined the police force in 1914, at age 25. While other young men were dying in the trenches of Europe, patrolman Brown learned to solicit bribes.

Sometime in the early 1920s, with Prohibition in full force, Brown secured a spot on the Purity Squad, charged with enforcing laws against prostitution, bootlegging, and gambling. Opportunities for bribery abounded. Brown's method was simple, he told his brother-in-law: "Go into taverns with your hand out." He was careful, though, never to take a bribe in the presence of another witness.

Brown matured into a hulking, formidable German-Irish detective. A lapsed Baptist, he married an Irish-Catholic woman, Mary Rafferty, and they raised four daughters and one son. Brown was an excellent provider who knew how to put meat on the table. For recreation, he fished and hunted: deer, walleye, duck, trout, goose, anything that moved.

Brown was promoted to detective on the Purity Squad, and by 1923, a grand jury was investigating charges that its cops were spectacularly bad at enforcing vice laws. That June, St. Paul mayor Arthur Nelson hired Chicago private eyes to investigate his own police department.

Meanwhile, in August, a young, dangerous rogue named Edwin Rust sneaked into St. Paul. He'd escaped from Folsom Prison, been captured, and was on a train in custody of the sheriff of Aberdeen, South Dakota. Rust shot the sheriff dead and leaped from the speeding train. In St. Paul, he rented a room and procured a job at a Catholic orphanage. Adept at stealing cars, Rust one day pulled over in a shiny sedan at a streetcar stop. He flirted with a pretty woman wearing a maid's uniform. Did she want a lift? She said: I'm going to church. He said: So am I, get in. They detoured to the movies.

"I never cared for him, I was lonesome, that was all," the young maid said later. She was Sigfrid Larson. Her husband had abandoned her and two babies, and she supported them by becoming a physician's servant. She began to tell friends about this new red-haired suitor, who showed up in a different car every time they dated.

This fellow claimed to be an undercover cop. A friend of Mrs. Larson's, Etta Tollefsen, was a Minneapolis cop. A real one. She checked on this flashy fellow.

The next day, Edwin Rust was in handcuffs.

But escape was oh so possible in those days, and despite being escorted to jail by three St. Paul cops, Edwin Rust, still in handcuffs, leaped out of the car. Or so the cops said. Rust retreated to his rented room. He wasn't there long before two plainclothes cops burst in: Stanley Cassidy and Tom Brown. Rust got off two shots; the cops killed him with three.

The *St. Paul Daily News* worked this into a front-page splash, with pictures of Tom Brown, his partner, and the erstwhile Edwin Rust. The *Pioneer Press* reported a subdued version, failing to mention the cops by name. But in the *Daily News,* Tom Brown was a front-page hero.

The glow soon faded. Mayor Nelson's Chicago hirelings nosed around the dicier parts of the city and discovered fifty-five bordellos, gambling dens, and speakeasies. "The Mayor's operatives reported that they had uncovered crime in cigar stores, pool halls, hotels, homes, cafes . . . even behind a dentist's sign," reported the *Pioneer Press.*

A typical setup was a store with a shallow front that sold cigars at a counter. A partition shielded the back room, where the real action took place. The men behind those partitions ran baseball pools, craps tables, and poker games and provided liquid refreshment. The mayor's spies described boys wasting their allowances on slot machines. One man they observed wandered into a cigar store, tried to buy a cigar, and was ignored until he departed. More typically, the proprietor of a "cigar store" would eye customers through a peephole and admit them to the inner sanctum if they seemed "all right."

Out on the street, prostitutes openly solicited passersby. The operatives noted a "so-called Chinese restaurant" that was a front for narcotics dealing. At 412 Wabasha Street, they found a "sporty" crowd at the "best patronized place" running the "biggest games in the city." It was owned by the man who would soon become the shadow mayor of St. Paul: Leon Gleckman.

Mayor Nelson winnowed this list of trouble spots from fifty-five to thirty-five. It is impossible to know his motive for that winnowing but easy to guess: St. Paul politics was highly factionalized, and the factions often suppressed some illegal businesses so that those owned by friends and benefactors might thrive. However it worked, the mayor seemed serious about enforcing the law against these thirty-five establishments.

So police chief Frank Sommer and his detectives, including Tom Brown, were required to call on each address on the mayor's list. Gosh darn it, they just couldn't find much illegal activity. Oh, two hapless guys were thrown in the clink for having moonshine, but the rest of those speakeasies were either closed when detectives arrived or were found to be clean. The Purity Squad visited Leon Gleckman's place "a half dozen times" and never found anything more sinister than "games of hearts and rummy." Chief Sommer proclaimed that Gleckman's club "was the only one in the city that served no liquor."

At Nina Clifford's, the city's most elegant bordello, detectives knocked but nobody had the courtesy to get out of bed to answer.

All this took place while the grand jury was preparing its report on corruption in St. Paul. If the mayor had been hoping for political cover from his police department, he didn't get it. On December 15, the jurors concluded that St. Paul police were so corrupt that Minnesota needed to establish a state police force. The county attorney noted that the jurors were intimidated by gangster threats, or they might have issued a bolder report.

The day after the grand jury's report, Mayor Nelson told Chief Sommer to resign or be fired. He also called in four detectives, including Tom Brown, for interrogation.

Brown, reporters noted, was in the mayor's office for thirteen minutes.

"Brown," the mayor said, "it's a remarkable thing that the only ones who look for gambling joints, moonshine parlors and disorderly houses and can't find them are St. Paul detectives." Then he announced that Brown and detective Austin McNeely would turn in their badges.

After a few days of blustering and waffling, Chief Sommer resigned. He had a backup job anyway, having been on leave from the Secret Service.

But within two days, the mayor changed his mind about firing Brown and McNeely. He couldn't come up with an explanation. When reporters asked if he really intended to retreat on a position he'd stated publicly and insistently, he said, "I refuse to answer that question yes or no at this time."

So Tom Brown, on the brink of disaster, had pulled his first Houdini.

In the mid-1920s, the federal government tried to snare the nation's biggest bootleggers in a trial centered in Cleveland. The main evidence came from the confessions of the Gleeman brothers, who were St. Paul bootleggers. The feds issued 112 indictments nationwide, and forty-one named residents of St. Paul, including detective Thomas Brown.

The indictment accused him of "covering up the operations of a syndicate." Brown lawyered up. He refused to go to Cleveland to testify.

The Gleeman brothers' case had hit the front pages when they were accused of a 1925 murder in St. Paul. Brown tried to persuade detective Fred Raasch to provide a false alibi for the Gleemans. "I told him I wouldn't, and that he could do it himself if he wanted to," Raasch later testified. "Brown called me up and said he'd get even with me."

In 1926, Brown was arrested in St. Paul on a federal warrant. It accused him of stealing a "large amount of alcohol" from the police station. The booze had been seized in a raid. U.S. District Judge John Sanborn chastised Brown after he testified that he didn't know bootleggers Leon Gleckman and Abe Gleeman. Brown's denials were "not worthy of belief," the judge said. But prosecutors could not muster enough evidence to convict him.

Brown was welcomed back to the force by George Sudheimer, the police commissioner. "Thomas A. Brown is an ideal police executive," Sudheimer said. "He is possessed of a remarkable breadth of vision." The police chief, Edward Murnane, said of Brown, "He's got courage, he's honest, he can use his head and he has always been a good officer."

By 1930, Leon Gleckman had mastered political bribery and gained a grip on St. Paul politics. "Big Tom" was Gleckman's choice for chief. Once appointed, Brown announced "drastic changes" in the police department. He doubled the size of the Purity Squad and stuffed it with corrupt cronies. He transferred honest cops, or those he simply didn't like, to the midnight shifts at substations.

When the position of chief inspector opened up, three men applied, including James Crumley, a Brown ally. Crumley got the job after the other applicants, detective Bertram Talbot and inspector Tom Dahill, withdrew. Both men told reporters they had dropped out under pressure

On January 30, 1931, the *St. Paul Dispatch* printed this photo of detectives John McGowan and William McMullen, inspectors James Crumley and Pat Larkin, and detectives Thomas Grace and Neil McMahon showing off a stash of guns seized in a raid on a citizen who was accused of murder and bank robbery. The charges were dropped, and the true story behind the seized arsenal was never explained.

from Chief Brown. When that story hit the newsstands, Talbot and Dahill insisted that reporters had misunderstood them.

Right from the beginning, Chief Brown found it easy to manipulate the press. Newsmen swallowed his pronouncements whole and disgorged them on page one. The first trick he played on the newspapers and the reading public was to call for a meeting of Minnesota law enforcement to coordinate a war on bootleggers.

None of his fellow cops could have been fooled. After all, this was Big Tom Brown, a man of dark reputation in a city flooded with illegal booze. His tenure on the Purity Squad had been a mix of bribery, shakedowns, and selective enforcement.

Brown was much the man to put on appearances, so he spruced up the city's traffic cops. They were dressed in new, snappy uniforms complete with epaulets. Traffic cops would echo the chief's stature: all would be at least six foot two. Their main accomplishment was to issue tickets for out-of-date license plates. Brown assured citizens he would "enforce all traffic regulations. We mean to make St. Paul as safe as possible."

Brown took another bold step to fight crime when he ordered tree sitters to climb down. This made front-page news. Four teenage boys in St. Paul were trying to establish an endurance record for staying up in a tree. Brown found that kind of crime intolerable.

Meanwhile, the O'Connor System began breaking down, and it was no longer taboo to commit crimes in St. Paul. Newspapers reported one frightening crime after another. Roadhouses, cafés, grocery stores, citizens walking down the street—all were robbed at gunpoint. Jewelry stores were regularly held up, as were banks outside the city limits. While today's bank robbers tend to be lone desperados armed with a note, these heists were pulled off by brazen machine-gun gangs who sometimes got away with the equivalent of $1 million or more.

In 1927, Minnesota's governor named a panel of distinguished citizens to investigate the bank robberies and gangland slayings. They concluded that local police had failed in their duties and echoed earlier calls for the establishment of a state police force.

How did a cop with such a blemished reputation become chief of police? The FBI eventually found the answer to that question.

When Brown was appointed chief, in 1930, there were three underworld power brokers, and he was allied with all of them. The kingmaker was Leon Gleckman, whose puppets sat on the city council. Brown also had connections to two criminal fixers, nightclub operators Harry Sawyer at the Green Lantern and Jack Peifer at the Hollyhocks.

But a more legitimate power broker also backed Brown. He was Adolph Bremer, a multimillionaire banker and brewer. He had made a fortune during Prohibition. His Schmidt's beer showed up in barrels at the Green Lantern and other speakeasies. His Commercial State Bank profited from the accounts of Leon Gleckman, Harry Sawyer, and many other gangsters and bootleggers. The FBI also learned that Bremer's bank had laundered stolen cash and securities.

Adolph Bremer had connections both high and low. He was a power in the Democratic Party and had a great many friends and allies. It was Adolph Bremer who made a behind-the-scenes push to get Tom Brown appointed police chief. The success of his brewery during Prohibition depended upon a corrupt police force. He eventually admitted that to the FBI.

Adolph Bremer would soon regret backing Big Tom Brown, his bitter tears illuminated by the flash of news cameras.

4

ROARING THROUGH THE OZARKS

As far as anyone knows, Tom Brown never met Ma Barker, although he would have a disastrous impact on her life. During the Roaring Twenties, while Brown was graduating from tavern bribery to wholesale corruption, Ma Barker's boys were roaring through the Ozarks. The boys were Scotch-Irish on both sides, with, some thought, a bit of Cherokee ancestry. The highest scholarly mark any Barker boy reached was eighth grade. But their father, a miner, gave them a backcountry education in fishing and hunting that would last all their lives.

George and Kate Barker raised their sons on Presbyterian revivals, but the light of the Lord soon faded to the beam of a burglar's flashlight. All four boys joined a variety of gangs, committing highway robberies, car thefts, burglaries, and sometimes murder. By all accounts Kate was a controlling mother, obsessed with her sons, and once they landed in prison she lobbied hard for their release. In Tulsa, her boys ran with the scourge of that oil boomtown, the Central Park gang. It proved to be a prep school for many future members of the Barker-Karpis gang.

In 1921, Arthur "Doc" Barker, age 25, set out with two other men to rob a safe at a hospital construction site in Tulsa. They were surprised by the night watchman, Thomas Sherrill, a man in his fifties who was the father of nine children. Two of those burglars shot Sherrill sometime around midnight and ran off. Police were clueless, but the Sherrill family hired private investigators to bring the killers to justice. In January 1922 a jury found Doc guilty of Sherrill's murder. Doc, protesting innocence, was sentenced to life at hard labor at the Oklahoma state prison. Upon hearing the judge pronounce sentencing, Ma Barker collapsed.

Volney "Curly" Davis, who ran with the Barker boys, had worked at the construction site where the murder occurred. Police figured him for an accomplice, and Davis, too, was charged with the Sherrill murder. As Doc Barker's conviction was being appealed, Ma Barker visited Davis in an Oklahoma jail. Her mission was to persuade Davis that, when his trial came up, he should tell the same story of that fateful night that Doc had told. "Otherwise," Ma advised him, "it would ruin" Doc's appeal.

Ma Barker had more trouble coming: the same year Doc was convicted, Lloyd "Red" Barker drew a twenty-five-year term at Leavenworth for mail robbery. By then, according to a family friend, "George Barker and his wife were having considerable difficulty over the fact that the boys were leading such a dissolute life . . . Ma Barker apparently countenanced their wrongdoings, which George would not stand for."

Papa George "refused to see [Lloyd] or aid him in any manner, feeling he was guilty of the crime," the family friend told the FBI. "As a result of this, Lloyd, without the aid of counsel or money with which to hire legal assistance, was convicted."

That split the family. "Kate and George Barker were separated," the family friend said, "she going to Tulsa to live with Fred and from that time on [her husband] refused to have anything to do with her."

At one point in the 1920s, every one of Ma's sons was behind bars: Lloyd in Leavenworth, Doc in state prison, Fred in a reformatory on burglary charges, and Herman in Minnesota after a jewelry theft. In 1925, Ma presided over a reunion of Herman, her oldest, and Fred, her youngest. Both had just been paroled and hadn't seen each other for years. Fred and Herman, free again to practice their trade, ran with their own gangs and earned their living by burglary and robbery.

On August 28, 1927, Herman Barker and accomplices robbed the safe of an ice-making plant near Wichita, Kansas, locking an employee in a freezer on their way out. They drove to the city for a nightcap of burglaries.

After midnight, two Wichita motorcycle cops chased and pulled over a car full of suspects. Officer Joseph Marshall dismounted to question the driver. Officer Frank Bush got out of the sidecar and approached the suspects' auto from the other side. The driver, Herman Barker, put Marshall in a headlock and shot into his mouth. As Barker's accomplices ran off, Bush fired at them. Herman Barker pushed Marshall's body into the middle of the road and sped away. He took a wild corner, his car hitting a telephone pole and then a tree. Too badly hurt in the crash to get away, Herman Barker put his gun to his head and pulled the trigger.

So 1927 was a terrible year for Ma Barker. She became a mother without a family when Fred was slammed into a Kansas prison for burglary of a butcher shop. Her husband George was off in Joplin, Missouri, where he opened a gasoline station. According to some, Kate Barker began living as a woman of "loose morals." Whatever the truth of that, she wasn't living swell. With three surviving sons in prison, and with scant education and no prospect of respectable work, Kate Barker sank into a miserable poverty. Her home was a dirt-floor shack with an outhouse, lit at night by the flicker of kerosene lamps.

In the spring of 1931, one of Ma's wishes came true: her baby boy Fred was sprung from prison. He had made new friends behind bars, among them a skinny, shrewd punk named Alvin Karpis. Ma would soon meet Karpis, whose parole date was coming up. This Karpis boy and Fred, they had adventures in mind.

5

MURDER AT THE GREEN LANTERN

At about the time that Fred and Ma Barker were reunited in Missouri, Chief Tom Brown confronted the first public crisis of his tenure.

It happened at the Green Lantern. This downtown speakeasy had originally been called Dapper Dan's and in the 1920s was run by the "Irish Godfather," Dan Hogan. Dapper Dan's was a criminal sanctuary under the O'Connor System and a place to launder money and fence jewelry. Out front, it was a hot dog stand.

If the Irish didn't have a monopoly on St. Paul corruption in the 1920s, they gave it a mighty try. The mayors, the police chiefs, and many of the crooked politicians were of Irish ancestry, and they paid homage to Dapper Dan. But their "Irish Godfather" had no Irish blood. He was a San Francisco Italian, an orphan adopted by an Irish family.

Hogan reigned until December 1928, when someone wired his car with a bomb. The ambulance men removed Dan from the smoldering wreckage, but minus a leg. In the hospital, the "Irish Godfather" rallied for a few hours, then was called home to that great speakeasy in the sky.

That was lucky for Dapper Dan's protégé, Harry Sawyer.

Many in St. Paul suspected Harry of more than good luck. At the time of Hogan's death, Sawyer had a money grudge against him. But Hogan had plenty of enemies, and there's no evidence pointing to Harry Sawyer as the prime suspect in his murder. Sawyer turned out, however, to be chief beneficiary. "After Hogan's death, I managed the business for his

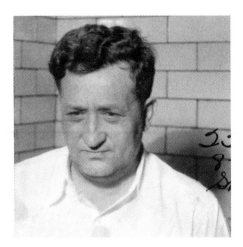

Harry Sawyer's mug shot, 1935.

wife for two or three months, then I took it over," Sawyer recalled. "I operated it until beer was legalized; then we had another room, ran sort of a cabaret and served meals."

Sawyer changed the tavern's name to the Green Lantern and stepped up to take Hogan's place in the system. Harry's game was fencing, money laundering, and criminal protection. None of Harry's boys would be arrested because he had the police chief on payoff. While many other speakeasies served home-brewed swill or spiked near-beer, the Bremer brewery delivered professionally brewed Schmidt's to Harry. The beer was secretly piped underground to a home near the brewery, barreled, and driven at night to the Green Lantern. Harry's deal with the Bremer family gave him distribution rights to other speakeasies.

So the Green Lantern became a watering hole for the soldiers of corruption. The tavern's reputation spread to the far edges of the American underworld. Journalists drank there frequently, but the Green Lantern was rarely identified by name in the local newspapers.

On a spring night in 1931, Frank Ventress escorted his wife Dorothy, "a striking brunette," to the Green Lantern. Ventress, a quick-tempered gangster, had no legitimate employment. He'd been married to Dorothy for five months, and the couple lived with the bride's parents.

Rubes took their women to this legendary tavern to impress them, but Frank was an insider who knew Harry Sawyer well enough to borrow his car. He took Dorothy for a joyride, then returned to the tavern around 10:00 PM. The Green Lantern's one-legged French cook prepared his signature spaghetti for them.

What a joint, this Green Lantern. The lights were low, the beer was fresh, and in the Blue Room, slot machines whirled. You never knew who might be drinking in the shadows: Machine Gun Kelly? Pretty Boy Floyd?

The Ventress couple settled into a booth when a man called to Frank: "Let's go outside."

Frank told Dorothy: "I'll be back in a minute, dear."

No, he wouldn't.

When Frank Ventress stepped out the back door a struggle erupted. Dorothy leaped up. "I just got to the door and I seen my husband got hit" over the head with a gun. "He was kind of slumped over, reeling and turning around. I heard a shot and jumped in and grabbed one of the men there. I don't know who it was I grabbed."

She snatched the hat off one man's head and hit him with it. "Then I heard another shot. I guess I got knocked down, I don't remember, I just kind of fell."

When she arose "everybody was running back and forth and I felt that someone was on the ground and I went over to see who it was. It was Frank."

Witness Carl Lund, whose apartment overlooked the Green Lantern's parking lot, heard four or five shots and saw flashes in the night.

A woman screamed, "My God! Help me get this man inside."

Lund watched two men run off.

A crowd gathered around Dorothy and Frank Ventress. Frank tried to speak, but both lungs had been pierced by a bullet. "I lifted his head," Dorothy said, "and he just coughed."

The Ventress murder and its attendant publicity threatened to expose the Green Lantern's role in St. Paul's protection racket. An investigation by state or federal officials might unravel the whole setup. The nightmare scenario was Harry Sawyer, who knew all, sweating in the federal hot seat.

Immediately after the Ventress shooting, Chief Brown closed the Green Lantern.

The murder had happened in a dark parking lot, and not even Dorothy Ventress got a good look at the killer. There were conflicting reports about how many shots had been fired and how many people had been in the parking lot. St. Paul detectives had no murder weapon, no motive, and no good witnesses, but they did have a couple of names, including Johnny Quinn and his friend Harry Kremer. Both had been seen at the Green Lantern just before the shooting.

Kremer, a 32-year-old family man, had been a newspaper ad salesman and then worked for the Sperry & Hutchinson Company, selling their Green Stamp incentive program to retailers. In 1929, he opened a "soft drink parlor" on a busy St. Paul street.

An hour or so after the Green Lantern murder, inspector James Crumley burst into Kremer's tavern and demanded, "Who is the boss?"

When Kremer stepped up, Crumley asked, "Did you see [Johnny] Quinn around here tonight?"

Kremer lied for Quinn, who was hiding in back. Crumley growled, "If Quinn comes here, you call the chief right away. If you don't I'll wreck this joint."

Later that night, Crumley returned and hauled Kremer to the police station. Crumley and Brown sweated Kremer, hated his answers, and locked him up. Crumley told him, "You're out on 7th Street selling rotten moonshine, and when we ask for a favor you're telling nothing but damn lies."

Kremer would be jailed for weeks, enduring what his attorney called "unlawful detention." He was never arrested, nor charged with any crime. He was dragged to show-ups seventy-six times, where he was viewed by citizens as a potential criminal, a process he found humiliating and intimidating. Kremer was interrogated not just by police but by Michael Kinkead, who had recently won election as Ramsey County attorney. Kinkead—tall, lanky, bespectacled, and gray-haired—was an immigrant from Limerick, Ireland, who would prove useful to Brown and his cronies.

After repeated interrogations, Kremer agreed to identify Johnny Quinn as the killer of Frank Ventress. Kinkead and Brown kept their star witness in jail through the end of the Ventress murder trial, and later Brown admitted he had locked up the witnesses for too long. "I was in a precarious position with the police department," Kremer said, because they could shut his business at any time.

Then Brown and Kinkead found another witness, although a questionable one. He was Harold White, a former Ramsey County deputy sheriff on the run from federal bribery charges. Crumley sequestered him at the Ryan Hotel under police guard. White agreed to testify that he had clearly seen Quinn, along with another man, murder Ventress. But there was no corroborating witness who placed White at the scene.

White claimed he fired shots in the air to chase the killers off. This would help account for the neighbors' reports of four or five gunshots. Ventress had only been hit twice.

With information squeezed out of Harry Kremer, police collected what they said was the murder weapon at the home of a Quinn relative. As the trial approached, they had the body, the weapon, and the witnesses.

After the Ventress shooting, Johnny Quinn knew he was in trouble. A 35-year-old veteran of the Great War, Quinn had been knocking around at a wild assortment of jobs, including oil-field roustabout, truck driver, and café counterman. He tried his luck as a speakeasy owner in Chicago, but that venture turned into an indictment, so in 1930, Quinn returned to his extended family in St. Paul.

Quinn had been in the parking lot when Ventress was shot, and he ripped his trousers leaping a fence as he ran off. He scrambled to his rented room and changed clothes, then met Kremer at the soft drink parlor. After Crumley's blustering visit, Quinn and Kremer drove to the Hollyhocks Inn. There Quinn spoke with his friend, bouncer Saph McKenna. Prosecutors alleged that Quinn asked McKenna to provide an alibi. Quinn testified that he'd only wanted McKenna to find out who was being sought for the murder. McKenna's testimony backed that up.

But McKenna didn't want Kremer and Quinn hanging around the Hollyhocks, so off they drove to Minneapolis, where Quinn's extended family lived. Quinn dropped a gun on the kitchen table and told his family he was in trouble. The gun was a six-shooter that had five bullets left in its cylinder. Quinn begged his brother-in-law to collect his clothes from his rented room. With his stuff packed into a car, Quinn drove to Winnipeg.

It's not known how authorities found Quinn in Canada, but Brown and Kinkead traveled to Winnipeg to bring him back to St. Paul. Frank Ventress had been a low-level gangster of the type that routinely met a violent early end. Why Chief Brown personally fetched Quinn from Canada is unclear. Why Kinkead, the county's top prosecutor, was along is equally mysterious. It was at least a seventeen-hour round trip on the highways of the time. Over the next few years, Kinkead would repeat this pattern, appearing in awkward situations that aroused the suspicions of cops and federal agents.

Indicted along with Quinn for the Ventress murder was one of his in-laws, Frank Fay. He supposedly accompanied Quinn to the Green Lantern that night. When cops started looking for Fay, he skedaddled to Florida and avoided prosecution for years.

Quinn's trial began in May. He and his attorney adopted a strategy of self-defense. The surviving documents from his trial do not answer the question of why they chose as they did. Did Quinn and his attorney feel that authorities were pressuring witnesses and that a self-defense plea would mitigate the inevitable prison sentence? Or was Quinn the lone killer? Or one of several shooters?

A Northwestern University ballistics expert testified that Quinn's gun had fired the fatal shot. Quinn's lawyers countered that ballistics was not yet a reliable science, and the expert admitted he was only offering an opinion.

Dorothy Ventress told her story but could not identify Quinn as the shooter. The unfortunate Harry Kremer was on the stand for hours and did identify Quinn, and he was then slapped back into his jail cell. Deputy Harold White also gave testimony blaming Quinn.

Quinn's lawyer charged that White, in return for his testimony, had been promised that the one-year bribery sentence hanging over his head would be reduced to probation. That accusation riled Kinkead. He told Quinn's attorney, "If you said that outside of that [courtroom] door, I would poke you in the nose." But a short time later, White admitted to the judge that, indeed, his bribery case had recently been fixed.

Despite reams of testimony and subsequent appeals, it never became clear what motive Quinn had to kill Ventress. It is not certain that he did kill him. Given Dorothy Ventress's description of the scene, the murder of her husband was most likely the result of a struggle among several men. Witnesses who were never called to court would have testified to multiple gunshots, and the possibility of more than one shooter. Dorothy did not identify Quinn as the man who had called her husband into the parking lot.

Quinn, in his own defense, said that on the night in question, he tried to enter the Green Lantern via the back door and Ventress stopped him. Ventress said, "What the hell are you doing here, you son of a bitch?"

Then, Quinn said, "I saw a gun in his hand."

Quinn testified that he grabbed the gun and slugged Ventress, who reached into his overcoat pocket as if to get another gun. That's when, Quinn said, he shot Ventress in self-defense. His lawyers put witnesses on the stand who testified that Ventress was volatile and dangerous, especially when drinking, and more who testified that Quinn, a slight man who suffered from tuberculosis, was easygoing.

The jury convicted Quinn of murder in the second degree, which earned him a life sentence at Stillwater Prison.

Although Brown had told the press he'd closed the Green Lantern "permanently," he soon changed his mind. "Chief Brown asserted today that the café will not be allowed to reopen as a place of its past character," one newspaper reported. "The premises may be used, however, for other legitimate business purposes. Police experienced trouble frequently at the café during its operation by George Hurley, whose wife took it over Jan. 1."

Pat Reilly, saloonkeeper
at the Green Lantern.

George Hurley was a thug and former boxer who'd twice been acquitted in murder trials. He and his wife were merely employees at the Green Lantern, convenient fronts for Harry Sawyer. The place had gone to hell under a woman's management, at least according to Brown's fiction.

This Ventress shooting and prosecution of Quinn left Harry Sawyer unscathed by scandal. His name never surfaced in the courtroom or the press. When the Green Lantern reopened, Sawyer hired a new front man, Pat Reilly, a batboy for the St. Paul Saints who was destined to become John Dillinger's little buddy.

In 1939, eight years after the Ventress murder, Frank Fay showed up in the Twin Cities again. By then the Gleckman-Brown combination had been broken up by federal authorities. Informed that Fay was looking to settle matters, Michael Kinkead, still the county attorney, dropped the indictment against him. In that affidavit, Kinkead admitted that the case against Fay had been weak and that supposed witnesses to the Ventress murder had been coached to lie.

Kinkead wrote that the case was weak because James Crumley, who'd conducted the investigation, was dead. The star witness, Harry Kremer, had repudiated, saying he was so drunk that night that he couldn't remember much at all and that Brown and Crumley had bullied him into lying on the stand.

The affidavit also noted that a cop named Ray McCarthy had been prepared to testify against Fay and Quinn. Now in 1939, McCarthy was saying that Harry Sawyer had "insisted that he tell the story to prevent further trouble with the police department, which might result in the closing of his, Sawyer's, place."

Although the Minnesota Supreme Court had refused Quinn a second trial, the governor commuted his sentence and he was released on parole in 1943.

Whatever Quinn's level of guilt or innocence, the outcome of his trial was good for Harry Sawyer. After the verdict, his tavern resumed flashing its Green Lantern sign, a beacon drawing crooks from all over the nation.

6

Summer in the Ozarks

In May 1931, as Johnny Quinn was led from a St. Paul courtroom into the dark vortex of his future, Alvin Karpis was driving away from a Kansas prison, free on parole. His immediate goal was to find his prison buddy, Fred Barker.

Together Karpis and Fred would become the stalwarts of the final, disastrous version of the Barker gang. Over the years many others joined, staying on for a job or two and then departing for another gang, or prison, or the grave. But the core was always Fred and Karpis. Karpis admired little Freddie tough-guy. A quiet, cautious worrier, Karpis had found in Fred "a natural born killer" who "never hesitated to shoot his way out of trouble."

In prison, Fred knew how to work the scams. When Karpis first met him, Fred opened a tin of Prince Albert tobacco and offered Karpis a smoke. It wasn't pipe tobacco but marijuana Fred had smuggled in. Fred was paroled first, and they vowed to team up once Karpis was free.

Days after his parole, Karpis checked in with the Slayman family of Neosho, Missouri, hoping they had a message for him from Fred Barker. They did not, but their 17-year-old daughter Dorothy developed a crush on Karpis. He promised to look her up again after he'd found Fred.

Ma Barker was living in Tulsa then, so Karpis went there to meet Fred, and the two drove back to Neosho two weeks later. Karpis began dating Dorothy, but there was more than romance involved. On June 10, 1931, Karpis, Dorothy, Fred, and three others were arrested for jewelry theft. Karpis, being on parole when he committed the crime, could not get out on bond. It took him more than three months to work a deal whereby Dorothy returned the stolen jewelry, satisfying the jeweler and getting Karpis released. On the day he was sprung, September 26, he celebrated by marrying Dorothy.

Three days later, Karpis bought a new DeSoto and drove Dorothy to visit his parents in Chicago. Emily Newbold, Karpis's sister, worked at the Eastman Kodak Company and helped Dorothy get a job there. It seemed that marriage, proximity to his parents and sisters, and a desire to stay out of prison were rounding over the sharp edges of Alvin Karpis.

But while "Dorothy enjoyed the quiet life in Chicago," he wrote, "I began to feel the old familiar restlessness."

Within a few weeks, he was back in the Ozarks with Fred, planning nighttime burglaries. Soon one of those break-ins would turn into a bloody crime that would follow Fred and Karpis all their lives, exile them from the Ozarks, and bring them into partnership with the corrupt police chief of St. Paul.

7

WHERE'S LEON?

In the fall of 1931, while Fred Barker and Alvin Karpis helped themselves to cash and merchandise in the Ozarks, Tom Brown confronted the second crisis of his tenure: the kidnapping of his patron, Leon Gleckman.

Gleckman's interests had grown during the 1920s to include partial ownership of a distillery in Havana. By 1931, Gleckman, aka "the little

Leon Gleckman, St. Paul's shadow mayor, at the police station in the late 1920s.

fellow," had graduated from mere bootlegging to become godfather of a home-grown protection racket. Where other cities had a Mafia, St. Paul had Gleckman's system. Bank robbers, thieves, and murderers slapped down protection money or risked arrest. Bordellos, gambling dens, and speakeasies paid a shadow tax or were shut down. Mayor William Mahoney, following his ouster from city hall, complained that the Gleckman system spread beyond the underworld to levy "a tribute on legitimate businesses."

Soon Gleckman's empire began to create victims. Saloonkeeper Frank Reilly described that process to federal agents.

At Gleckman's prompting, Reilly opened a "hotel" in downtown St. Paul. Its "guests" would never have to sleep alone or, for that matter, sleep at all. A week after the hotel opened, Tom Brown's Purity Squad arrested its prostitutes and clients.

So Reilly visited the third floor of the Hotel St. Paul and the luxurious offices of "the little fellow."

"Gleckman gets on the phone," Reilly said, "and tells Brown to lay off, or pretends to." Then Gleckman advised that, for a price, he could teach the police some manners. Reilly realized he was a patsy and that Gleckman had encouraged him to open a bordello for the express purpose of cleaning him out.

Thus, Gleckman's rackets didn't just tolerate crime. They invited it to town.

Mayor Mahoney said that Gleckman worked his political magic through his men on the city council, Irving Pearce and Clyde May. They supported the mayor's pet projects, and in return, Gleckman got the secret power to name the police commissioner, and hence the police chief, making some of the St. Paul cops his goon squad.

It was soon after Tom Brown's ascension to chief that Michael Kinkead was elected county attorney. Once Kinkead was in office, these men enforced such tight control over the city that, as Reilly put it, "even candy companies had to pay bribes" in order to put their products in stores.

The system was working, maybe too well. That kind of power was bound to antagonize someone.

On the morning of September 24, 1931, Gleckman's car was forced to the side of the road not far from his home in St. Paul's Mac-Groveland neighborhood. Sam Cimin leaped into the car, leveled a sawed-off shotgun at Gleckman, and took over the driving. Albert Tallerico slipped taped glasses over Gleckman's eyes. Gleckman begged his abductors not to take him out of the city. They tried to calm him and drove. And drove. And drove.

They were trailed into the Wisconsin countryside by another car containing Joe Jurley and Tony Scandale.

Sam Cimin, the boss, was the only career criminal among the four kidnappers. Albert Tallerico was hardly more than a boy burglar. Joe Jurley was a witless follower, and Tony Scandale an ex-con and family man in desperate financial trouble. They were all unemployed and lived in St. Paul but had been born in Italy.

It took eight hours for the kidnap caravan to reach Rest Lake, deep in the woods, between Lake Superior and the resort town of Woodruff. In late September, the vacation crowd would have already hauled their boats out of the water and retreated to Chicago and Milwaukee.

At Rest Lake, the kidnappers consulted "The Finlander." He, innocent of conspiracy, helped row them and their victim across the lake. The kidnappers had rented a two-room cabin, heated by wood stove and lit by kerosene lamps, that was nearly impossible to reach by road. Sam Cimin took $1,400 from Gleckman, then shut him in the back room and demanded two letters: one reassuring his wife and another asking his partner, bootlegger Morris Roisner, to raise $200,000 ransom.

So on Thursday evening at sundown, Gleckman lay alone in a rustic room, relieved of his goggles but not his anxiety. Joe Jurley and Tony Scandale guarded him and cooked his meals. Sam Cimin and Albert Tallerico drove all night to St. Paul, arriving on Friday morning.

It's not known what Cimin did for the next twenty-four hours or how he got the notes to Rose Gleckman and Roisner. The official investigation left that and many other aspects unexplored. Tallerico later testified that "Cimin said he was talking to Gleckman's partner [Roisner], who only offered $7,000 or $8,000."

Cimin rejected that offer, telling Roisner he "didn't care to talk business."

On Saturday, Cimin and Tallerico drove back to the hideout. Cimin demanded that Gleckman write a letter reducing the ransom demand to $75,000. Letter in hand, Cimin took the train for Chicago. Tallerico, Jurley, and Scandale guarded Gleckman and drank wine all weekend.

Tallerico and Gleckman played cards. Gleckman was encouraged to fish from the dock, but he couldn't relax. He found $2.10 in his clothing and asked the kidnappers to buy him a bottle of moonshine, which he sipped as a tranquilizer.

Tallerico was assigned to meet every train that arrived in Woodruff from Chicago, and on Tuesday, Sam Cimin alighted. After being driven to the cabin, Cimin paid off his partners in varying amounts, no more than $200 each. Tallerico drove back to St. Paul and gave his wife money to pay the household bills.

That left Gleckman at the cabin, guarded by Jurley and Scandale. On Thursday they heard "The Finlander's" dog barking across the lake. A rowboat appeared at the dock, containing Sam Cimin, a "big man," and Albert Tallerico. The kidnappers later testified that they did not know the "big man." He wore a topcoat and had a handkerchief draped across his face. The "big man," Cimin, and Tallerico took Gleckman away in the rowboat.

Their job done, Scandale and Jurley hitchhiked thirty-three miles to the mining town of Hurley, Wisconsin. There they drank, bought new clothes, and took the train for Duluth and ultimately home to St. Paul.

The next day, the fellows were drinking wine when "Cimin come in and said lay low of everything," Tallerico later testified. "He promised they would get $44,000 within 10 days . . . from either [Roisner] or some other friend of Gleckman's."

In the morning newspaper on Friday, October 1, St. Paul police announced that Morris Roisner had phoned from Chicago, promising to bring Gleckman home. But Gleckman was in fact delivered by night-club owner Jack Peifer and police chief Tom Brown.

How the press reported this kidnapping comprises a twisted and curi-ous tale. For the first five days, not a whisper of Gleckman's disappear-ance hit the newspapers. Then on September 29, a reporter for United Press, checking on a rumor, queried Chicago police: had they been asked to look for Gleckman? They replied that they hadn't heard he was missing. The newsman found this curious, since Chicago gangs were presumed to be involved in bootlegger kidnappings. If reporters were hearing rumors, weren't St. Paul police hearing them too?

Suddenly, the case burst into the headlines.

Chief Tom Brown told reporters he had learned that Gleckman was missing from a "St. Paul physician whose name he would not reveal."

The doctor had treated Rose Gleckman for a "nervous breakdown" after she received "a letter from Leon Gleckman postmarked Chicago which said he was being held for ransom." Brown added, "The fact that Leon Gleckman disappeared after taking a phone call at home proves he went out at the bidding of a friend and that the trap for the kidnapping was laid in Chicago."

It proved no such thing.

No reporter challenged that logical leap. No reporter brought up the fact that Brown blamed Chicago gangs yet had not called Chicago police.

Newspapers not only handled the police gingerly, they treaded quietly around wealthy criminals. They referred to Gleckman as the "head of a finance company" and a "politician." But Gleckman had already served time for federal tax evasion, had never run for office, and was a celebrity-gangster, known far beyond St. Paul.

While Brown blamed the kidnapping on Chicago gangs, his top man, inspector James Crumley, arrested a "Minneapolis negress." The pretext was that the woman "claimed she had known all along that Gleckman would be kidnapped." She was soon released.

Chief Brown's blame-Chicago story held up until Friday, October 1, the day Gleckman was delivered home. One newsman followed a tip and drove to St. Paul's Keller Golf Course. "Leon Gleckman," he wrote, "was grabbed at Keller Golf Course . . . two caddies saw him drive up in his car between noon and 12:30." One caddy shouted, "There's Leon, better get his clubs."

But when Gleckman's caddy lugged his clubs into the sunshine, neither Leon nor his car was in sight.

The reporter discovered that "attired in golf clothes, Leon Gleckman had gone to the barber shop of Jacob Perlman for a shave" before his tee time. That story contradicted the one Chief Brown had told the press, but all was obliterated by the explosion of headlines the following day:

I WAS FISHING SAYS GLECKMAN
$75,000 EXTORTED BY KIDNAPPERS

Underneath those headlines, the *St. Paul Daily News* printed a picture of Leon, daughters on his lap, wife in the background. The story said: "Leon Gleckman, political leader, kidnapped eight days ago in St. Paul, returned to his home at 2168 Sargent Ave. in time for late breakfast today."

Gleckman insisted he'd been on a fishing trip. He chose a curious location for this fictional trip: Crane Lake, Minnesota, where Tom Brown owned vacation property.

"That's my story," Gleckman said. "I can't help what the public believes."

"But why did you leave so suddenly?" asked the *Daily News* reporter.

"What's all the fuss about?" Gleckman asked. "If I broke a golf appointment . . . it couldn't be helped."

Confused reporters scrambled to their typewriters and clanked out contradictory rumors: a St. Louis mob was behind the abduction, one wrote; another theorized that Roisner had made a deal with Chicago mobsters for Gleckman's release.

The chief was no help. "I have talked to Mr. Gleckman," Brown said, "he says he was fishing. There is nothing further I can do."

On Saturday, October 2, the day after his release, Leon Gleckman, trailed by reporters and photographers, showed up at Keller Golf Course in St. Paul. The resulting headline said:

GLECKMAN, BACK FROM FISHING TRIP,
KEEPS 10-DAY OLD GOLF DATE

Gleckman had decided to reinforce the golfing version of his kidnap story. He teed off with his buddies, criminal attorneys John DeCourcy and John Dwyer. Reporters recorded a slapstick conversation.

"You know," said DeCourcy, "some people think you'd been taken for a ride."

Gleckman sank a twelve-foot putt.

"Well, that gives me a birdie," chirped Gleckman.

It was the kind of wink-wink story few reporters can resist.

But no reporter tried to resolve the many contradictions. Brown said Gleckman had been called on the phone, then abducted outside his house. What about the caddies at Keller Golf Course? What about the barbers in Perlman's shop? Why were two contradictory stories told, one by Gleckman and another by the chief of police?

On Sunday morning, newspaper readers saw a banner headline that at first seemed to have no connection to the Gleckman kidnapping:

ST. PAUL HOTEL PROPRIETOR IS BEATEN, SLAIN

The body of Frank LaPre, age 37, an Italian-born owner of the sleazy Evans Hotel, had been discovered Saturday evening. He'd been shot three times in the head. His face was so badly beaten that he could only be identified by receipts found in his pockets. Robbery was suspected, since his pockets contained only receipts, keys, cigarettes, and an obviously dysfunctional good luck charm.

That Sunday, the morning after LaPre's murder, police arrested Jurley, Tallerico, Cimin, and Scandale. "When I was first arrested," Scandale later told a judge, police "examined me orally. Then they tapped up on me, beat me up, and after that I made another statement which they took down in writing. They said that Sam and Tallerico and Scandale had all confessed."

Joe Jurley also testified that St. Paul cops beat him until he made a statement. Sam Cimin brooded in silence, demanding a trial. Albert Tallerico, 23, youngest of the kidnap crew, swore that the cops neither beat nor threatened him.

Only after interrogating the four men did police arrest a new conspirator, Albert Robbins. A home-taught paper chemist who conducted lab experiments on his front porch, Robbins, curiously enough, had been indicted in the same 1926 Cleveland rum-running case that had ensnared Tom Brown. Now he was awaiting sentencing for defrauding investors in a failed fur-farm venture. Robbins's defense in that case was that he had been hornswoggled by state officials who'd muscled into the business.

Robbins lived across from the Gleckmans and had gone to high school with Leon. Robbins claimed he had been coerced into joining the conspiracy by Frank LaPre. Robbins's role was to signal the kidnappers by drawing a window shade when Leon left the house.

So the story was wrapped up. Four men admitted the conspiracy, another would stand trial, and the sixth, the supposed mastermind Frank LaPre, was dead. The newspapers printed a picture of him: He looked like a movie villain, with a fat face, a trimmed mustache, and a dark scowl underneath a bowler hat.

Five other mugs on that page belonged to LaPre's accomplices. Also pictured were eight cops who "had worked day and night to solve the case." The biggest picture showed the proud chief, Tom Brown.

When viewed in the flash of the news cameras, Brown was looking good. The conclusion of the kidnapping seemed satisfying, even heroic. Brown invited newsmen to his office to photograph himself and Gleckman in their mutual triumph. He praised his detectives. The newsmen bubbled over.

The contradictions—the supposed Chicago connection, the mention of Crane Lake, the golf course version of events, the roles of the go-betweens Jack Peifer and Morris Roisner—were never explored.

8

THE SHOW

On Monday, October 4, one day after the kidnappers' arrests, Tom Brown, Leon Gleckman, and Michael Kinkead, followed by newsmen, took Albert Tallerico on a 750-mile round trip into the Wisconsin woods to re-create the kidnapping. In its next editions, the *Daily News* ran a story and photo under the headline:

BELIEVE IT OR NOT HE WAS FISHING,
AND HERE'S THE PROOF

The "proof" was a photo taken by a *Daily News* photographer as Gleckman sat fishing on a dock at Rest Lake, outside the kidnap cabin. "Police returned from Rest Lake armed with indisputable proof," a *Daily News* reporter wrote. Proof of what, he never said.

On page four, the newspaper pictured Albert Tallerico, his face masked by a bandana, sitting on a bed with Gleckman, playing cards. In hundreds of pages of court testimony, no kidnapper mentions wearing a mask. Putting a mask on Tallerico for the photograph was a dramatic flourish invented for the news story.

The legal implications of this public relations drama are worth pondering: The police chief and the prosecuting attorney took an accused

man to the scene and had him reenact the crime for reporters and photographers. This took place before the case reached the courts. The
grand jury heard testimony on the following day, with this staged event
appearing on every front page in town.

Back in St. Paul, while two hundred of Frank LaPre's friends, relatives,
employees, allies, and enemies were riding in his funeral procession,
Brown sent inspector James Crumley to search for the gun that had
been used to murder the man. Crumley found a gun that he said belonged to Sam Cimin. Despite this supposed evidence, neither Cimin
nor anyone else was ever charged in the murder of LaPre.

As a final act in the Gleckman drama, Jack Peifer's supposed role as
rescuer was revealed. The story broke into print that Peifer, carrying the
ransom, had been blindfolded by Gleckman's kidnappers and taken to
the remote hideout. The newspapers praised Peifer for his "errand of
mercy."

But it was an errand that made no sense. Why would Gleckman's kidnappers create a witness by inviting Peifer to their hideout? Anyone who
could locate the hideout could link its renters to the abduction. Peifer
could have dropped his ransom payment anywhere. There was no need for
him to meet the kidnappers, as such a meeting endangered both parties.
But Peifer's "rescue" makes sense if the story was being stage-managed.

A few years later, when the FBI discovered that Tom Brown was more
than just a bootlegger's best friend, they interviewed Albert Tallerico
in Stillwater Prison. He recalled helping to row Jack Peifer out to the
cabin where Gleckman was held. He told the FBI that Peifer had said
"I'd better put this blindfold on" to make his hero act convincing. Tallerico added that St. Paul's crooks lived in mortal terror of Peifer, who
was thought to have written the death warrants of a number of gangsters. He told the FBI that Cimin and LaPre had told him Peifer was to
get a 50 percent cut of the Gleckman ransom.

Tallerico also said that he and the other kidnapping suspects had been
beaten by police until they signed confessions. Police "suggested" the
answers. Tallerico said that back then Kinkead and Brown had visited
him in jail. Their message: "If you mention [Jack] Peifer's name before
the grand jury, we will know about it and you will not get one year but
40 years."

Tallerico's attorney told the FBI his client had introduced him to a woman who knew enough about the Gleckman kidnapping and the torture-murder of LaPre to "blow the lid off St. Paul." But if the story came out, that attorney said, everyone would know she had talked. He told the feds he had to keep her identity a secret or put her life, Tallerico's, and even his own in danger.

Eventually, the FBI uncovered a motive for Peifer's involvement. Saph McKenna said that gambling began at the Hollyhocks in 1929 and that he was Peifer's partner then. That year, the casino's "license" was stamped by county attorney Chris O'Brien in return for a bribe, according to McKenna.

But in 1930 a new St. Paul regime swept in, with Gerhard Bundlie as mayor and Tom Brown as police chief. Bundlie's powers were limited because the city was really run by Gleckman's little empire. When Michael Kinkead was elected top prosecutor for Ramsey County, the empire acquired a court system of its own.

"When Kinkead went into office we closed" the casino, McKenna said.

In an effort to connect with the new regime, McKenna called on Leon Gleckman at the Hotel St. Paul. Gleckman said, "See Billy Dunn and it will cost you twenty percent." So McKenna met Dunn, Gleckman's bagman, and complained that the Hollyhocks wasn't making much money. "Well, Saph," Dunn replied, "you are running out there . . . you will have to pay us $100 a week regardless."

The payments "kept up until Gleckman was kidnapped," McKenna told the FBI. "After Jack Peifer brought Gleckman back I did not have to make any more payments to Dunn, but what the circumstances were I don't know."

The circumstances, the FBI soon learned, included Gleckman canceling a debt Peifer owed him and rescinding his $100-a-week "tax" on the Hollyhocks.

It would take Gleckman years to realize what the FBI and some in the underworld had concluded: that Jack Peifer had the motive, means, and opportunity to engineer his kidnapping. Peifer's motive was to relieve himself of the tax and become a lord, not a serf, in Gleckman's kingdom. By using Italian gangsters, Peifer could distance himself from the abduction.

The more the FBI heard, the darker the story grew. After LaPre's murder, Chief Brown went to LaPre's hotel, opened his safe, and pocketed the ransom. He used it in his campaign for sheriff, Albert Tallerico told the FBI. Agents heard a similar story from Brown's brother-in-law, cab driver George Rafferty. Brown admitted in court that he had taken $5,500 from LaPre's safe. He and Morris Roisner wrote their names on every bill, Brown said, and then he locked the cash in his safe at police headquarters. LaPre's widow sued Brown for the return of that cash but never recovered it.

Saloonkeeper Frank Reilly told the FBI that LaPre had been "killed by Brown and others and planted in an automobile to make it look like a gangland killing."

When the Gleckman kidnapping came to court, County Attorney Kinkead pleaded for leniency for the kidnappers. The exception was Sam Cimin, who demanded a trial. At age 41, Cimin was a loner, abandoned by his wife and by the parents who had brought him over from Italy. After a perfunctory trial and twenty-five minutes of jury deliberation, Cimin drew a forty-year sentence. Bootlegger Morris Roisner was never called to testify, although he had gotten the ransom notes from Cimin.

Albert Robbins, the finger man, pleaded guilty and blurted out in court unprompted: "I do not know any of the circumstances surrounding the death of Mr. LaPre or who was responsible for his death and have no suspicions."

His sentence was reduced from a possible forty years to twenty-five.

Joe Jurley, 35, had emigrated from an impoverished Italian village at age 18 and was nearly illiterate. "I can read a little American," he told the judge, who realized he was dealing with a man of "limited intelligence" who was "easily influenced." Kinkead lobbied for leniency, citing Jurley's cooperation. Jurley got fifteen years and would soon die in prison.

Tony Scandale, 33, had come from an Italian village at age 15 and worked at a variety of jobs including bootlegging, which had earned him a trip to Leavenworth. He had a wife and three children and had only been out of the federal lockup for a year or so. "I owe $2000 on my home, we are just about ready to lose it. The doctor garnishes my wife's wages," Scandale told the judge. Kinkead asked for clemency, claiming that Scandale had been "vouched for by very respectable, decent citizens." He never named those citizens, nor did the judge inquire. Scandale got a fifteen-year term.

Finally came Albert Tallerico, who had been brought to the United States from Italy as a toddler. He told the judge the lie he'd been rehearsed to say: "Chief Brown . . . did not threaten me with any physical punishment . . . I was not struck in any way or promised anything if I did confess."

Kinkead urged the judge to be "as lenient as possible" with Tallerico. "Police and myself had no idea whatsoever of the identity of the kidnappers until Mr. Tallerico confessed his part in it and implicated the others," he said.

Tallerico got the lightest sentence of all, two-to-twelve years.

But Kinkead's plea for Tallerico was a fabrication. Prosecutors are certainly aware of what has been in the newspapers, and Chief Brown had described to reporters how he had called in his best men on a Sunday morning to arrest the kidnap gang. The detectives split up into teams to make simultaneous arrests of Tallerico, Cimin, Jurley, and Scandale. So Brown knew the names *before* Tallerico was arrested. Albert Robbins could not have been the source, since his role was only discovered after the four Italians were in custody.

That narrows the source to Frank LaPre, murdered the night before the arrests of the other four. The informers who told the FBI that LaPre had been tortured by police until he gave up the names, and then murdered, may have been holding the dragon of truth by the tail.

Sam Cimin was defended by criminal attorney John DeCourcy. Notorious for getting drunk in downtown bars and blabbing the confidential details of his clients' cases, DeCourcy was also legal adviser and golf buddy of Leon Gleckman.

So the four Italians and Albert Robbins had gotten themselves into a trap from which there was no escaping. The police chief who arrested them and the man who prosecuted them were both Gleckman soldiers. Their confessions were beaten out of them, and men in high office were bearing false witness in the courtroom. In the only case that came to trial, the defendant's legal counsel was suspect. The murder of Frank LaPre, and the nature of Jack Peifer's involvement, were never probed.

Jack Peifer and Tom Brown would work together on another kidnapping, which would be pulled off in eighteen months. Stage-managing a kidnapping, and hand-feeding the press, would become a Tom Brown hallmark. The patterns of Frank LaPre's murder would show up again too, in a 1934 shooting involving Brown: a dead suspect, conflicting stories fed to the press, the implication of Brown by underworld informants, and the disappearance of the dead man's money into Brown's pockets.

9

THEY SHOT THE SHERIFF

In October of 1931, an older, well-dressed, and somewhat inebriated gentleman arrived in Thayer, Missouri, looking to rent a farm. His name was Arthur Dunlop. He'd been a billboard painter but had retired to drink full time. The woman pretending to be his wife was named Kate Barker. The young man who posed as his son was Fred Barker.

Dunlop settled on an "out of the way place" and moved in with Kate and Fred. "Dunlop was generally assumed to be a retired farmer," neighbors said, "who had made money from his oil lands in Oklahoma. He always bought the best and always paid cash."

But crude oil was not the source of Dunlop's prosperity. Thayer is a convenient drive to the borders of Kansas, Arkansas, and Oklahoma. Convenient, that is, for robbers. In an era when the law was enforced by

Alvin Karpis, about 1925.

local cops, bandits often dashed across state lines to safety. One of those dashing bandits was Fred Barker, the family's breadwinner.

Shortly after the Dunlop family moved in, a new DeSoto sedan began appearing in the farmhouse driveway. It belonged to Alvin Karpis, fresh from Chicago.

In 1931, this new configuration, the Barker-Karpis gang, was hardly the formidable outfit they would become. Burglary was their specialty, but they often bungled safecracking, and so left the big prize behind. Whatever it takes to pull off daylight machine-gun bank robberies—courage? lunacy?—the 1931 version of the Barker gang didn't have it.

On December 18, Karpis and Fred pulled one of their signature punk burglaries. In the deepest part of the night they drove to West Plains, Missouri, and broke into McCallon's, a clothing store. Their technique was to get into the apartment or storage space above a store, drill a hole, and lower themselves in. Failing to find much money at McCallon's, they stole dresses, coats, and ties. They drove this loot twenty miles back to Thayer and piled it inside the farmhouse. Hence was the mystery solved of how the unemployed Arthur Dunlop could dress in sartorial splendor.

The next day, Karpis fired up that DeSoto and he and Fred paid an ill-advised visit to the scene of the crime. Karpis, posing as a typewriter

Fred Barker, from the wanted poster issued in Missouri after the killing of Sheriff C. Roy Kelly in 1931.

repairman, poked his head into the office of an attorney but was really casing the bank next door. Then he drove his car into the Davidson Motor Company to get a couple of tires repaired.

Sheriff C. Roy Kelly was across the street getting a cup of coffee. Kelly was a popular sheriff, a macho man with a reputation for bringing down tough gangsters single-handedly. A garage worker ran up to tell him that a DeSoto had pulled in that looked like the car involved in the previous night's burglary.

Sheriff Kelly was wearing an overcoat, which covered up his belt and pistol. He approached the DeSoto from behind. The tires matched the tread marks left outside McCallon's. The sheriff asked the driver to get out.

Karpis pulled a .45 and shot the sheriff in the abdomen. The sheriff grabbed Karpis. Fred shot the sheriff in the arm. Kelly fell to the greasy floor, Karpis firing at him. Karpis "ran out of the garage and across a vacant lot" and "disappeared, carrying a pistol in his hand." Fred roared away in the DeSoto, while one townsman took potshots with a .22 rifle. Outside of town, Fred abandoned the DeSoto, stealing a red Chevy to replace it.

A posse traced Karpis and Barker to the farmhouse. Angry citizens burst in, but Karpis, Fred, Ma, and Dunlop had vamoosed. They left the looted clothing behind, except for, inexplicably, fifty neckties. The sheriff's widow pinned her husband's badge to her blouse and vowed to hunt down his killers.

From the gang's point of view, the episode was a disaster. Karpis lost a hideout and a new DeSoto and had gained only a pile of neckties. Worse, a sheriff's wife and her posse were vowing vengeance via the gallows, and the Barker "family" was running scared. That two-bit burglary also cost Karpis his marriage. Dorothy Slayman Karpis had decided to track down her husband and, by strange coincidence, on the day of Sheriff Kelly's murder took the bus from Chicago to West Plains. The cops, quizzing all arrivals at the bus station, figured out Dorothy's connection to Karpis and threw her in jail.

The gang's next refuge was the farm of Herb "Deafy" Farmer outside Joplin. Deafy was tagged with his nickname because he was hard of hearing. But his other senses were alert to the local underworld, where he was a well-connected fixer. He had known the Barkers for years, and during rough patches between Ma and Pa Barker, Deafy's mother had taken young Freddie in.

So during Christmas week, Ma, Karpis, Fred, and Dunlop cooled out at Deafy's place. But the sheriff's widow was determined and furious, and Deafy advised the Barkers to leave the Ozarks. He knew a safe place: St. Paul, Minnesota. In that so-called Holy City it was possible to buy protection from any crime committed anywhere. Check in at the Green Lantern, Deafy said. Tell Harry I sent you.

10

CAMBRIDGE, SADIE, AND ROSE

The exact circumstances of the Barker gang's arrival in St. Paul are not known, but it is certain they had to pay for the privilege of residency. One prison inmate, Robert Newbern, told the FBI that he had been a cellmate of a thief named Larry DeVol, and that DeVol had claimed that he had been paying Harry Sawyer $100 a week for protection, and that the money went to Brown and Crumley. "DeVol also told him that ten percent of all the money the Barker-Karpis gang made in their robberies was turned over to Brown and Crumley for protection services." Newbern added that he had direct experience with St. Paul's system. In the summer of 1931, he said, he "paid $80 to Harry Sawyer, which was ten percent of a sum obtained through a confidence game," and Sawyer had told him "that this money was to go to the police department." In this way, St. Paul's protection racket managed to turn predatory criminals into its prey.

Besides the price of police protection, the Barkers needed cash so they could replace the DeSoto Karpis had abandoned and rent respectable lodgings. Ma hated the hotel rooms and the constant moving. With Arthur Dunlop along to pose as the father-husband, they could pretend to be a normal family. This made, in Karpis's estimation, for a "nearly foolproof cover." Shortly after their arrival, they rented a home a few minutes' drive from St. Paul's vibrant downtown.

Having been advised by their new mentor Harry Sawyer to commit their crimes outside St. Paul, Fred and Karpis led a raid on the village of Cambridge.

Fifty miles up the road from St. Paul, Cambridge was home to 1,200 people and one bank. Fred and Karpis, along with accomplices who have never been identified, raided that town at about 3:00 AM on a January night. After failing to crack the bank safe because it wouldn't open, they broke into the Gillespie Auto Company and were confronted by Mart Dunning, a fellow "somewhat along in years" who roomed on the grounds as a night watchman. Dunning's dog charged the burglars. "Call the dog off!" one bandit shouted. "I said sic 'em," Dunning later told police, "and that's when I got this lump on the head." The bandits moved cars out of the building in order to get to a Buick Karpis particularly wanted. Again they fumbled at safe-cracking but managed to jimmy $35 out of the auto company's till. Meanwhile, other members of the gang disarmed patrolman Frank Whitney. "One fellow came walking along and when he met me he shoved his gun in my face and said hands up," Whitney said. The gangsters took $50 from Whitney and marched him along as they stole $21 from the Fairway Market and $85 from the Runyan Drug Company. They attacked the door of the Lewis Department Store with a sledgehammer. The noise spooked one gangster: "Let's get out of here, it will have the whole town up." His partner said: "To hell with the town."

The bandits drove their own car, and the purloined Buick, to the department store and began loading them with clothing. Then they forced Whitney and Dunning into a back seat, jammed in with all the loot. About twenty miles out of town, the gangsters let their captives go. "You fellows go and keep going," one gangster said. At the first farmhouse the men came upon, the farmer had no phone. He had drained the water from the engine block of his car to keep it from freezing. "So it took a while to get to a phone," Whitney said.

Karpis drove the stolen Buick back to St. Paul. But as much as he loved to speed down dark roads at night, the gang had taken big risks and returned with little. These early Barker-Karpis jobs amounted to a "long string of small deals," Karpis later admitted. This Cambridge heist was just the kind of bush-league job they'd been pulling in the Ozarks, sledgehammer tactics and all.

The Barker gang's next home stood on Robert Street, the main road through West St. Paul. It belonged to the Hannegraf family, who owned three houses in a row: two occupied by family and one for rent to strangers.

It was winter, 1932, when the Barker gang moved in. The yard would have been drifted over in sparkling snow, the windows frosty. Ma was accustomed to a gentler climate, but winter lost its bite after Fred gave her a purloined fur coat.

In West St. Paul, the Barkers called themselves the "Andersons." They seemed a touch exotic, speaking in gentle Okie drawls. They got along well with the neighbors. The two "brothers," Fred and Ray, seemed quite different. "Ray" was Karpis, going by his middle name. He was quiet and reserved and talked softly, with the hint of a lisp. His eyes had a cold, spooky look. Ray was an avid reader of newspapers and detective magazines. Fred was Ray's opposite: energetic, cheerful, and friendly. He was even smaller than Ray, maybe the size of a jockey, and had three gold teeth up front. He wore his hair cut savagely short on the sides, long and greasy on top. Fred never read anything and rarely sat still. Except that they were both skinny, they didn't look much like brothers.

Ray was smarter than any of Ma's sons. Ma admired him, craved his company, and maybe (who knows the heart of another?) loved him like a son. In the fairy tale Ray invented for the landlord and neighbors, he and Fred were speakeasy musicians. This would account for the odd hours and the violin cases.

Ray and Fred, both in their twenties, called the shots in this criminal enterprise posing as a family. It was Ray and Fred who planned to augment the gang with other proven criminals. It was Ray and Fred who dreamed of big-time bank robberies. It was Ray and Fred, skinny fellows, pipsqueak tough guys, who stood at the cliffs of infamy and decided to dive off.

The old man, "George Anderson," dressed like a gentleman: bowler hat, suit, vest, watch fob, and chain. He had distinguished salt-and-pepper hair and a mustache. Some days he got into his liquor too early and began shouting at Kate or the boys. By all other measures the family seemed swell: they spent freely, dressed fashionably, and drove shiny new cars.

As in many families, there was internal tension. Fred called Dunlop "the old bastard," and Ray called him a "worthless drunk" and an "ingrate." Ma Barker had always lived amid quarreling men, and that wasn't going to change just because they'd moved north. In fact it was never going to change, and Ma would be shot dead during the ultimate form of male argument.

But in that winter of 1932, Ma was living a swell life. She didn't need a dreary job, nor would her menfolk allow her to work. She loved to listen to the radio, hillbilly music mostly, and was most fond of *Amos 'n' Andy*. She had brought a little bulldog with her from the Ozarks, and now she walked it along the icy streets and chatted with neighbors. She delighted when people fussed over her fried chicken with Ozark biscuits and gravy. She spent hours with her lifelong companion, the jigsaw puzzle.

But she never put it together, Ma Barker.

The real-life Ma was hardly the cigar-chomping, bank-robbing maniac she became in the national imagination. That fiction was created by the FBI. "She ruled like a queen. Her word was law," Melvin Purvis wrote, "She could handle a machine gun as well as the next man." J. Edgar Hoover wrote that Ma was "the most vicious, dangerous and resourceful criminal brain of the last decade," an "animal mother of the she-wolf type" and a "veritable beast of prey."

That was propaganda, meant to justify her killing by federal agents. The FBI hardly knew who Ma Barker was. In March 1934, an FBI memo informed Hoover about "a woman referred to as 'mother,' who evidently goes around with the Barker boys." Ten months later, in January 1935, she was dead.

Nearing 60 when she moved to Minnesota, Ma was a plump, square-built, homely rube. Karpis described her as "superstitious, gullible and cantankerous." She was so short she needed a booster seat to keep her head above the car dashboard. She gave herself home permanents, so her surroundings reeked of noxious chemicals. Ma Barker was extraordinary only in that she raised four criminal sons. Her spectacular death brought her notoriety, but in life she was known only to family and friends.

Ma's restless boys were always moving, stashing her in apartments, leaving her lonesome for weeks at a time. Ma was a complainer, a gossip, and a troublemaker, so few people enjoyed her company. For much of her life, she had endured dirt-floor poverty. But her youngest, the vicious mama's boy Fred, had raised her status. Thanks to his nighttime activities, she wore beautiful clothing now. The icebox was crammed with good food. This house in West St. Paul had coal heat, running water, a warm bathroom, and electric lighting. Her menfolk chauffeured her in a fancy new Buick. She saw the latest movies, played bingo whenever she pleased, and had wads of cash for shopping. Never again would her feet scrape the dirt floor of a tarpaper shack.

Ma was reborn in a frostbitten heaven.

The Hannegrafs, their landlords, owned a speakeasy, the Drovers Tavern. It was so named because of the stockyards down the hill in South St. Paul. The Drovers' clientele were the hardworking, bloodstained men from the Swift and the Armour slaughterhouses.

Although the movement to repeal Prohibition was gaining, selling alcohol was illegal in 1932. The Hannegrafs bought booze from bootleggers who produced or imported it. The bootleggers paid protection money that flowed through the system and spilled over into the police department and beyond.

After the Andersons had been living next door for a few weeks, Ray and Fred rode with Nick Hannegraf to look over the Drovers Tavern. The boys were thinking about buying a business. They said they might make Nick an offer for it. Spring was coming. They were beginning to like it here.

A few weeks after the "Anderson" family moved to Robert Street, two young women were released from the workhouse in Duluth. Their names were Margaret Perry (she was more commonly called "Indian Rose") and Sadie Carmacher. Rose was half-Indian and Sadie was Jewish. Rose hatched the plan; Sadie was a busted prostitute, just tagging along. Rose wanted to find her 10-year-old son, Bobby. Her husband, being in prison, could not help her. She was broke and needed quick cash.

From the Duluth train station, Rose called the Filben house in St. Paul and asked for Tom.

Tom Filben, too, was a soldier for the little empire and had plenty of cash. He owned slot machines all over St. Paul. Tom, a churchgoing Catholic, had volunteered to look after Bobby while Rose served time in Duluth.

But now when Rose called, Jim Filben answered. His brother Tom wasn't home.

Rose begged Jim for fifty bucks. Jim said he didn't know her and certainly wasn't going to wire money to a stranger.

So Rose called the Hollyhocks in St. Paul.

She had known Jack Peifer, host of the Hollyhocks, for a long time. Jack's years of hustling had paid off. His nightclub was the classiest gambling, drinking, and whoring spot in St. Paul. Jack had a safe full of cash, and sure, he said, he would wire Rose fifty bucks.

With that money, Sadie and Rose took the train to St. Paul and registered at the swank Ryan Hotel.

Rose and Sadie began drinking and telling stories at the Green Lantern. Rose had been living in North Dakota with her husband when some hick sheriff dug up a bag in their backyard. It was filled with money and marked DENVER MINT.

The Denver Mint robbery had been one of the most sensational crimes of the 1920s. The robbers snagged $200,000, or about $4 million in today's money. The federal government, rankled by the notion that its mints were vulnerable, came hard after the perpetrators but never solved the crime. They traced much of the loot to St. Paul, where it subsequently disappeared. About $500 of it turned up unexplained in the bank account of Jack Peifer's lawyer.

Rose, out of jail after a six-month stint, told friends she was fixing to marry a local fellow, whom she secretly despised, because he could provide for her and Bobby. However, she had schemed up an alternative. She and Sadie knew an underworld secret. They knew who the Cambridge robbers were.

And the Cambridge town fathers were offering a reward for their capture.

In return for a reasonable amount of underworld money, Rose and Sadie said, they would keep their mouths shut. They told this to Tom Filben, Mr. Slot Machine. They told this to Jack Peifer, grand host of the Hollyhocks. Those two guys knew every crook in town. One of them, Rose figured, could scare up some hush money.

But Filben and Peifer weren't buying.

So Rose and Sadie, hoping to collect a reward, walked into the St. Paul police station and revealed that Fred Barker and Alvin Karpis were the Cambridge ringleaders.

The St. Paul cops called Cambridge and talked to the mayor and to patrolman Frank Whitney. The cops invited the Cambridge men to St. Paul. They wanted the men to hear what Sadie and Rose had to say.

That never happened. Word of Sadie and Rose's visit leaked out of the St. Paul police station. Unfortunately for them, the two women were unaware of the deep connections between certain St. Paul cops and gangsters.

On the evening of their visit to the police, Rose and Sadie were called for at the Ryan Hotel. They drove away in the company of Jack Peifer. The next morning, on March 7, 1932, two passing motorists noticed a flaming automobile near Balsam Lake, Wisconsin. While attempting to quench the flames, they discovered bodies in the rear seat. Police found that the two women inside had been shot dead. Their faces had been disfigured with nitric acid. The car, a new Buick, had been set afire.

The women were identified from their fingerprints as Margaret "Indian Rose" Perry and Sadie Carmacher.

Back in St. Paul, chief Tom Brown took charge of the investigation, even though the murders had been committed in Wisconsin. Brown told the press that "no one from St. Paul had anything to do with the murders." But if he didn't know who the culprits were, how could he know they weren't from St. Paul?

Neither of the logical suspects, Tom Filben and Jack Peifer, had a thing to fear from a Tom Brown investigation. Filben and the chief were "very good friends," Filben later acknowledged. They owned adjacent lakefront vacation property on the Canadian border and "often went north to their lake cottages together."

As for Jack Peifer, he and the chief had friendly chats on the night-club's lawn. Peifer provided bags of cash to keep the chief, his cops, and political cronies happy. Ultimately, the FBI and state police would conclude that Peifer had Sadie and Rose murdered to silence them. Filben admitted that whoever killed them had done so to shield St. Paul's criminal protection racket. The little empire would crumble if gangsters like Barker and Karpis were no longer safe in the city.

A day after the gruesome murders, Alvin Karpis was shocked when he fetched the morning paper. Its front page featured a picture of a burnt car with the corpses of Sadie and Rose inside. Karpis had let a friend borrow that car. It was the Buick he'd stolen in Cambridge.

11

"MA, PUT YOUR GLASSES ON"

It didn't take long for the murders of Rose and Sadie to fade from the headlines. Chief Tom Brown's investigation was going nowhere. Meanwhile the nation was transfixed by the Lindbergh kidnapping. The obsession was only deeper in Minnesota, the great aviator's home state.

It was a cold spring in Minnesota. Cars were temperamental, and Nick Hannegraf's wouldn't start until the weather warmed. So when he closed the Drovers Tavern at 1:00 AM, he walked the muddy, icy streets toward home.

Nick nestled into bed and paged through *True Detective Mysteries* magazine. Each month, it highlighted some notorious criminal for whom there was a reward. This month, April 1932, the magazine featured two desperados.

They looked familiar.

The tiny kid with the gold teeth.

The young fellow with the creepy eyes.

Nick gawked at the pictures. These boys were wanted for bank robbery. Wanted for murder of a Missouri sheriff.

Nick leaped out of bed and tapped on his mother's bedroom door.

"Two in the morning! Nicky, what is it?"

Nick flicked on the lamp. He sat on the edge of his mother's bed and pushed a magazine into the light.

"Ma, put your glasses on."

His mother, shaking off sleep, looked over the faces in the magazine. One was labeled Fred Barker; the other, Alvin Karpis. For sure, they were the tenants next door. The total reward for their capture was $1,200. That was a year's pay at the stockyards.

The Hannegraf houses in West St. Paul were not in the jurisdiction of the St. Paul police. Nick called at the West St. Paul police station, but he'd been sampling his own moonshine and didn't make a great impression. Undaunted by the rejection, he borrowed a relative's Essex and drove to downtown St. Paul.

Officer Roy Coffee was working the night desk. "Nick Hannegraf came to him about 2:30 or 3 A.M. and reported that Barker and Karpis were living in one of their houses. It being outside the city and also rather a startling report, Coffee wanted to talk to his superior before taking action."

So Nick Hannegraf sat on a bench at the police station, clutching pictures torn from the magazine. He asked passing cops to check out his tenants. No luck. He sat on that bench, or paced the hallways, for five hours.

Enter detective Fred Raasch, who had known Nick for years.

"I arrived at work about five minutes to 8," Raasch later testified. "I met Nick Hannegraf. He showed me a clipping from a detective magazine containing pictures of Barker and Karpis." Raasch "went into Inspector Crumley's office and told Crumley I would go" check out Nick's tenants.

"Crumley said 'All right, just a minute.'"

Brown revived the practice of the "show-up" in December 1930. Four times a day, patrolmen, witnesses, and detectives (wearing masks to avoid identification) viewed prisoners in the city's jail. This image from the *St. Paul Dispatch* carries an inset of John Tierney, police Bertillion expert, conferring with detective Charles Bragg, who is masked.

Instead of dealing with Nick Hannegraf's inquiry, Raasch and Crumley trudged upstairs to the morning "show-up" to look over the riff-raff hauled in by the night shift.

Upstairs at the show-up, Crumley told Chief Brown "there was a sucker downstairs" who had clipped pictures of Barker and Karpis out of a magazine.

"Brown said 'Jesus Christ,' and walked for his office," Raasch later testified.

"After the show up," Raasch said, "I returned to the detective room and sat down and started to talk to Nick. He stated that he had been at the station since 2:30 that morning making the complaint . . . Crumley returned from upstairs and went into his office. He was followed in a few minutes by Chief Brown. Chief Brown came out of Crumley's office, and Nick went to him and said, 'This fellow will go with me.'"

"Chief Brown called me aside and said, 'Duck up on the third floor,'" Raasch testified later. "So I turned and left." Raasch hid in the third-floor Bureau of Records room, where he passed the time reading newspapers.

Hours went by. Nick's mother called the police station. Hurry Nick, she said, the "Andersons" were packing their cars. At eleven in the morning, Raasch said, "Inspector Crumley came in and told me to go over to the West Side. I went downstairs, met Nick again, and as he had his car, he drove over alone. Officer Brennan and myself went over in a police car.

"When we arrived at the house, the doors were open, a radio was playing and the house appeared as if it had been hurriedly vacated," Raasch continued. Coffee was burning in a pot on the stove.

"Some hats were still there and in searching the place we found some shotgun shells and a box of .380 automatic shells," Raasch reported.

Clothing left hanging in the closets had the labels deliberately cut off. The cops also found a fur coat left by the Barker lady. But the Barkers and their little bulldog were gone.

Later testimony by Gladys Sawyer indicated that the warning was sent to the Barker gang through Harry Sawyer. After relaying Chief Brown's warning to the Barkers, Sawyer popped in at the police station. At about that time, Fred Raasch returned from the failed raid.

"I went in and reported to Inspector Crumley," Raasch said. "He told me to go up and report to Chief Brown direct. In the anteroom to Chief Brown's office, I met Harry Sawyer coming out of the Chief's private office."

"Sawyer said: 'Hey you were over on the west side, weren't you?'"

"I answered yes."

"Sawyer said, 'You found everything all right, didn't you?'"

"I said we found everyone gone, there was nobody there."

Raasch showed Harry Sawyer the shotgun shells he had taken in the Barker raid.

Sawyer asked if he could have those shells. He wanted to show them to Fred Barker and Alvin Karpis. "I want to show these guys that that thing was all right," Sawyer told Raasch. "I want to show them their own stuff." Even though the shotgun shells could have been evidence against sheriff-killers, Raasch handed them over. Then he "reported to Chief Brown and told him that we had found the place vacant."

Harry walked back to the Green Lantern with the shotgun shells in his pocket. They were proof of his power over the St. Paul police. They would bond the Barker gang to him and show that he was the power in St. Paul, not his rival Jack Peifer.

Meanwhile, Karpis didn't know how his gang had come to the attention of police. So he focused suspicion on Arthur Dunlop, who'd been drinking and gabbing with the Hannegraf men.

12

DUNLOP'S LAST RIDE

It's not known exactly what happened to the Barker-Karpis gang in the days immediately following their exit from Robert Street. Apparently, Fred Barker was in Kansas that week, and that left Karpis to deal with Ma.

Karpis later wrote: "Dunlop admitted he had talked too much. He excused himself by saying he was drunk. I called him a rotten son of a bitch. I told Ma she'd be better off without him. I said I'd ship him off to Chicago and give him some money."

Ma fumbled and foot-dragged. She and Dunlop had been together a long time. But soon Arthur Dunlop went for a ride.

Drinking and blabbing with Nick Hannegraf would be his last transgression. Whoever drove off with Dunlop probably got him drunk and told him comforting lies. Nobody wants to endure a three-hour ride with a squirming man who knows he's about to be executed.

Dunlop's killers drove him to a lake in Wisconsin, up in bog country, where cranberries and wild rice are harvested. At that time of year it would have been muddy and newly green. Dunlop's executioners had apparently planned to shoot the old man on the shoreline, weight his body, and toss it into the lake. They had not counted on squishy lakeshore and spring mud.

Their car bogged down a hundred feet from the lake. So they pushed the old man out and shot him in the head with a .45 automatic. They shot him again and again.

The local sheriff soon got a call that a boy had spotted a body on the lakeshore. The sheriff followed tire tracks to a trail of blood. At the lake he found a bloody woman's glove and then the corpse.

Minnesota's state police would report that "one person had taken [Dunlop] by each arm and dragged him through brush. They found it so boggy that it was not possible for them to get the body out into the lake, and they dropped it where it was partially submerged on the shore." The body was "naked," and near it was a "bottle of alcohol."

Attendants at a gas station near the lake, shown photos of Karpis and Fred, said those men had stopped in for gas that morning. The Minnesota state police soon quit pursuing the murder, saying it was Wisconsin's problem. FBI public-enemies hunter Earl Connelley concluded years later that it was "very probable" that Karpis killed Dunlop.

Karpis would claim in his autobiography that he had nothing to do with the murder, saying Jack Peifer had his thugs kill Dunlop as a favor to the Barker gang. But Karpis's autobiography is filled with evasions, especially in regard to murder. For one example, Karpis lied in his autobiography when he denied culpability for shooting Sheriff Kelly in West Plains. There were multiple eyewitnesses who said he fired the first shot. Karpis had a motive for this evasion: even when he was an old man, freed from Alcatraz, he might have been prosecuted for any number of killings.

Whoever pulled the trigger, Arthur Dunlop, like Rose Perry and Sadie Carmacher, was murdered to protect the Barker-Karpis gang. But Dunlop's murder demonstrated that the gang was blind to politics. This blindness would someday contribute mightily to their destruction. The gang consisted largely of grade-school dropouts who got most of their information via the speakeasy grapevine. Fred and Karpis could not imagine that the murder of a helpless old man would cause a political earthquake that would rattle their world.

Politician William Mahoney used the Dunlop murder, and the escape of Barker and Karpis, as fuel for his campaign for mayor. Mahoney told voters the Barker-Karpis gang had escaped because they'd been "mysteriously tipped off" by police.

Mahoney's opponent was the incumbent, Gerhard Bundlie, a lawyer who claimed he knew nothing of corruption and had never seen a slot machine.

Mahoney scoffed. Bundlie "doesn't know what's going on in the city," he charged. "The real world, and its problems, are alien to his gentle mind." Mahoney said Mayor Bundlie could learn who really ran the city by visiting "the racketeer king" (Leon Gleckman) at his headquarters at the Hotel St. Paul.

Mahoney, a sworn enemy of chief Tom Brown, was a progressive and a founder of the state's farmer-labor party. He had come to prominence as editor of the Minnesota *Union Advocate*. In the 1930s, the progressives were riding a wave of anger emanating from dispossessed farmers and unemployed workers. The farmer-labor party would soon sweep to its biggest victories ever, winning the 1932 elections for governor and for mayor of both of the Twin Cities.

As the election approached, Mrs. W. O. Clayton, a candidate for St. Paul's city council, charged that the underworld enjoyed the "passive if not active support of the police department."

Clayton, a leader in the Women's Christian Temperance Union, challenged the city to address its gambling habits. She cited the case of a boy whose family had saved $1,000 for a homestead. The boy had stolen the family's life savings and poured it into slot machines. She appealed to Leon Gleckman to make the family whole.

Gleckman shrugged.

Clayton complained that Gleckman "openly boasts of his control of the council" and that mayor Bundlie "knows nothing."

She handed the police commissioner a list of twenty establishments that ran slot machines but got no response. Gambling and booze are harming our youth, she lamented, and parents of kids who'd lost money in slot machines were constantly calling her.

Gleckman said he was waiting for reformers to make "specific charges."

Chief Brown said his department "stands on the record made."

At a conference on Prohibition, the Rev. Melvin Eidson of Temple Baptist Church complained that police were protecting bootleggers, gamblers, and prostitutes. He said he had witnessed police leaving speakeasies without making arrests. He had seen prostitutes waving merrily as cops left houses of ill repute.

Brown and county attorney Michael Kinkead sent cops with subpoenas looking for the Reverend Eidson. Kinkead thundered that any citizens making such outrageous charges would find themselves standing before his grand jury.

Brown agreed. "Let him tell his story to the grand jury," he said.

After the pastor testified before the jury, Brown called him a publicity hunter and said he'd failed to give the jury "one single fact." Eidson's motive, Brown said, was "filling his church on Sunday, when the collection plates are passed around."

Kinkead said one address Eidson had given the jury had already been raided by police. Another address was the "home of a respectable colored family."

The Reverend Eidson problem quietly faded away.

But the escape of the Barker gang became such sensational newspaper copy that reformers gained public support. The underworld began to panic. Bootleggers ginned up a smear campaign against Mahoney. St. Paul godfather Jack Peifer "squeezed everybody for money" to fund Mahoney's opponents, Alvin Karpis acknowledged, "as the Dunlop murder strengthened the reformers' case."

Chief Tom Brown defended his department, noting that the Barker escape took place across the Mississippi in West St. Paul, "where we have no jurisdiction."

Publicly, Brown dismissed Barker and Karpis as "so-called killers," although there's no doubt he knew they were wanted for the murder of a sheriff.

A week after Tom Brown tipped off the Barker gang, William Mahoney was elected mayor of St. Paul. Brown would soon be demoted to detective. The Barker gang, spooked, abandoned St. Paul.

It was a victory for clean government.

Or so it seemed.

13

WHITE BEAR LAKE

Mayor Mahoney elevated Tom Dahill from the ranks of the St. Paul police. Dahill was described in an FBI memo as "honest, dumb and afraid of his own soul."

Chief Dahill wanted to fire Brown, but civil service protections were too strong, and Brown had influential friends. So he assigned Brown to

In a photo retouched by the *Pioneer Press* for printing in 1927, Tom Dahill, then a "junior captain of detectives," smashes slot machines.

the auto theft squad. But Big Tom did not need to be chief to work his game. He had dark money to pass around and remained the feared boss of an entrenched clique of St. Paul cops.

Brown kept an office on the third floor of the luxurious Hotel St. Paul, a few steps from the office of his "little friend" Leon Gleckman. To both offices came a parade of bootleggers, gamblers, con men, saloonkeepers, pimps, and hustlers. The cheerful Mr. Dunn was a frequent visitor. By day, he was W. W. Dunn, sales manager of the Hamm's brewery. By night, he was Billy Dunn, St. Paul's preeminent bagman, shuttling illicit cash all over town.

There was plenty of cash to carry. Breweries could legally produce only a punchless, half-percent beer and soft drinks. So the two big St. Paul brewers, Hamm's and its crosstown rival Schmidt's, were in a tough spot. Half the nation's breweries had already closed. Many of the survivors found sneaky ways to produce real beer, and naturally, this required payoffs.

But by the summer of 1932, the end of Prohibition was in sight, with the Democrats promising to open the taps if elected in fall. Their presidential candidate, Franklin Delano Roosevelt, vowed to sweep away federal dry laws and let the states decide. In St. Paul, Adolph Bremer, brewer of Schmidt's beer, donated $350,000, a fabulous sum at the time, to FDR's campaign. Adolph and his brother Otto knew FDR personally, and there were rumors of an ambassadorship if Roosevelt won.

So it was imperative that the brewers, who had hung on for so long, not give up now. Both Hamm's and Schmidt's played along with bootleggers and gangsters. In St. Paul, the system worked through Harry Sawyer and Jack Peifer.

"I didn't ever deal directly with the police and politicians who made St. Paul so congenial," Karpis wrote. "I didn't have to. I was friendly with the middlemen . . . Harry Sawyer and Jack Peifer."

Even demoted, Tom Brown was valuable to Peifer and Sawyer. The old guard of St. Paul cops and politicians, enriched by the Brown clique's dark money, frustrated Chief Dahill's reform moves. When the new administration replaced Brown operative James Crumley as the head of a special crime squad, it settled on William McMullen. But McMullen, too, was a member of Brown's clique.

Dahill kept trying. He had his men make a couple of arrests at the Green Lantern, which had long been sacred ground in the criminals'

Holy City. The shock waves of Dahill's arrests spread far beyond the Green Lantern.

Prohibition had made criminals out of people who today would be considered good citizens. Off-track horse-race betting, casinos, poker rooms, and the liquor and beer trade were criminal enterprises during the 1920s and early '30s. So the legitimate world became hopelessly tangled with the underworld. In St. Paul, the Jacob Schmidt Brewery secretly owned a piece of the Green Lantern, and its illegal beer was sold there. The Green Lantern's Harry Sawyer was also in charge of bootlegging Schmidt's beer all over St. Paul.

So when Chief Dahill's men violated the sanctity of the Green Lantern, another power broker made a countermove. Schmidt's uberboss Adolph Bremer bailed out the crooks Dahill had arrested at the Green Lantern. One of these was "Lapland Willie" Weaver, who had run with the Barker boys since their Tulsa days. He, too, was a thief and murderer enjoying protection in St. Paul.

Bailing out Weaver was another move Adolph would bitterly regret.

Even after these criminals were bailed out, Harry Sawyer was steamed. Arresting guys in his tavern? That violated the unwritten rules. He walked to the police station and looked up detective Fred Raasch. He said: Hey, Fred, what the hell's going on here?

Raasch shrugged.

For a few weeks that summer, St. Paul was free of the Barker-Karpis gang Following the murder of Arthur Dunlop, they split for Kansas City. There, Fred and Karpis reconnected with Larry DeVol, whom they'd first met in prison. He was older and far more experienced, "a great teacher" in Karpis's opinion and a lunatic in the opinion of many others.

Fred, Karpis, and DeVol hooked up with Francis Keating and Tommy Holden, two prison escapees who were legendary bank robbers. Along with Bernard Phillips, a cop gone bad, this gang robbed the bank at Fort Scott, Kansas, of $47,000. This kind of robbery would become a signature of both the era and the Barker gang, complete with a Tommy-gun shoot-out and women hostages clinging to the getaway car's running boards.

On July 8, Keating and Holden were arrested by the Kansas City FBI while playing golf. The Barker-Karpis gang scrambled back to their safe haven in Minnesota and this time rented a cottage at White Bear Lake, a resort outside St. Paul. There were good reasons to vacation at White

Bear Lake. Karpis was an avid fisherman; the climate was breezy and cool; they'd get warnings from Harry Sawyer if the cops cooked up a raid. Also, the gang needed to fence $200,000 in stolen securities, and Sawyer and Peifer were reliable underworld bankers.

The gang settled in but grew restless. Karpis and Fred were addicted to the excitement of planning and pulling off robberies. In late July, they rounded up a gang and zipped down to Concordia, Kansas, to rob a bank, then drove back to White Bear Lake. Concordia was a big score, and Karpis and Fred had finally proved they could lead, and not just go along on, a big-time daylight bank robbery. They cased the banks, planned getaway routes, recruited gunmen and lookouts, and then strode boldly in, pulled out their Tommy guns, and demanded cash. They made their getaways in fast, expensive cars that could outrun any police junker. They engaged in shootouts with citizens and cops. They tossed nails from their speeding getaway car to flatten the tires of their pursuers. Eventually, they armored their cars and equipped them with smoke-screens. Every success made them bolder.

At the lake cottage, the Barkers told neighbors that they were Mrs. Hunter and her boys, Fred and Ray. Shy, quiet Ray went fishing all day. Fred drove into St. Paul often, to shack up with a woman he'd recently met. She was a blond-haired, cross-eyed Texan named Paula Harmon.

Paula bore the marks of a damaged childhood. She was still in her teens when she became a prostitute, hanging around the pool halls and taxi stands of Beaumont and Port Arthur. She also brewed bootleg beer with friends in Galveston. First married at age 15 or 16, she put herself in the hands of one bad man after another. Perhaps the worst was her second husband, Charles Harmon. She was arrested as helpmate when he and his gang robbed and torched an Iowa shipping company. After Charles Harmon was killed in a Wisconsin bank robbery, Paula cashed his insurance policy and went on a spending spree. Her next boyfriend helped her party away the cash and then dumped her. A horrible car crash in Lake Charles, Louisiana, cracked her skull, crushed her nose and cheekbones, and knocked out her front teeth. She used the insurance settlement to get plastic surgery and then wasted the balance with yet another boyfriend, who left her when the cash ran out.

Paula's reconstructive surgery was not successful, and when she met Fred her face had a strange, flattened appearance. People alternatively described her as "rather attractive" or "funny looking." Her upper dentures often popped out when she talked. She was a tiny woman, weighing less than one hundred pounds, and addicted to both liquor and golf. Karpis dismissed her as a "rotten choice" for Fred and a "drunk."

At the lakes, the Barker gang seemed to their neighbors to be a well-behaved family who were "expensively dressed and drove expensive autos."

The state police agency, known as the Bureau of Criminal Apprehension, followed up on the Barkers' escape from West St. Paul. Agent Earl Rodgers wrote to his boss in May that he had interviewed the Hannegrafs. Nick, badly frightened, had been receiving threatening letters. Nick had burned the letters.

"Nick had been drinking during the day," the agent noted. Soon Nick would be beyond gangster retribution, dying after complications from surgery.

The state cops also noted that a certain Mrs. Hannegraf had tried to cash a $500 bond that had been stolen from an Iowa bank. The cashier called the police. Mrs. Hannegraf said she had found the bond under the rug at the house she'd rented to the Barkers. Agents noted dryly that during their investigation, they had turned over all the rugs.

By August, the state police, following citizens' tips, had determined that the Barkers were at White Bear Lake. The agents began preparing a raid. Suddenly, the Barkers packed up. Neighbors said they began rushing around after being visited by two strangers in a car.

There was an illness in the family and they had to leave, Ma explained to the landlord. Once again, the Barkers displayed astonishing powers of intuition and rolled out of town just in time.

14

A ROBBERY AND THREE MURDERS

It was "like working in a greenhouse," Alvin Karpis recalled.

He was describing the robbery of the Third Northwestern Bank in Minneapolis. The bank stood at a busy triangular intersection. It had plate-glass windows. A streetcar stop was planted outside the bank's front doors. Karpis said that in planning this broad-daylight robbery, the gang was seeking "excitement" and a "challenge."

They got it.

The robbery was planned in typical Karpis detail. The gang stole a Lincoln specifically for the job. They parked a "switch car" in Como Park. Its lakes, golf course, zoo, and amusement park would be depopulated in this, the frozen time of year. The robbery was timed for 2:40 on a Friday afternoon to maximize the take and to coincide with the shift change of the Minneapolis police.

The Barker gang was strengthened by the addition of Larry DeVol and Freddie's brother Doc. Both had been greased out of prison via bribery. All fall the gang had been robbing midwestern banks, but this Minneapolis job was going to be big league.

Doc was a dimwit and a drunk, but he was family and could be counted on. He was the same height as his younger brother, five foot three, but huskier. He answered to the nickname "Shorty." A stone-eyed killer and compulsive gambler, Doc was the only Barker gangster who generally abjured female company. Said one woman who knew him, "Doc has been in the pen so much he does not associate with women."

Larry DeVol, whose specialty was dynamiting safes, was described on his wanted poster as "a paranoid maniac who suffers from persecutory illusions and is apt to kill associates suddenly without warning." A cold, grasping psychopath, Karpis found impulse killers like the Barker brothers and DeVol useful. They possessed a lunatic courage that Karpis lacked.

On the afternoon of December 16, 1932, the Barker-Karpis gang surrounded the Third Northwestern Bank. An armored car pulled away, its guards having unwittingly delivered a $19,000 bonus to the gang. The streets and sidewalks were icy and crowded with Christmas shoppers. A poster in the bank window urged patrons to sign up for next year's Christmas club.

Larry DeVol stood outside the bank, boldly brandishing his Tommy gun. A boy and a girl wandered over from the streetcar stop to admire his weapon.

"Beat it," growled DeVol.

The rest of the gang, exquisitely dressed in overcoats, business suits, and hats, walked into the bank lobby, passed the big Christmas tree, and pulled out pistols and Tommy guns.

"Stick 'em up!"

The gang looked like bankers themselves, with the exception of Fred Barker, who had fitted himself with an absurd set of dime-store false teeth. This disguise was meant to hide the gold teeth featured in his wanted poster.

Sixteen people were inside the bank, ten of them employees. Teller Paul Hesselroth was ordered to open the grill on the main vault. He stepped on the silent alarm, then claimed he didn't know how to open the grill.

"You son of a bitch, open it!" ordered Fred Barker, and then knocked him cold with a pistol. With resistance in the form of Hesselroth lying stunned on the floor, Fred persuaded another teller to open the vault. The gang rushed in and stuffed loot into canvas bags.

DeVol walked in to help keep the tellers and customers covered. Outside the bank, a streetcar pulled up and idled. Passengers could see into the bank, where customers and tellers stood, hands raised. A mailman on board clanged the bell and shouted, "Bank robbery!" Riders pressed their faces to the streetcar windows, gawking.

A few blocks away, Minneapolis patrolmen Ira Evans and Leo Gorski were driving their squad car to the police station. They were a few minutes overdue for the shift change when they got a call about a disturbance at a bank. This was a Friday, the first of the "payless paydays" meant to balance the city budget. The cops had every right to shirk the call. They decided to answer it anyway. By the time they pulled up in front of the bank, a crowd had gathered on the sidewalk.

Leo Gorski, shotgun in hand, jumped out of the squad car.

Suddenly, the bank's windows were shattered by machine gun fire. Gorski was knocked to the icy sidewalk. His partner Evans slumped dead in the driver's seat of his squad car.

After a moment of eerie silence, Larry DeVol walked out of the bank and finished off the cops with another burst of machine gun fire.

People on the street screamed, ran, and ducked for cover. DeVol slipped on the icy sidewalk, his Tommy gun spraying bullets everywhere. One punctured a front tire on the getaway car.

The gang hopped into that crippled Lincoln, and Verne Miller drove toward St. Paul. Miller was a sheriff and war hero gone bad, a bank robber and murderer freelancing with the Barkers for this one job.

Getaways to St. Paul were so common that Minneapolis cops routinely blocked the Mississippi River bridges after a bank robbery. But there is one sector where the Twin Cities join directly on land, and Karpis picked that route for the getaway. Miller drove like a madman, sixty miles an hour down icy industrial streets, swerving, skidding, throwing sparks, losing first a front tire, then a wheel, dragging the smoking Lincoln into Como Park.

Miller pulled up next to the switch car, which was parked at the zoo, between the monkey house and the buffalo pen, and transferred the loot in canvas bags from the battered Lincoln to a Chevy.

It had started as a good day for Oscar Erickson. He was feeling optimistic, he told his wife. Erickson was 29, a laid-off cook whose last job had been in a railroad dining car. He'd been married two years. Lately he'd been shoveling snow for rich people to earn a few coins. He was excited at the prospect of making money by selling Christmas wreaths door to door. He and his pal Arthur Zachman had loaded wreaths into the back of the car.

The two young men knocked on doors in Como, a prosperous "streetcar suburb." But Como had been "worked" by wreath salesmen, so they drove Erickson's jalopy across the park toward another neighborhood.

Near the monkey house, they saw two cars surrounded by five or six men. These were well-dressed young fellows. One of their cars was obviously broken down. Erickson stopped to offer help.

A little guy with gold teeth barked at them. Keep going, he said.

Erickson took a moment to size these guys up.

It was the last conscious moment of his life.

The guy with the gold teeth whipped out a pistol and fired. The first shot hit Oscar Erickson in the head. He slumped on the wheel. His foot jammed on the clutch, and his jalopy rolled past the buffalo pen. Arthur Zachman pulled his bleeding friend into the passenger seat, wriggled behind the wheel, and drove for the Como firehouse.

At the hospital, as Erickson's wife waited in an anteroom, doctors examined a bullet wound in Erickson's head. He was in a coma, bleeding from his mouth and nose. "Patient was restless, thrashing around in his bed," noted the attending physician. "Pupils did not react to light."

Before dawn, Oscar Erickson was dead.

The murderous bank robbery took place on a Friday. That evening, the gang retreated to Larry DeVol's apartment to divide the loot. Then they split up. Nobody wanted to stay with DeVol. He was dangerous under any circumstances and now a wanted cop killer. As Karpis knew, "A cop murderer is the number one target for policemen."

By Sunday, Larry DeVol was lonesome, liquored up on gin and orange juice in his apartment on St. Paul's Grand Avenue. Psychiatrists would later diagnose DeVol as suffering from "dementia praecox." His symptoms were said to be "unbalanced judgment, delusions of persecution, hallucinations, apathy and indifference alternating with violent excitement."

None of which was helped by heavy drinking.

St. Paul's Grand Avenue was, and still is, a quality part of town, the commercial street that serves the city's most elegant homes. The avenue is lined with hundreds of apartment units, and in one of these Associated Press wire operator Haskett Burton was playing bridge with friends.

He'd been up all Saturday night, telegraphing news about Friday's bank robbery and triple murder.

Now it was approaching midday Sunday. For the last hour or so, somebody had been causing a commotion in the building. Burton and his bridge partners played on until trouble came pounding on the door. Burton opened it as far as the security chain allowed.

The knocker wore only underwear and a fur coat. He looked "all doped up."

He told Burton, "I'm looking for a friend."

"There's no friend of yours here, get going," said Burton.

"Oh yeah," said DeVol.

But he kept making a ruckus in the hall, so Burton went out to confront him. DeVol whipped out a pistol. Burton retreated to his apartment and dialed the cops. St. Paul patrolmen George Hammegren and Harley Kast showed up a few minutes later and found DeVol careening drunk around his own apartment.

Hammegren said, "Why you're nothing but a drugstore cowboy. Little boys like you shouldn't be playing with guns."

DeVol aimed a pistol at Hammegren. The cop grabbed at it. "Hey," Hammegren shouted to his partner, "this guy has a rod and I can't get it away from him." The two cops wrestled the crazed DeVol, and Hammegren knocked him on the head with his service revolver. The cops handcuffed their prisoner, locked him in their squad car, then searched his apartment. They found cash wrapped in bundles, marked: THIRD NORTHWESTERN BANK, MINNEAPOLIS.

At the police station, Minneapolis and St. Paul cops interrogated DeVol. In the beginning, still drunk, he admitted he was the shooter who had sent two policemen to their graves. He said Oscar Erickson's killing was the work of Fred Barker. "He lost his topper and just started to fire," DeVol said. "I tried to stop him but it was too late."

Then DeVol was interrogated by St. Paul detective Charles Tierney, who proved shrewd and effective, asking simple, open-ended questions rapid fire. Tierney started by asking what DeVol knew about the Minneapolis bank robbery.

"I would rather not answer that at this time."

But he admitted that the .45 and .38 found in the apartment were his, and so was a watch and a big diamond ring. He acknowledged that the bonds and securities in his apartment had been stolen from the Minneapolis bank.

"What do you know about those?"

"They were left there," DeVol answered, meaning in his apartment.

"By whom?"

"I won't say, only I was supposed to burn them up."

"Tell me what is in the trunk of the car."

"Oh I had some shirts and hats."

"And in the rumble seat?"

"Oh I had two rifles."

"What were you doing in the apartment [the afternoon of the bank robbery]?"

"Oh, I transacted some business."

"What business?"

"Money."

"Where was this money and securities from?"

"I couldn't say positively."

"Have you any idea?"

"Yes, I found out since then. It was supposed to come from a bank in Minneapolis."

"Do you know which bank?"

"The Northwestern."

"Who did you find out from?"

"They charged me with it."

After a while, Tierney summed it up. "You know that your statement has been evasive," he told DeVol, "and the facts . . . are mythical and imaginary. You know that."

"Yes, but they are not."

DeVol would plead guilty to the murder of policemen Evans and Gorski and be sentenced to life in prison. But no prison could hold DeVol.

By Christmas of 1932, the body count was mounting. Sheriff Roy Kelly. Ma Barker's companion Arthur Dunlop. The female desperadoes Perry and Carmacher. The unemployed and unlucky Oscar Erickson. Minneapolis cops Evans and Gorski.

The wives of Erickson and those Minneapolis cops faced a bleak Christmas. Mrs. Gorski had heard the news while at the beauty parlor listening to the radio. Mrs. Evans was at work at a factory three blocks from the bank when her supervisor called her into his office. Gorski also left behind a young son.

All the while, there were at least two cops in the St. Paul hierarchy who could have solved all these crimes. Tom Brown not only knew who carried out those robberies and murders; he knew where they could be found.

But it was not just the Barker gang Brown could have fingered. The FBI would discover that Brown and his buddy, slots king Tom Filben, had entertained bank robber and cop killer Verne Miller at their lakefront resort. The FBI was also told that Brown had gone hunting and fishing with Harvey Bailey, a fellow West Virginian and one of the most infamous bank robbers of the era.

So even the murder of brother officers in a neighboring city failed to move either Brown or Crumley to their duty. Nor were they apparently bothered by the murder of Erickson, an innocent civilian who lived in their jurisdiction. In that week before Christmas, did Brown and Crumley wrestle with their demons? Weren't they among the hundreds of cops who attended the funerals of patrolmen Evans and Gorski? Did they reflect on the tormented Christmas that their criminal friends had brought upon the families of Evans, Gorski, and Erickson?

15

THE LAST NEW YEAR'S EVE

Among St. Paul's first European residents was Pierre "Pig's Eye" Parrant, a French trader who discovered that whiskey sold better than beaver pelts. He peddled his hooch to the soldiers at Fort Snelling, which had been erected on the bluffs in 1819 to guard the confluence of the Mississippi and Minnesota rivers.

But Fort Snelling's commanding officer, not amused by his soldiers' drinking, enforced a prohibition of his own. Banned from the fort, Pig's Eye Parrant moved downriver and hacked out a clearing that would eventually grow to become St. Paul. His whiskey hut was the mother of St. Paul speakeasies. A century later, that niche was occupied by Harry Sawyer's Green Lantern.

Harry's tavern became a legend during Prohibition, but nothing could protect it from greater political realities. By New Year's Eve, 1932, the Democrats and Franklin Roosevelt were about to take power, and Prohibition was to officially end the next day. Bootleggers' cash had been the lifeblood of Harry's system, and Tom Brown's too. They needed another source of income, and so cultivated that gang of homicidal hillbillies known as the Barkers. The gang had been pulling off midwestern bank robberies all that fall, strengthened by the addition of Fred's brother Doc and an old pal from the Central Park gang, Volney "Curly" Davis. Fred Barker had paid bribes to free both Doc and Curly from Oklahoma's prison system.

It may have unsettled Harry that the Barker gang had murdered two cops and a civilian in that Minneapolis holdup. But they were generating tremendous amounts of cash and securities. Harry laundered that cash, not just for himself, but to keep the payoff system going.

New Year's Eve 1932 would be the last at the Green Lantern as a speakeasy, and everybody knew it. When Prohibition formally ended, taverns sprung up all over St. Paul. The competition was destined to destroy Harry's business, so this New Year's celebration had an edge to it.

"There was probably never as complete a gathering of criminals in one room," Karpis wrote, remembering that last great Green Lantern party. "If the cops had arrested everyone there, there would have been no crime spree of 1932–33."

For the big evening, Fred was accompanied by Paula Harmon. Doc Barker, never much of a ladies' man, just got drunk. Karpis, chronically sick to his stomach, celebrated only by eating a couple of the tavern's boiled eggs. He marveled at the connections he was making at the Green Lantern. He called it "a rogue's gallery or hall of fame, depending on your point of view."

At midnight, Harry Sawyer bellowed. He bellowed so loudly, so often that bartender Pat Reilly had nicknamed him "the sea lion." Karpis too disdained Harry for "always spouting off."

And now to greet 1933, Harry bellowed for silence, so the crowd could hear Ben Pollack's orchestra, via the radio, play "Auld Lang Syne."

In the first hours of the new year, the Barker gang discussed their plan to leave town. They would decamp to Reno, to escape the Minnesota winter and blow the loot from the Third Northwestern robbery. The Barker brothers would lose "quite a bit of money" at Reno's Bank

Gladys Sawyer, July 16, 1936.

Club casino, while their women "drank heavily" and enjoyed "the wild excitement of night life."

The gang would bring Ma to Nevada; Fred insisted on that. Fred, a stone-eyed killer, was kind to his mother. Old Kate Barker suffered from heart palpitations, panic attacks, fits of loneliness, and worry. Her baby boy couldn't leave her behind in cold St. Paul.

Harry Sawyer, too, had big plans for the new year. His wife Gladys had become captivated by a 5-year-old girl with curly blond hair. Her name was Francine. The child had been, for all practical purposes, orphaned when her father was sentenced to a long term at Stillwater Prison. Gladys, with no children of her own, had bottled up her motherly instincts and now was letting them flow.

Harry was the son of a respected Nebraska family of Orthodox Jews who shunned him as his criminal reputation grew. Perhaps that rejection accounts for his desire to start his own family and retreat to his farm. He and Gladys began keeping chickens and hogs. New Year's resolution: they would raise Francine out in the healthy countryside.

16

TARGET: WILLIAM HAMM

If the Green Lantern was the rough, dirty downtown speakeasy for low-lifes, the Hollyhocks was a bucolic casino. It had a dress code. Its waiters were Japanese men who'd learned their trade in railroad dining cars. Nightclub maestro Jack Peifer preferred Japanese employees and felt they could be depended upon to shut the hell up.

The Hollyhocks was set behind a broad lawn in a spectacular location on the banks of the Mississippi. It was landscaped with its namesake plant. All its neighbors were mansions. It was renowned for its steak, its frog legs, its slot machines, and its mixed clientele of socialites and gangsters. Any rube could take the lurching streetcar to the Green Lantern, but to get to the Hollyhocks you needed a car, and in 1930, most Americans didn't own one.

A police car would do. Big Tom Brown was seen often at the Hollyhocks, conferring with Jack Peifer. According to several witnesses, Brown and Peifer liked to chat while standing out on the lawn. A suspicious soul might wonder whether they chose the outdoors to prevent their conversations from being overheard. And a suspicious soul may have been right, because the Hollyhocks was soon to be wiretapped by the FBI.

As the chief and Peifer stood talking, they had a leafy view across the Father of Waters to Minneapolis and its lone skyscraper, rising twenty-eight glorious floors. It was early summer of 1933, and during at least one of these talks, they were planning a kidnapping.

Jack Peifer had been too restless to follow the path his family had set out for him, as a turkey farmer in a small Minnesota town. An eighth grade dropout, he was drafted in 1918 and served as an army engineer in Massachusetts and France. After his discharge, he drifted to the Twin Cities and became a "barker for a carnival and Hawaiian show."

A heavyset young man with dark hair and big eyes, he became a hotel bellhop, the perfect job for a hustler. According to an FBI background report, he pimped by day, hijacked liquor by night, and soon bought a speakeasy. He ran a gambling den at a Minneapolis hotel for a while, then moved across the river to St. Paul and opened a "chop suey" joint, employing Japanese help for that supposedly authentic touch. He learned how to launder money, and the FBI suspected him of cleaning the cash from a Kansas City kidnapping. He also handled cash that Machine Gun Kelly had liberated from midwestern banks.

His personal life was as erratic as his criminal career. A Chicago woman the FBI identified only as "Mrs. Ogilvie" met Peifer in 1928. She had a friend who was being married in Indiana and "casually asked Peifer to go along." Mrs. Ogilvie was single at the time of this particular adventure. During the journey, "Peifer suddenly suggested that they likewise be married and for some reason Mrs. Ogilvie cannot explain she agreed."

So it was a double wedding. The newlywed Peifers returned to St. Paul, where Jack bought the Senator hotel and moved his bride in. Guests were beside the point at this hotel, a front for prostitution, gambling, booze, and money laundering. Mrs. Ogilvie told the FBI that "during this time she went out very seldom, met but a few friends of Peifer's, that Peifer was quite illiterate and spent a great deal of time at home."

She also told the FBI that "Peifer drank quite heavily." One night with his wife he was driving drunk and "narrowly escaped colliding with a telephone pole." Jack became "greatly inflamed" at this cosmic injustice, a temper tantrum that frightened his wife so much she fled to Chicago and filed for divorce.

By the late 1920s, Jack had become a rising power in the criminal under-world. He "made his bones," an informant told the FBI, by confronting Leon Gleckman in a car, sticking a gun in his ribs, and telling Gleckman to quit hijacking his booze.

That worked for a while, but by the time Jack became the host of the Hollyhocks, Gleckman had taken control of St. Paul's shadowy politics and was squeezing protection money out of Peifer's casino. By late 1931, however, Gleckman was fending off federal charges of income tax eva-sion, as well as threats from St. Paul's gangsters. Tom Brown assigned city cops as his bodyguards, but even so, in the months following his own kidnapping, Gleckman's daughter was abducted, then released when the scheme went wrong. "My children can't sleep . . ." Gleckman complained. "My wife is constantly under tension. I am planning to sell my house and move to another to rid them of the associations and thoughts of the kidnapping. In the meantime I'll move to a hotel."

As Gleckman's power faded, Harry Sawyer and Jack Peifer filled the vacuum. Harry became chief fence and crime coordinator. Jack took over the rackets, especially slots and prostitutes. Both men laun-dered money. No longer able to count on bootlegging for cash flow, both men coveted the cash and securities brought in by the Barker-Karpis gang. If counted in today's currency, the bank and payroll robberies the gang executed from their St. Paul base sometimes exceeded $1 million per job.

Early in the planning stages of the Hamm kidnapping, Peifer called in Alvin Karpis. Outwardly, Karpis seemed like anything but a thug. Many who met him remarked on his dignity and manners. He seemed more like an accountant than a gangster. He was a skinny young man who wore rimless octagon eyeglasses. He wasn't put together quite right, with those creepy eyes, stooped shoulders, and a shuffling gait. Peifer had once hired Karpis to oversee the transportation of a booze shipment and was impressed with the way it had been handled.

But now, Peifer had something much grander in mind.

"Ray," Peifer said, "how would you boys like to work on a kidnapping?"

They talked in Peifer's office for "a couple of hours," Karpis later re-called. They discussed the Lindbergh kidnapping. After that sensation ended with the discovery of the baby's corpse, Congress had passed a law giving the FBI authority over kidnapping cases.

Karpis told Peifer he feared the FBI because they couldn't be bought off. Peifer waved that away. He told Karpis he could "put the fix in with a couple of cops."

Peifer had a genius for accomplishing multiple objectives with one ruthless act. His objective now was to gain ascendancy over his rival Harry Sawyer, to set himself up to survive the demise of Prohibition, and to repay a favor he owed to Al Capone.

Even with Scarface in prison, the Chicago criminal organization he had built, known as "the Outfit," was going strong under the ruthless Frank Nitti.

A couple of Capone's boys are going to join you on this snatch, Peifer told Karpis. The ransom, Peifer said, would be $100,000. By today's standards, that might be as much as $2 million.

Karpis fretted over every job. He was the tough one to persuade. Fred Barker, all guts and no brains, would follow Karpis's lead. Doc Barker, a daylight drinker, would follow his little brother. So it was Karpis who counted.

Karpis suspected complex motives behind this proposed kidnapping. With Prohibition over and his brewery thriving, Hamm would have been able to pay much more in ransom. According to a front-page item in the *St. Paul Daily News,* the estate left by Hamm's father in 1932 was worth more than $4 million.

"I never understood the [Hamm] kidnapping," Karpis wrote later, "because less money was demanded than the victim was able to pay, and for that reason I felt there was some reason besides the ransom. I thought it political and had something to do with the [St. Paul] police and Ramsey County officials."

He was right. But with the perspective of history, it seems that Karpis, who considered himself shrewd, was used by Jack Peifer. The Barker-Karpis gang was composed of young men. For Doc and Fred Barker, the bulk of their crimes were committed in their twenties. Karpis was 26 the year of the Hamm kidnapping. His gang had been spectacularly successful at bribing their way out of trouble. Blinded by greed, his youth, his limited education and sophistication, Karpis could not see that Peifer was leading them all down the dark alley of destruction.

When Karpis gave a tentative okay to the snatch job, Peifer sent a message to a man in Chicago, Fred Goetz, better known by his nom de guerre, Shotgun George Ziegler.

Ziegler had been a prime actor at the St. Valentine's Day Massacre, one of two shooters who'd posed as cops. By the early 1930s, Ziegler was among the Chicago gangland elite, receiving a monthly cut of the profits of the Capone syndicate. The Outfit used Ziegler as an executioner in its war against rival mobs and once sent him to New York to pull off a murder.

Shotgun George was a gentleman-monster. One of the most sophisticated gangsters of his era, as Fred Goetz he'd been an engineering student and football player at the University of Illinois. He trained as an army flight officer in the Great War. But one summer, while a lifeguard at a Chicago beach, he'd been arrested for the rape of a young girl. A friend said that Ziegler was perplexed by this crime and wondered what kind of demons had possessed him. His mother posted a $5,000 bond, but Fred Goetz never showed up in court. He began living as Shotgun George.

He was soon hired as a Capone bootlegger and graduated to executioner. He lived in disparate worlds, attending lectures, concerts, and plays with his middle-class friends, then descending into the shadows to shoot gangsters who'd displeased the Outfit. Between executions, he took a correspondence course in landscape architecture. His dream was to develop a resort on lakefront land he owned in Wisconsin. His neighbors in the Chicago suburbs believed him to be a cultured professional.

Because of his role in the St. Valentine's Day Massacre, Ziegler had a huge reputation in the underworld. It's a testament to Jack Peifer's power that he could summon such a figure to make the all-day drive from Chicago to the Hollyhocks.

It wasn't hard to persuade Ziegler to join the plot against Hamm. He needed the money. Shotgun George was chronically broke, spending money recklessly or losing it in stock schemes. After consulting with Peifer, he returned to Chicago on a recruiting mission.

Every big shot needs an errand boy, and in Ziegler's case the role was played by Byron Bolton. People often took them for brothers. Bolton, "very sickly and delicate," suffered from tuberculosis he'd contracted in the navy. A golf pro turned criminal, Bolton had been recruited by Ziegler to be a lookout at the St. Valentine's Day Massacre. As the victims arrived, Bolton panicked, sent the shoot signal too early, and caused the ambush to miss its prime target, Bugs Moran.

Bolton also left behind a medicine bottle that had been fingerprinted by the cops. The Chicago Outfit held both these lapses against Bolton. They weren't pleased with Ziegler lately, either. He'd been boasting of his St. Valentine's role. So in Chicago in the summer of 1933, Ziegler and Bolton both needed underworld redemption.

Ziegler asked Bolton whether he wanted to work on "snatching a brewer." He promised it would be "easy money." Bolton's assignment was to drive to the suburb of Bensenville, Illinois, and find a hideout appropriate for stashing a kidnap victim.

In early June, responding to a second summons from Peifer, Ziegler and Bolton drove a new Chevy coupe to the Hollyhocks. They arrived at nine in the morning. Peifer's headwaiter, a Hiroshima native nicknamed Sam Tanaka, served them breakfast and then woke up his boss. Peifer, Ziegler, and Bolton then drove out to lake country.

In those days, the Father of Waters was more like the Father of Sewers, and no homes had air conditioning. People with money escaped St. Paul for the summer. It was only a few miles to the lakes by auto or trolley. The lakes were surrounded by summer cottages, boathouses and fishing docks, pavilions, taverns, and dance halls.

Jack Peifer directed Bolton to drive to Bald Eagle Lake. They parked at a summer cottage that had a name engraved on its screen porch: IDLEWILD. There Peifer introduced Capone's boys to Karpis, the Barker brothers, and an older gentleman nicknamed Fitz. They drank beer and discussed the kidnapping. Fitz argued for $250,000 ransom. Shotgun George agreed. Peifer said that was unrealistic and they should settle on $100,000. Peifer reassured them that the St. Paul police would actively help them.

Once Peifer drove back to St. Paul, his six recruits sat around at Idlewild, ordered notable quantities of ice and beer, and worked out the kidnapping details. They got daily visits from various young women, who drove out from their apartments in St. Paul. A jealous Ma encouraged kitchen table gossip among the women, then carried those tales back to the men. She seemed to enjoy instigating squabbles and took no guff from younger, prettier females. "She wanted to be the only woman who counted with her boys," Alvin Karpis noted. Every other woman was dismissed as a "hussy."

So Fred stashed her in the Commodore Hotel, up on Summit Hill, where the rich people lived, overlooking downtown St. Paul. Fred was always hiring someone to be Ma's keeper, and this time it was Helen Fergusen, girlfriend of Earl Christman, who'd been shot dead while freelancing on a Barker bank robbery. Fred gave Fergusen money and told her to keep Ma amused. Trapped with Ma, Fergusen "gradually developed a dislike for her company."

At the lake, the Barker gangsters impressed their neighbors as friendly and generous most of the time. They tipped big. At the resort bars, these young hoodlums and their girlfriends would often buy a round for everyone in sight. On hot days, Jack Peifer would drive out and go swimming with the Barkers. But sometimes the men of Idlewild seemed withdrawn, even hostile, staying indoors behind drawn shades. Most of them were pale and rarely seen at the lake. The exceptions were Karpis, who often went fishing, and Shotgun George, who sometimes sunbathed nude. The gang enjoyed the services of Henry Maihori, a Japanese cook hired by Peifer.

The gang made regular trips to St. Paul, including stops at the Hollyhocks. On June 12, according to gangster-turned-informer Byron Bolton, Shotgun George and Peifer left Idlewild cottage to meet with a big, beer-bellied plainclothes cop, the former police chief Tom Brown. Peifer introduced Brown and Shotgun George. This is the man who will run interference with the St. Paul police, Peifer said. Detective Brown gave Ziegler helpful kidnapping hints. He also warned him to keep phone conversations short, as calls could be traced in two minutes.

Even Ziegler, Al Capone's hit man, was astonished at the depth of corruption in St. Paul. He told his buddy Byron Bolton that "in return for the money this officer was to keep us advised on the developments at the police department" during the kidnapping. Ziegler was "greatly pleased about making connections with this police officer," Bolton said, "saying there was very little chance of a slip up. It was like getting money from home."

Meanwhile, a curious scenario played out for Bobby Perry, son of the ill-fated Rose Perry. The boy had been left in the care of slots kingpin Tom Filben, who admitted that Rose Perry had been killed to protect St. Paul's rackets.

Filben, a rosary-praying Irish Catholic, lived at a luxury address on the St. Croix River. He ran the Federal Acceptance Corporation, a car loan scam that specialized in hiding gangster transactions. His downtown St. Paul store, the Patrick Novelty Company, sold radios, supposedly, but was a front for his slot machine business. Never known to have committed a violent act, Filben nevertheless had dark dealings all over town. Jack Peifer made a big show of running the Hollyhocks casino, but it was Tom Filben who held the real estate title.

Filben apparently had some remnant of a Catholic conscience. He was now responsible for a 10-year-old boy whom he'd helped make an orphan. Filben was "a very good friend" of Shotgun George Ziegler and his wife Irene. He had helped Ziegler get into the slots business, and now Shotgun George owned machines here and there in Chicago. So one evening after Irene and Shotgun George dined at the Hollyhocks, they agreed to take custody of little Bobby.

The Zieglers' motives are unknown. Perhaps they liked the boy and truly wanted to adopt him. Perhaps Shotgun George thought Bobby would be good camouflage and make them look like a "normal" family. The Barkers used their mother in just this way. Whatever the motive, Ziegler and Irene took the boy to Chicago. They told Bobby that Ziegler was an architect, but the boy noticed that his new "dad" spent most of his time golfing.

Filben, lying to the FBI, later claimed he knew nothing of Ziegler's background; otherwise he would not have let him keep the boy.

In any event, Bobby proved too much trouble for the flighty Zieglers. They had grandiose plans, as gangsters so often do. They began dreaming of a new and luxurious life in Florida, and Bobby, clunking along in Chicago's parochial schools, didn't fit in.

The Zieglers phoned Filben and said come for the boy at once. Tom flew down and returned to St. Paul with Bobby, leaving the boy with Jack Peifer and his paramour Violet Nordquist at the Hollyhocks. Thus, Bobby was in the care of the man last seen with his mother before she was shot, disfigured, and incinerated.

Bobby's stay in a room above the nightclub lasted three weeks, and then Lillian Shultz took him home. She was the sister of Tom Filben's wife. When the FBI began investigating Bobby's case, Lillian Schultz admitted that Tom Filben was paying the boy's expenses. The payments, perhaps, helped Filben calm his conscience.

The early summer of 1933 was a pleasant time for the Barker gang. In early May, they had taken a joyride to Louisville to bet on the Kentucky Derby. Now they were partying in their lakeside bungalow and planning the most audacious crime of their careers. This gang, street toughs and petty burglars not long before, was about to enter the big leagues, targeting rich men for ransom.

Alvin Karpis lived to steal, to drive fast, and to fish. That summer, he would have been out on the lake in a rented boat, reeling in a musky, a lit Chesterfield bobbing in his lips. Fred Barker and his crazy, smash-faced girlfriend Paula would be drinking Hamm's beer and playing cards at a Formica kitchen table. Doc Barker would be lying in a whiskey stupor on the front porch. Ma Barker might visit from her luxurious exile in a St. Paul hotel. Did she miss Arthur Dunlop? Had Karpis ever told the truth about the fate of her old man?

As the planning progressed, the core of the gang was regularly visited by the outsiders, Bolton and Ziegler and Charles "Fitz" Fitzgerald. In contrast to his boyish co-conspirators, Fitz was a dignified 57 years old, with "fishy blue eyes." The FBI description of Fitzgerald reads: "5-11, 175, complexion ruddy, nearly red, hair very gray about the edges, close trimmed gray mustache, very noticeable heavy bull neck."

He must have been a wily crook indeed, to have survived so long. The Barker gang held him in awe. Here was a man who'd played by the criminal's code but largely escaped punishment, living wild and free. Fitzgerald was a genuine freelance criminal, but had deep connections with the Outfit and was a longtime friend of Chicago arch-criminal Gus Winkler. The FBI would attribute more than fifty bank robberies to Fitz. Karpis recruited him for the Hamm abduction because "he looked like a gentleman and could stop Hamm on the street without suspicion."

Fitz, the designated "greeter," began hanging around Swede Hollow, the St. Paul neighborhood dominated by the Hamm mansion and brewery. Karpis tagged along to observe the habits of the victim. "I was sick of him long before the kidnapping," Karpis said.

17

"YOU ARE MR. HAMM, AREN'T YOU?"

On June 14, 1933, William Hamm Jr. walked home for lunch, as was his habit. He was a slender, handsome man, six foot two, his hair parted in the middle, in the style of the times. Divorced and 38 years old, Hamm was a prince of St. Paul. He was planning to marry Marie Hersey Carroll, the daughter of a prominent St. Paul family. She had been a childhood friend of the greatest writer St. Paul ever produced, F. Scott Fitzgerald.

"I think of you as my oldest real friend, and my first true love," Fitzgerald once wrote Marie.

William Hamm had inherited the brewery from his father and grand-father. A huge, steaming hunk of Teutonic architecture, the brewery was bubbling around the clock now, making beer legally. The Hamms' business had survived the double hit of Prohibition and Depression, which had killed most of America's 1,345 breweries. Of all those, only thirty-one were operational enough to resume beer making immediately after Prohibition. Hamm, and many other brewers, had survived by doing business with bootleggers and speakeasies. It was either that or go broke. America had only so much appetite for root beer and ginger ale.

One informant told the FBI that "Mr. Hamm had engaged a mob, paying them $6,000 to $8,000 a year through [St. Paul fence] 'Frisco Dutch' to keep another mob off his brewery during the Prohibition days . . . after the legalizing of beer, Hamm cut loose from the gang protection."

By snubbing the underworld, Hamm unwittingly set himself up for a kidnapping.

Uphill William Hamm walked, toward the family estate, perched on a rise overlooking the brewery and Swede Hollow. His late father had con-structed a fantasy world behind a stone garden, alive with peacocks and captive deer.

At one street corner, Hamm noticed two fellows leaning against a building. He wondered about them "casually," then dismissed them as loafers. The next day, on his walk home for lunch, he saw the same two men. One of them was an older, well-dressed gentleman. The other was a skinny young man. Had Hamm been a reader of detective magazines, he might have recognized that young man as Doc Barker.

The older gentleman stepped in front of Hamm and offered his hand. "You are Mr. Hamm, aren't you?"

The gentleman tightened his grip and grabbed Hamm's elbow.

Hamm said, "What is it you want?"

Doc Barker grabbed Hamm's other elbow.

They threw him to the curb.

A black Hudson sedan drove up, driven by a kid wearing a chauffeur's cap. Underneath that was another face from the detective mags: Alvin Karpis. Fitz shoved Hamm down on the back floor of the Hudson. Doc Barker roughed a white pillowcase over his head.

Off they drove. Nobody said much for a while. Thirty miles out of St. Paul, the Hudson stopped in the countryside. Lying on the floor, sweating under his hood, Hamm heard other voices. The hood was lifted so he could see the ransom notes he was ordered to sign. Holding those notes was Shotgun George Ziegler, the gang's secretary of communications.

Hamm didn't bother to read the notes but scribbled his name in a shaky hand. Meanwhile, his kidnappers chatted about musky fishing.

Hamm, listening to the voices, sensed that the dramatis personae had changed. Indeed, Fitz, Shotgun George, and Fred Barker were to return to St. Paul to work the ransom angle. The FBI would later determine that for the drive to Chicago, Karpis and Doc Barker were joined by Byron Bolton in the Hudson. Bolton was the only man who knew their exact destination.

If they were true to their natures, Karpis would have been nervous and quiet, the tall and tubercular Bolton would have been coughing, and Doc Barker would have stunk of gin and been compulsively chewing gum. Somewhere in Wisconsin, the Hudson pulled over in a field. Asking whether he was hot in that hood, Bolton fitted Hamm with goggles that had been taped over to create blinders. During the exchange of hood for blinders, Hamm saw that the car was being refueled from gas cans.

They drove off again. Hamm somehow glimpsed a road sign that gave the mileage to Janesville and Beloit—Wisconsin towns on the road to Chicago.

After a long time, they turned off the pavement onto a gravel road, stones ticking off the undercarriage. Blinders in place, Hamm was hustled into a house and upstairs into a bedroom. He was ordered to sit facing the wall. Always working behind his back, or so he later said, his captors brought him a magazine, a pork sandwich, and a glass of milk.

Goggled, Bill Hamm slept in a bed with a headboard inscription: MOTHER.

In the morning Bolton removed Hamm's goggles and, staying behind his back, asked him to choose who would gather the ransom for him. Hamm threw out a few names, one of them a bootlegger he'd gone to the university with. When the gang rejected those ideas, he named brewery sales manager W. W. "Billy" Dunn.

Dunn was a born wheeler-dealer, a smiling Irish cherub whose family had known the Hamms for many years. He operated a pool hall in the basement of the Hamm building downtown. Billiards wasn't the only game played there: There was a back room for dice games and a horse-racing wire.

Among Dunn's many roles was serving as the Hamm family's emissary to the underworld. A few steps from Dunn's pool hall stood the Hotel St. Paul, the *grande dame* of Twin Cities hostelries, then and now. The hotel's third floor was lined with offices rented specifically to receive bribes and graft. One of those offices was rented by Big Tom Brown. For years,

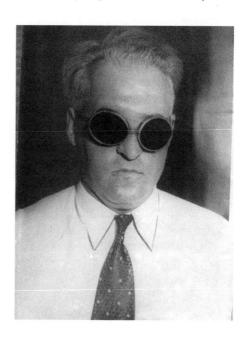

A St. Paul cop demonstrates the kind of goggles used to blindfold Hamm.

Dunn had shuttled money and messages among the crooked police chief, bootlegger Leon Gleckman, Harry Sawyer at the Green Lantern, and Jack Peifer at the Hollyhocks. Ma Barker, obsessed with jigsaw puzzles, would have loved Billy Dunn. He was the piece that completed St. Paul's puzzle. He had deep connections with the elite and lived among them up on Summit Hill. He also knew the players in the dirty lowdown game.

Hamm spent hours facing a bedroom wall, on which was drawn a crayon sketch of three flamingos. His guard, usually Bolton, sat in a rocking chair behind him. The room was "quite warm," so his kidnappers purchased him a Westinghouse fan.

He was being held in the home of Edward Barthelmy. A candidate to be his town's postmaster, Barthelmy involved himself in this most serious of crimes and set himself up for a long prison sentence in return for $500.

Barthelmy cooked meals for the captive and for the gang and otherwise sat drinking beer in the kitchen with Karpis and Doc. Those two would sometimes relieve Bolton of guard duty. Karpis tried to convince Hamm that he was merely a hanger-on, paid $100 a day for guard duty. Bolton later recalled Karpis and Doc "having a good laugh" over that.

Downstairs, Barthelmy, Doc, and Karpis avidly followed accounts of the kidnapping in the Chicago papers. They were surprised to read about a shootout in Kansas City where two cops and two federal agents had been killed. They did not know yet that Verne Miller, their driver during the Minneapolis bank robbery, was the primary shooter and that this event would become known as the Kansas City Massacre. They could not foresee that the FBI would be energized by the killing of their agents. All the gang worried about was that somehow, the crime would be pinned on them.

Upstairs, Bolton and Hamm were talking.

"I used to ask them every night how the stock market was doing," Hamm recalled. "I asked about American Can once. They gave me the closing quotation."

His captors brought him an occasional bottle of beer, with the label washed off. It was a Chicago beer, and they didn't want Hamm to know where he was.

Once, delivering a beer, Bolton said, "I see advertisements for your booze, Mr. Hamm, is it really special?"

No, the brewer admitted. "It's all pretty much the same under the label."

But that friendly tone changed late Friday night when Shotgun George mounted the stairs. He scolded Bolton for removing the victim's goggles. Then he stood behind Hamm and asked, "What kind of man is Mr. Dunn?"

"Why?"

"The first thing he did was go to the police. The police set a trap for our man but we were too smart for them."

Shotgun George Ziegler was the ransom negotiator, shuttling between St. Paul and Chicago by car, train, and airplane. His original demand was that a Hamm's brewery truck deliver the ransom. But St. Paul detective Charles Tierney came up with a plan to ambush the kidnappers. Tierney—a small, wiry man—planned to hide under canvas in the truck bed. He would pop up, Tommy gun blazing, when the kidnappers tried to collect the ransom.

It might have worked, except that Brown leaked that plan to the kidnappers.

As Bolton later confessed to the FBI, "an officer of the St. Paul [police] Department had tipped [Ziegler] off about the trap." Ziegler told Bolton this tip alone proved that "the payoff [to Brown] was worth it."

Working with Brown's leaked information, the gang revised its ransom strategy. They demanded that delivery be made in a vehicle that had its sides and trunk removed so that no machine-gunning cops could lurk there.

18

"TOO BAD FOR HAMM AND YOU"

On the day of the kidnapping, Billy Dunn was working in his office at the brewery. It was a stifling afternoon. The brewery stank of boiling grain.

The phone rang.

"Is this W. W. Dunn?"

"Yes sir."

"I want to talk to you and I don't want you to say anything until I get through."

"All right."

"We have Mr. Hamm. We want you to get $100,000 in 20s, 10s and 5s, and goddamn you, see that they are not marked."

"Hey! Hey, what the hell is going on here?"

"Now shut up and listen to what I have to say. You are to get a Hamm's truck, and take off the sides so that we can see there is nobody concealed in the truck and follow the instructions you will receive over the phone at 5 o'clock tomorrow night. And if you tell a soul about this, it will be too bad for Hamm and you."

Click.

It wasn't unusual for William Hamm to take the afternoon off, so Dunn checked his haunts, including the golf course. No Bill Hamm here. No Bill Hamm there. Dunn and his office mates debated how to deliver the news to Hamm's ailing mother. Then Billy Dunn called the Lowry Hotel downtown, reserved a room, and arranged to meet the police chief there.

By June of 1933, Tom Dahill had succeeded Tom Brown as police chief. He had been appointed by new mayor William Mahoney but "did not have a free hand" to clean up the police department.

After meeting Dunn at the hotel, Dahill put two men in charge of the Hamm kidnapping case: his friend, detective Charles Tierney, and the former chief, Big Tom Brown. Dahill knew that Brown had underworld connections but considered them an asset in police work, he would later say.

After his meeting with the police chief on Thursday night, June 15, Billy Dunn went home. The FBI, alerted by Chief Dahill, tapped Dunn's phones at home and at the brewery. It is not clear how much Dunn knew, at this point, about who had set up the kidnapping. His immediate interest would have been to get his boss and benefactor home alive. Take away his connection to the Hamm family, and Billy Dunn might be selling apples at the streetcar junction.

At 1:30 AM, Dunn's phone rang. It was that same voice.

"You must realize by now," the voice said, "that the call was not a joke as you thought. Now Dunn, remember what I said about the police department. Or we'll get you and Hamm too."

Click.

Meanwhile, at the parking garage at the Lowry Hotel, Yellow Cab driver Leo Allison was approached by a well-dressed stranger, whom he'd describe as "6-foot, 180 lbs, 48–50 years, exceedingly sunburned, big nose, snappy talker, straw hat, dark brown suit, big ears."

In other words, Barker gangster Charles Fitzgerald.

Fitz told the cabbie, "I don't want a ride."

He handed Allison a note to deliver.

"How much?" Fitz asked.

"A dollar," said the cabbie.

Fitz paid two dollars.

Allison drove up Summit Hill, its new-fangled electric street lamps shedding light on the broad lawns. He shined his spotlight on number 1916 Summit Avenue.

Two men leaped out of the shadows. One pinned him to the taxi. The other snatched the note out of his hands. These were plainclothes cops. Three hundred pounds of cop muscle pinned Allison against the taxi. Big Tom Brown twisted his arm, demanding answers. Detective Charles Tierney ran up the stairs to show the note to Dunn. In part it said:

YOU KNOW YOUR BOYFRIEND IS OUT OF CIRCULATION. YOU ARE TO PAY OFF $100,000 IN THE MANNER EXPLAINED TO YOU THIS AFTERNOON.

On the next afternoon, Dunn waited in his brewery office for the kidnapper's call. The five o'clock deadline passed, but the phone never rang. A few hours after the deadline, Dunn drove his Chevy to town and went about his business, seeing this guy and that guy, moving and shaking, fixing and pitching. Then he went home, ate dinner, and sat around in his living room with detectives Tierney and Brown.

They were like Laurel and Hardy, these cops. Brown the blubbery lunk and Tierney the wiry little guy, five foot three on a tall day.

Brown would work as a double agent during the entire Hamm kidnapping and its investigation. He had been consulting with Chief Dahill, the FBI, and Tierney and then relaying the gist of those conversations to the kidnappers. He had lobbied the chief to minimize the FBI's role. He fed the newspapers stories he wanted to see in print. Now after sundown on Friday, Brown sat in Billy Dunn's lavishly furnished living room, knowing far more about the kidnapping than he would ever reveal. His bagman Billy Dunn knew that major crimes in St. Paul usually had Brown's approval. That left Detective Tierney, alone in his ignorance, staring out the big windows at broad, leafy, lamp-lit Summit Avenue.

The three of them would be in that living room when the kidnappers' next message came, via drugstore delivery boy.

In the age before the chains took over the business, drugstores were neighborhood gathering places. They often had a soda fountain, along with booths and lunch counters. People stopped in for coffee, ice cream sundaes, and gossip. During Prohibition, drugstores had also been covert liquor stores, dispensing doctor-prescribed booze in pint bottles.

Around eleven o'clock on the night of the Hamm kidnapping, six customers loitered in the Rosedale Pharmacy, three men and three women, all gathered around the pinball machine. In walked a blond-haired stranger. None of the pinball players recognized Shotgun George Ziegler, author of Al Capone's greatest hits.

He wore white pants, white shoes, a dark shirt, and a straw boater. He had a pronounced potbelly. He was of average height and perhaps 40 years old. He was quite sunburned. He seemed nervous. He ordered a pack of Camel cigarettes. He also asked for 25 cents-worth of sulfur ointment, which sent pharmacist Clarence Thomas to the back of the store.

Ziegler then wandered past the pinball players and toward the booths. He surreptitiously dropped an envelope in a booth and turned for the cash register. He paid for his ointment and walked toward the door. Pharmacist Thomas called to him: "Hey, mister, you forgot your cigarettes."

Shotgun George snatched the Camels off the counter and hurried away.

A few minutes later, the drugstore's phone rang. It was answered by Art Kleifgen, a delivery boy. The caller claimed to be W. W. Dunn.

Well, Dunn was a regular customer at the Rosedale Pharmacy, and to Kleifgen's ears this caller did not sound like Dunn.

I left a lighter in a booth at your store, the caller seemed to say. I wonder if you could bring it to me.

Young Kleifgen peered into the booth. He told the caller he didn't see any cigarette lighter.

This annoyed the caller. "I did not say a lighter, I said a letter."

Indeed, an envelope lay in the booth. Art Kleifgen delivered it to Dunn's home at 11:30 PM.

Detective Tierney snatched the typewritten note out of Dunn's hand. In part it said:

> YOU'RE SO GOD DAM SMART THAT YOU'LL WIND UP GETTING YOU BOTH KILLED. FURTHERMORE WE DEMAND THAT YOU PERSONALLY DELIVER THE MONEY SO THAT IF THERE IS ANY DOBLE CROSSING, WE WILL HAVE THE PLEASURE OF HITTING YOU IN THE HEAD.

The cops summoned druggist Clarence Thomas to the Dunn home. Tierney listened to his story, then dispatched both druggist and ransom note to Chief Dahill at the police station.

Sometime after that, Big Tom Brown left for the night. His wife and kids were fever sick at home, but he made a detour to the Green Lantern. There, at that Western Union for crooks, he left the Barker gang a message about how the kidnapping was going.

On Saturday morning, the Hamm kidnapping took an unexpected turn. A call came in from Mr. L. J. Sullwold, who helped run the Hamm realty business. A note had been left in his car, addressed to Dunn. Sullwold brought the note to the brewery.

Dunn read the note, which told him to drive home and await instructions.

At 9:00 AM, Dunn's home phone rang.

"I know this line is tapped. Don't try to stall. Go to Sullwold's house on Wall Street and you will receive your instructions."

Dunn drove to Wall Street in downtown St. Paul, and Sullwold said he'd been phoned with these instructions: Drive Highway 61 toward Duluth, go no more than 20 miles per hour, have all the money in a bag, wait for five flashes of our headlights, drop the ransom on the side of the road, keep going to Duluth, get a hotel room, Mr. Hamm will meet you.

Dunn, "dressed in a Palm Beach suit and straw hat," drove to the Hamm garage. A swarm of reporters and photographers surrounded it. Big Tom Brown opened the garage door and Dunn drove in.

In that garage was the ransom car, modified as the kidnappers had wanted it: doors off, trunk removed so it could not conceal any cops.

"I lighted a cigar, got into the car, and drove toward Duluth," Dunn later wrote. Outside the town of Wyoming, he was tailgated. Near Rush

City, he was tailed and passed four times by the same car. Finally, head-lights behind him flashed five times. He grabbed a rope attached to the suitcase and flung the ransom out.

"It seemed as though the minute I dropped it," he said, "there was a man there to grab it."

In Bensenville, at around 3:00 PM on Sunday, Ziegler entered the bed-room where Hamm was held captive and said, "I have good news for you. We can start tonight."

Hamm shaved. He changed into fresh clothes Byron Bolton had bought him. Homeowner Barthelmy was "busting around, anxious for us to go," Bolton said.

The gang strapped the goggles on Hamm again, hustled him to a car, and told him to sit low in the back seat. Bolton guarded Hamm on one side, Doc the other, and Karpis drove. They rode into the night, conversing amicably. They discussed President Roosevelt's policies and whether those would help end the hard times.

Crowds wait outside the gates of the Hamm mansion after William Hamm's return, hoping to see the drama inside.

At dawn, his captors abandoned William Hamm in a farm field. He lifted his goggles, walked to a farmhouse, and called St. Paul. His friends drove his touring car to the Minnesota river town of Taylors Falls to meet him.

Dressed for Palm Beach, Billy Dunn had driven an open car across the night prairie and arrived in Duluth feeling "very cold." He registered as instructed at the Hotel Duluth. "Imagine my disappointment when I got to Duluth and did not find Mr. Hamm there," Dunn wrote later.

Dunn plunged into a warm bath. While he was in the tub, someone pounded on the door. Dunn expected to open it and see Bill Hamm, but in burst detectives Brown and Tierney, firing questions at him.

It was a restless night for Billy Dunn, as the three of them waited in that hotel room for the kidnap victim to show up. Tierney and Brown slept sideways on the lone bed, and Dunn had to curl up on the floor. When the sun rose, still no William Hamm. Then Brown called the police station and learned the victim was already home.

After the kidnapping, left to right: Tom Brown, police chief Tom Dahill, Charles Tierney, Billy Dunn, and William Hamm Jr.

19

Hidden in Plain Sight

The day the Hamm ransom was paid, detective James Crumley phoned Myrtle Eaton "more or less to have some fun." Catching kidnappers was not, it seems, a Crumley priority.

Myrtle, hard-boiled at 31, was a habitué of the Green Lantern and was "known among hoodlums as a superb shoplifter." Her specialty was fur coats. She had taken the name Eaton from her husband Doc, a notorious bank robber. She and Doc Eaton were the parents of "two girls whose whereabouts were not revealed." When her husband went to prison, Myrtle found a sugar daddy, a married St. Paul saloonkeeper named Andy Rothstein. Although Rothstein paid the rent on her high-class apartment, eventually Barker gangster William Weaver muscled him out.

A longtime friend of the Barker brothers, Weaver, aka "Lapland Willie," was on parole after killing a member of a posse that had hunted him in the Ozarks. He was one of the two criminals arrested by Chief Dahill's men at the Green Lantern but bailed out by Adolph Bremer.

According to FBI informant Bess Green, "Myrtle disliked Bill [Weaver] very much . . . Bill would on occasion kidnap her or force her to go on trips at the point of a gun. Once he had held her up in her bathroom at the point of a gun and wrapped her up in clothing and carried her away . . . Myrtle Eaton would welcome Bill Weaver's apprehension because she is desperately in fear of him."

Myrtle didn't know it, but James Crumley had lobbied Dahill to arrest her as a suspect in the Hamm case.

Ring ring. Inspector Crumley calling.

Myrtle answered. Crumley asked: "Don't you have a red car?"

"Yeah," Myrtle said. "What about it?"

"Well, Mr. Dunn saw a red car circling his home during the kidnapping," Crumley said. "Don't say a word until I get through talking. You sure had a fast ride Saturday night, didn't you, in that red car. There's going to be plenty of heat in this town, and those fellows should have known better than to try a kidnapping."

Crumley, recounting this phone call to the FBI years later, said he expected Myrtle Eaton to "bawl him out."

Instead, "She said 'that's right' in a low voice and hung up."

After the kidnapping, Crumley said, Myrtle "came to his house one night." Crumley "noticed that when she moved her handkerchief she had a roll of bills in [her pocket] and he presumed that she had a little money for him."

Then what? asked the FBI.

"Oh, I shooed her out of the house," Crumley said.

He never bothered to ask about Myrtle's connection to the kidnappers.

Tom Brown was even less serious about investigating the Hamm kidnapping. A few days after Hamm's return, he led a diversionary raid on a cabin at Lake Minnetonka. Instead of kidnappers and captive, the raid only managed to surround and terrify a couple of vacationing women. Then reports of suspicious behavior kept coming out of a certain St. Paul neighborhood, and Dahill, chief without a clue, sent Big Tom to check it out.

The target was 204 Vernon Street. The house stood in a professorial neighborhood, bordering the elite Macalester College. It had been rented by Mr. and Mrs. Stanley Smith.

They were a lively young couple. Mrs. Smith was barely five feet tall, a skinny "rather attractive" blond with a crushed nose. She was cross-eyed and spoke in a drawl. She wore spectacular diamond jewelry, rings on every finger. Mr. Smith was just as skinny and hardly taller. He had gold teeth. He was a personable guy who said he was a machinery salesman.

A neighbor, Mrs. Lester Quick, suffered from cancer. She could hardly sleep. She spent a lot of time staring out the windows, and what did she witness? Men and women coming and going at all hours. Slamming car doors. Shouting. Always carrying suitcases. Mrs. Quick suspected some of those suitcases contained guns. This town had been a criminal haven for thirty years.

Mrs. Quick's daughter had a boyfriend, Charles Bradley, who visited quite a bit. Charles grew suspicious of these renters too.

On the day of the Hamm kidnapping, activity at 204 Vernon stopped. Cold. Shades drawn. Total shutdown. Nobody was home because the Barker gang was working out the kidnapping and their women were keeping each other company. Gladys Sawyer told the FBI that Fred's girlfriend Paula and Jack Peifer's lover Violet went for long bike rides during Hamm's captivity.

Other neighbors had grown suspicious of "Mr. and Mrs. Smith." These Smith people went through beer and ice like they were throwing a frat party. Delivery boys were met on the porch and kept out of the house, but the Smiths tipped so extravagantly that people began to gossip about it.

Chief Dahill lived in the neighborhood. He was a backyard neighbor to Harry Sawyer. Charles Bradley phoned Dahill, but the chief wasn't home. So Bradley took his suspicions to the parish priest, who drove him to police headquarters.

Along the way they cruised past 204 Vernon and noticed milk bottles souring on the porch and newspapers piling up. So downtown they drove, parish priest and earnest young man, on a mission to help capture the Hamm kidnappers.

At the police station they talked to detective Tom Grace and then to John McDonald, the police commissioner. McDonald was "blind drunk at the time and only semi-conscious," Bradley said. Other cops, presumably sober, seemed "only mildly interested." Bradley left headquarters after signing a statement, which the cops soon lost.

Bradley then drove to Vernon Street "expecting to see a kill." No police raid materialized, and at midnight, he went home disappointed.

The FBI would later judge that Bradley was "quite talkative" and one of those people who "claims to be a witness to all manner of spectacular events." So even an honest cop may not have believed him. Bradley next tried the newspapers, in the person of *St. Paul Dispatch* reporter Glenn Harrison. The newsman listened to Bradley's story, then lobbied Chief Dahill to check out 204 Vernon.

The next morning, no police action. Harrison felt "exasperated that a tip should be left lying around like an old egg."

The tenants, Mr. and Mrs. Stanley Smith, had come recommended, with references from a doctor and a lawyer. James McLaren, the landlord, was a hardware salesman and didn't know that the lawyer specialized in defending thugs or that the doctor had dark connections and would someday tend the wounds of John Dillinger. All the McLarens wanted was a little rental income. They were at the lakes that summer, so why not take tenants in their city house?

But at some deeper level, the McLarens harbored suspicions. James McLaren returned from the lakes on the excuse of fetching his daughter's bike. His wife Gertrude showed up a few days later on the pretext of gathering her bridge cards and score sheet. Paula Harmon, alias Mrs. Smith, "appeared greatly upset" by this visit, Mrs. McLaren later told the FBI.

Gertrude McLaren noticed that the table was set for breakfast, and it was nearly noon. If "Mr. Smith" really was a machinery salesman, why did he have the luxury of a late breakfast? She also noticed three men's hats and wondered exactly how many people were staying at her house. On the way out, she locked her china closet. As her husband drove her away, she jotted down the license numbers of the cars parked at her home.

She also remembered glimpsing a skinny fellow in the living room, not the tenant, but a young man with creepy eyes. She did not notice him hide his pistol under a newspaper, but Alvin Karpis would recall it that way in his memoirs.

A few days later, as Karpis was setting Bill Hamm free in a country town, Fitz and Fred carried suitcases jammed with the $100,000 ransom to 204 Vernon. Neighbors noticed and joked that they were carrying the ransom money.

Shotgun George Ziegler, Fred Barker, Charles Fitzgerald, and Paula Harmon, along with the ransom money, stayed one more restless night at 204 Vernon. According to Bolton, Ziegler "was spooked because while the woman [Paula Harmon] had not seen the money she had 'seen the bag' and 'certainly would know what was in it.'"

The suffering Mrs. Quick could hear the "Smiths" phone ring into the night. At some time after 2:00 AM, somebody finally answered. A few minutes later, the "Smiths" scrambled to pack their cars.

That morning, reporter Glenn Harrison finally persuaded Chief Dahill to send a cop to Vernon Street. Tom Brown drew the assignment. According to Byron Bolton, "[Jack] Peifer said that Brown had called him that evening and told him to go out to the house and see if there was anyone there and to tell them to get out . . . that [Brown] had received a report that there was something suspicious about the house and that he

Inside 204 Vernon Street, the home rented by the Barker gang in a quiet
neighborhood near Macalester College.

would have to investigate it and would not do so until the following
morning."

Peifer sped to Vernon Street and hustled Fred, Fitz, and the ransom
money out to the lake cottage. Then he drove back to clean up any
evidence. Brown reported to Chief Dahill that the occupants of 204
Vernon had "nothing to do with the Hamm kidnapping."

Tom Brown may have convinced Dahill he had investigated, but the
Daily News made a public fuss and St. Paul police begrudgingly dusted
204 Vernon for fingerprints. Eight months later, they sent those fingerprints to the FBI.

Five days after Fred Barker fled the house, the FBI searched it. But
Peifer had whisked away the evidence. FBI agent Oscar Hall concluded
that "Tom Brown had again warned the Barker gang." Hall also passed
on an informant's story that "on at least one occasion" Tom Brown had
gone duck hunting with Doc and Fred Barker and Alvin Karpis.

Werner Hanni, head of the St. Paul FBI, long suspected that someone
in the police department was betraying them. And now he had a name.

20

THE FBI'S WRONG TURN

At the time of the Hamm kidnapping, the FBI, in the modern sense, barely existed. Its agents had only recently been authorized to carry guns and make arrests. There had been political resistance to empowering a national police force. As it happened, the Hamm kidnapping occurred on the weekend that the modern FBI was born. The trigger event was the so-called Kansas City Massacre.

The main actor in this bloody drama was Verne Miller, who had driven the Barker gang's getaway car after that deadly Minneapolis bank robbery. In Kansas City, Miller was joined by two men who have never been satisfactorily identified, but one was probably Pretty Boy Floyd. Their purpose was to free Miller's friend Frank Nash from custody. Nash, a legendary bank robber, had escaped prison, had been recaptured, and was being transferred through the Union Depot in Kansas City.

Verne Miller's story is among the strangest of the public enemies era. A parachuting World War I hero, he had been elected sheriff of a South Dakota town but was jailed for embezzlement. After his release, he became a bank robber and mad gunman feared by cops and crooks alike. Miller botched the Kansas City plan about as badly as possible. He murdered two cops, two FBI agents, and his buddy Frank Nash, whose last words were a shout: "For God's sake, Verne don't kill me."

The death of two agents galvanized the FBI and J. Edgar Hoover. He staked his reputation on nailing the outlaws, and the term *public enemies* was born.

The Hamm kidnapping, presumed to be the work of the Chicago mob, got second priority to the Kansas City Massacre, but still, Hoover expected a quick arrest.

Hoover seemed infatuated with his subordinate in Chicago, Melvin Purvis. A South Carolina lawyer who had drifted into police work, Purvis was a tiny man with a squeaky voice. By taking on the public enemies, he would become a newsreel hero, for a while more famous than Hoover. His public image inflated when he and his men shot down John Dillinger. A raging, jealous Hoover would ultimately drive Purvis out of the FBI and hound him for life, for the crime of upstaging the boss.

But in June of 1933, Purvis was in Hoover's good graces and focused on the Hamm kidnapping. An honest cop, Purvis nonetheless fumbled case after case. Hoover's men, handpicked by the director, were derided as "college boys" who lacked street sense. Purvis never understood that he'd often been used by Chicago's corrupt cops. In the Hamm case, Purvis let an Illinois prosecutor's detective convince him that the kidnapping had been pulled off by Chicago bootlegger Roger Touhy.

History would reveal that this prosecutor's detective, Dan "Tubbo" Gilbert, was a Capone operative. Newspapers would come to mock him as "America's richest cop."

Acting on Tubbo's tip, Purvis brought William Hamm, cab driver Leo Allison, and pharmacist Clarence Thomas to the FBI's Chicago office. Also traveling to Chicago were St. Paul police chief Tom Dahill and Tom Brown.

Brown watched in treacherous silence as Purvis built a case against men who were not guilty of the Hamm kidnapping. For Brown, the framing of Touhy was a stroke of luck. A Touhy conviction would protect the Barker gang and make it more likely that Brown's role in the kidnapping would never be revealed.

Purvis put Touhy and his men behind a one-way mirror. The St. Paul visitors made a tentative ID of Roger Touhy and three of his gangsters. Well, Hamm was less sure as the day wore on and would later say he never positively identified Touhy's men. But Allison, the cabbie who'd delivered one of the Hamm ransom notes, confidently fingered the Touhy boys.

That was enough for Purvis. He wired Hoover that the Hamm kidnappers were in custody. "Splendid work," replied J. Edgar.

Chief Dahill developed a fixation on Touhy's guilt. Hamm's identification may have been shaky, but Dahill predicted, "When the case comes to trial we will have plenty of identification, you will see."

Decades later, a federal judge would conclude that Tubbo Gilbert was working for the Chicago Outfit, which had cleverly destroyed their rival, Touhy, by manipulating Purvis.

When federal agents brought William Hamm to Chicago, they flew him down on the Northwest Airlines mail plane. It was a tiny plane by today's standards, a Lockheed Orion, with a single engine, a wooden frame, and six passenger seats.

On that weekend, most of the actual Hamm kidnappers were running around Chicago, in a frenzy over how to launder the ransom money. Shotgun George thought he could wash it through friends who had a concession at the World's Fair, which was drawing huge crowds. That scheme didn't work, so Fred Barker and Charles Fitzgerald agreed to hustle the cash by train to Reno, hiding in their sleeper compartment for the entire ride.

When they detrained, they hit the taverns and casinos. Fitzgerald got drunk, climbed atop a bar to do a fan dance, fell off, and "hurt his tailbone." When it came to business, they found only one bank they could trust, a gangster-owned institution, and even then, they fed the money through a little at a time. The cash would eventually be laundered as payment to rum-running ships lying off the West Coast, carrying their last loads of bootleg liquor.

In the meantime, other Barker gangsters waited at a cottage in Long Lake, Illinois. They blew off fireworks for the Fourth of July, they drank, they argued. Paula Harmon was "downcast and drinking because Fred was in Reno." Volney Davis, assigned to watch over the gang's women, gave the fragile Paula a pep talk to keep her from going over the edge.

On orders from Ziegler, Byron Bolton flew to St. Paul to "get Jack Peifer so he would be in Chicago when the money was split up." Bolton stayed overnight at the Hollyhocks, but Peifer declined to leave the next day, "wanting to be in St. Paul for the celebration of an important politician's birthday." That politician was Clyde May, a Gleckman-affiliated member of the city council, "important" only in St. Paul's shadow politics.

Bolton, Peifer, and his girlfriend Violet left May's birthday party for the late show at the Plantation nightclub. Somewhere during that excursion, Bolton picked up a woman identified as Mrs. Harry Heide. This group stayed out all night, returning after dawn to the Hollyhocks to sit in lawn chairs on the banks of the Mississippi.

Finally that afternoon, a Sunday, the four of them drove to Holman Field in St. Paul for the flight to Chicago.

Operating on little sleep, and either drunk or badly hung over, it took Bolton about fifteen minutes of flight time to notice something familiar: the back of William Hamm's head. "I had become very familiar with [the] back of Hamm's head" while guarding him, Bolton told the FBI later.

Sitting with Hamm on that plane was his FBI handler, Rufus Coulter.

"I told Peifer about it," Bolton said, "and said as we neared Madison that I was getting off the plane."

By strange coincidence, five of the six passengers on that plane had some connection to the Hamm kidnapping. The FBI would later waste a lot of time trying to tie that sixth passenger to the case. But Mrs. Harry Heide fooled the FBI into believing she didn't know any of these characters and was merely a blackout drinker flying to Chicago for no sober reason.

Peifer, "half drunk," was relaxed because Hamm could not have identified him as a kidnapper. But Bolton, hacking with tuberculosis and terrified of discovery, felt trapped on this small airplane bouncing through the midwestern skies. When the plane landed in Madison, Bolton slipped out of his seat harness and ran for it.

Walter Walker was pulling his car up to the airport. He'd brought his wife and kids out to watch planes land. A tall thin man, gasping for breath, ran out of a hangar and up to the Walkers' car. He begged for a ride uptown and offered to pay.

The Walkers let him in. The stranger sat up front, coughing, doing most of his talking to Mrs. Walker in the back seat. He said he had gotten sick on the plane. He asked about trains and car hires. The Walkers dropped him off at the Lorraine Hotel downtown after he paid them five dollars off a huge roll. Walker and his wife later agreed that the man appeared more frightened than sick and seemed to be running from something.

Back on the tarmac, the copilot checked the list of passengers and found one missing. Flight attendants and airport officials tried to find him, gave up, and flew off.

A few days later, while Purvis and Hoover were exchanging congratulations over the Touhy arrests, the real kidnappers were dividing the laundered ransom money in a Chicago apartment. "Fred [Barker] put the money in a briefcase on the bed, and started handing out $100 and $500 bills," Bolton recalled.

The gang had paid a 7.5 percent fee to the money launderers and so worked out on paper how that would affect the shares.

"Mention was made of Brown's share," Bolton said. "Not recognizing the name I asked, 'Who is Brown?' Someone . . . said he was the man in the St. Paul Police Department who provided Peifer with information during the time of the kidnapping."

The gang debated whether to discount the laundry fee from Brown's share but paid him the whole $25,000. Peifer and Brown claimed $36,000 between them.

The six men who actually abducted and held Hamm got $7,800 each after expenses. That would translate to more than $100,000 each in today's money.

But it didn't last long. Shotgun George blew his share speculating on wheat futures. Fred Barker treated Ma and Paula to jewelry and furs. Gamblers soon parted Doc Barker from his money. Bolton moved his family to Phoenix, where the dry air might be easier on his wheezing lungs.

Only Alvin Karpis was prudent enough to stash money in secret bank accounts. After the kidnapping, he rented a glamorous summer cottage overlooking Lake Michigan. There he befriended a neighbor, Lester Gillis, who would soon become world famous under a nickname he hated: Baby Face Nelson.

The beach cottage, complete with Steinway piano, must have impressed Karpis's teenage lover, Dolores Delaney. She was sixteen when they met, but not a sweet sixteen. Tough and rebellious, Dolores was the daughter of a Chicago railroad detective and, to judge from her letters, a chronically ill, neurotic mother. Dolores "didn't like school, didn't like her mother," Karpis recalled. "Her mother had put her into a Catholic school for wayward girls," but Dolores ran away to St. Paul to live with a sister. That sister, "Babe," was married to Pat Reilly, the Green Lantern's bartender. When Karpis met Dolores, his infatuation was evident to Pat Reilly. The family had standards, Pat warned Karpis. "Nobody gets into her pants until she's seventeen."

The arrest of Touhy took the heat off the Barker gang. St. Paul was becoming a magical place for them. It seemed they could get away with any crime in the Holy City, as long as the keys were held by Harry Sawyer, Jack Peifer, and Tom Brown. Barker gangsters began drifting back to St. Paul, visiting Sawyer at his farm and sharing a laugh at the ineptitude of the federal government.

In his autobiography, Melvin Purvis observed that criminals were compulsively restless. Certainly that applies to the Barker gang, whose members seemed driven by the need for excitement and money. Only a few weeks after dividing the Hamm ransom, Karpis staked out the next job. His target was the Swift and Company payroll, which every week moved from a downtown Minneapolis vault to the South St. Paul stockyards.

If Karpis felt comfortable in St. Paul, that feeling may have been accentuated by his troubles in Chicago. His girl Dolores, now 17, announced that she was pregnant. Karpis arranged for an abortion and heartlessly suggested she also have a tonsillectomy, since she'd be under anesthesia anyway.

Around that time, Karpis was also delivered a warning from the Chicago Outfit. They grudgingly ceded the Barker gang the right to rob banks but warned that they'd pay with their lives if they stepped into Frank Nitti's rackets.

So why not go back to St. Paul, where the Barker gang had it made? Karpis paid a Chicago mob mechanic to armor-plate a car especially for this next job. He timed the payroll delivery, drew the getaway maps, and laid in a stock of bandages and morphine. Harry Sawyer helped him set up the job and guaranteed police cooperation.

On the morning of the robbery, Karpis drove the armored car into downtown South St. Paul, and Fred occupied the front passenger seat. He would be the navigator, reading the getaway map Karpis had drawn. Shotgun George was not invited on this job. His acolyte Byron Bolton was given a machine gun and assigned to kill cops if they showed up. Thus Bolton took over the role once played by Larry DeVol, who was now a madman rattling the bars and screaming all night in Stillwater Prison.

South St. Paul was a muddy riverfront town whose stockyards employed thousands. Meat from its slaughterhouses traveled by icebox cars all over the Midwest. On the day of the robbery, just before Labor Day weekend, patrolmen John Yeaman and Leo Pavlak escorted the payroll via train from the Federal Reserve of Minneapolis to the Swift and Company stockyards. Yeaman and Pavlak were relatively new hires and did not belong to the old guard of South St. Paul cops loyal to just-deposed chief Truman Alcorn.

It was approaching ten in the morning. Doc Barker and Byron Bolton drank beer at the Depot Café on Concord Street downtown. Doc's shotgun and Bolton's Tommy gun lay in suitcases underneath a pinball machine that stood near the door. Outside the Depot Café, Charles Fitzgerald impersonated a man innocently awaiting a streetcar.

Two messenger boys carried the payroll down the main street, passing the post office with bags of money. Inside the Depot Café, the "shorter bandit [Doc Barker] kept going to the window," the bartender said. Fitzgerald, watching the payroll procession, moved his leg in an odd circular motion. Doc Barker "grabbed his pal by the arm and said, 'Come on.'"

Karpis and Fred drove up in the armored sedan. Doc Barker stepped in front of patrolman Leo Pavlak, his sawed-off shotgun pointed at the cop's head.

"Stick 'em up," Doc shouted, and took away Pavlak's pistol.

The messengers were ordered to drop the money bags. They did, then hid underneath a parked livestock truck. Pavlak, hands in the air, told Doc to keep him as hostage but to let the others go.

Doc suddenly screamed, "You dirty rat, you son of a bitch," and fired a shotgun blast, killing Pavlak instantly.

Doc's shot caused the gang to start panic shooting. Bolton raked the street with machine gun fire. Lapland Willie Weaver shot officer John Yeaman, who was in his car at the head of an alley. The gang dragged the bleeding cop out of his car and shot him again. Yeaman caught bullets directly and by ricochet but would survive. Charles "Fitz" Fitzgerald was also hit in the wild shooting, which had bystanders diving and ducking. The gang grabbed the money bags and took off, leaving Fitz bleeding in the street.

"Goddamn it, don't leave me here," begged Fitz. Karpis backed up his armored car and Doc Barker dragged the bleeding Fitz in. They raced down Concord Street, emitting a smokescreen, swerving to avoid a trolley car. When they could safely pull over, Dr. Karpis administered Fitz a shot of morphine.

Their haul was $33,000. As in the Minneapolis bank robbery, no cop had gotten off a shot.

Deposed South St. Paul police chief Truman Alcorn stood safely behind the counter of a liquor store as the attack erupted just down the street. "There is no question Alcorn and Tom Brown were in on the Swift robbery," James Crumley would later tell the FBI. But Crumley, too, played a role, muddying the waters in the aftermath, in the opinion of Dakota County attorney Harold Stassen. Crumley, interviewing wit-nesses, left them "so confused that they became useless."

The family of the surviving policeman, John Yeaman, tried to prove that hunting buddies Truman Alcorn and Tom Brown had conspired with Harry Sawyer to set up the robbery. Their theory was that Alcorn and Brown had convinced themselves that the robbery would be blood-less, that the patrolmen, overwhelmed by the gang's firepower, would drop their weapons. But even if Tom Brown had no role in planning the Swift robbery, his deal to protect the Barker gang had resulted, again, in the death of a fellow officer. There were now three Minnesota police-men in their graves as a result of Tom Brown's secret partnership with the Barkers.

21

HARRY'S HARVEST

While his restless criminal friends moved from hideout to hideout, Harry Sawyer settled on his farm. In the fall of 1933, he gathered his only harvest. The Sawyers and their hired help kept chickens and pigs and grew a vegetable garden. Harry's wife Gladys and little Francine lived out there full time, with their maid Miss Betty Baerwold and a couple of handymen. The move to the farm may have been motivated by Harry's desire for respectability. It may have been a way to escape FBI surveil-lance. Or it may have been a ruse to fool the social services people, mol-lify Gladys, and set the scene for Francine's adoption.

Francine was a ward of the Ramsey County Child Welfare Agency. Harry asked his lawyer to find a softie on the staff who would allow the Sawyers to adopt her after a minimal background check. The lawyer sent Harry to an agent named Mrs. Crawford, who was wary of "contradic-tory stories of residence" and after "subsequent checkups" denied for-mal adoption.

Harry complained to his lawyer. Didn't this rube bureaucrat know how to play the St. Paul game?

Whatever Harry's motives for this move to family, fatherhood, and farming, he could not escape himself. The farm became a hangout for criminals and their girlfriends. Tom Brown and other St. Paul cops were frequent visitors too. Brown had purchased his own farm acreage just across the road.

That Thanksgiving, Harry, Gladys, and Francine ate turkey with Shotgun George and his wife Irene at the Zieglers' Wisconsin lake resort. Soon after, "All the 'heavies' began showing up in St. Paul," said the Barker gang's Edna Murray.

That fall, the nation's sense of financial crisis intensified. Agriculture prices fell so low that midwestern farmers fomented a strike. Banks were failing, breadlines growing longer. As reflected in FDR's famous comment about "fear itself," the public seemed to lose confidence in government. At the FBI, this translated into pressure to subdue the public enemies. It was Verne Miller's time to be "put on the spot." In November, police issued a shoot-to-kill order on Miller, engineer of the Kansas City Massacre and one-time Barker gangster. Soon after, Miller shot his way out of a Chicago police ambush and vowed he'd never be taken alive. The Chicago cops blamed that escape on their favorite patsy, Roger Touhy, even though he was in jail at the time.

Harry and his hoodlums eagerly followed the Touhy prosecution. In jail, Tubbo's cops had brutally beaten Touhy and his friends. Touhy lost twenty-five pounds in a few weeks and had seven teeth knocked out. The four Touhy gangsters were indicted and moved to the St. Paul jail. There the beatings stopped, but one of Touhy's men, Willie Sharkey, lost his mind, screaming all night. He would eventually hang himself, using neckties his brother had sent him as a gift. When the news of Sharkey's suicide broke, Minnesotans began sending neckties to Touhy in prison, an invitation for him to join his pal.

Prosecutor Joseph Keenan's life was threatened in anonymous phone calls. Police feared the mobs that gathered around the courthouse. They worried that Touhy's friends might try to free him, in an encore of the Kansas City Massacre. Those gory shootings had happened during the simple transfer of a prisoner.

The *Pioneer Press* reported that "30 guards manned the jails with machine guns, rifles, tear gas bombs. Guards surrounded the defendants at all times. Nightly, a radio station broadcast a summary of the trial" to a public that had been roused against kidnappers. "Scores were turned away" from seats at the trial, the *Pioneer Press* reported.

U.S. marshal Bernard Anderson, right, and Frank Lorenzi of the marshal's office guarding the eighth floor of the Ramsey County courthouse during the Roger Touhy trial, November 13, 1933.

"We were manacled and chained" throughout the trial, Touhy recalled. His nemesis Tubbo Gilbert attended each court session.

The star witness, William Hamm Jr., was a "broken man after the kidnapping." He became morose, and at company meetings often seemed lost in thought.

It wasn't just the memory of the kidnapping that disturbed Hamm. Jack Peifer had recently sent him a message through his bouncer, Saph McKenna, a half-blind former boxer. "The boys" had advice for Hamm. He'd better "go easy" if ever asked to identify the Barker gang. McKenna, rather than deliver the message himself, sent it via Herbert Benz.

Benz was part of the nexus of gangsters and legitimate businessmen common in St. Paul at the time. His real estate company held the mortgage on the Hollyhocks, so at least in a business sense he was partners with Jack Peifer. He had other friends throughout the underworld. A first cousin of Bill Hamm's, the two had become estranged after business disputes.

Benz delivered his warning to Hamm as they played golf before the trial began.

It's no wonder reporters at the trial described Hamm as "shy and aloof." He didn't know who his kidnappers were, or whether these Chicago gangsters on trial had anything to do with it. He didn't know exactly who had threatened him through cousin Benz. But obviously, the less he said, the better. On the witness stand, Hamm was "suffering from a heavy cold," so his physical misery matched his emotional torment.

A writer for the *St. Paul Dispatch* described the scene when Hamm was asked to identify his kidnappers.

"The long white finger of William Hamm points at Eddie McFadden as the man who seized his hand and pushed him into the car."

"'This resembles the man.'

"And then.

"'That is the man.'

"'McFadden squinted back with steely eyes through large steel rimmed glasses and a look of testy dissatisfaction.'"

Hamm was mistaking McFadden for Barker gangster Charles "Fitz" Fitzgerald. Under cross-examination, Hamm admitted he wasn't sure about McFadden. He thought his abductor was "taller and had finer features." He also said he did not recognize the other Touhy men: Gus Stevens, Gloomy Gus Shaefer, the doomed and unraveling Willie Sharkey, or the supposed mastermind Roger Touhy.

St. Paul dentist Horace LeBissonierre, who'd been playing pinball that fateful night at the Rosedale Pharmacy, was also a member of the state legislature. He boasted about what a fine observer he was, given his scientific training. He said the Rosedale Pharmacy had been robbed several times, so he'd made a long study of the stranger who'd wandered into the drugstore. He positively identified Eddie McFadden as the man who had dropped the ransom note in the booth that night.

Cabbie Leo Allison took the stand, far more humble than the politician-dentist. He said he was "not so sure" that the shadowy man who had passed him a note in the Lowry garage was McFadden.

Prosecutors, infuriated, turned on Allison and impeached their own witness. The cabbie began to "squirm in his chair" as the government pressed him on his previous identification of McFadden. But Allison stood firm. Finally, the government gave up.

"Are you now assured that McFadden is *not* the man?" prosecutors said. "I am."

A Chicago printer testified that he'd happened to be in St. Paul on the day in question and witnessed the abduction of William Hamm. He identified all the members of the Touhy gang. That proved to be a flimsy perjury. Touhy's lawyers produced the man's payroll timesheet, showing he'd been at work in Chicago on the day Hamm was abducted.

Touhy's alibi for that day was that he had been in Indianapolis, staying at a hotel. His lawyers said a man flashing a federal badge had requested the registration card from the hotel clerk, then walked off with it.

A friend of Touhy's who testified to back up his alibi told the court he'd been threatened by federal agents: "If you go to St. Paul to testify for Touhy, you'll be sorry, and maybe you won't come back."

The trial's tone, Touhy wrote in his autobiography, was "let's pretend we're all nuts."

Defense attorney Thomas McMeekin presented evidence that Gloomy Gus Shaefer and his wife had been in King City, California, on the weekend of the kidnapping. The evidence was an auto camp registration card signed by Gloomy Gus. A pilot testified that he had flown Shaefer and his wife back from that trip.

On November 29, the jury returned a not guilty verdict for all four Touhy defendants.

On hearing the verdict, a reporter wrote, observers were "stupefied." They sat "open mouthed, looking at one another in frank amazement." Filing out past guards armed with shotguns and teargas rifles, "the observers left the room in a daze. They couldn't, most of them, believe it."

Among the stunned observers was Tom Dahill. "Chief Dahill's face was white, his jaw set and his face clenched" reported the *Pioneer Press.* "People spoke to him. He didn't reply."

During the Touhy trial, two men in San Jose, California, were lynched in response to a kidnap-murder. Embittered by the Touhy acquittal, Dahill told reporters, "If that [the acquittal of Touhy] is the attitude that American citizens take toward kidnappings, I applaud the San Jose citizens for taking justice into their own hands."

The Touhy acquittal unleashed demons. Wrote Touhy: "There was a howling mob in the streets around that jail that night. I figured we were going to be lynched, all of us." His attorney appealed for police protection when a mob surrounded his home.

T. O. Sundry, a 69-year-old farmer who was jury foreman, was among those threatened by a furious public. One letter called Sundry "an old fool."

"How much did Mr. Touhy paid you to tell lies? You sure made a mistake, you Judas. Watch out for you are going to be taken for a ride."

Another citizen wrote: "A whole jury boarded at a high class hotel for three weeks and living on the fat of the land, all expenses being paid by us taxpayers, and a bunch of gangsters turned loose?" Another letter said: "You will long be remembered and despised by many thousands of our citizens for your incompetence." Sundry was called "chief nitwit in a jury of nitwits" and leader of a "bunch of cowards."

But the old farmer stood strong. He told the *Pioneer Press* the jury had done its duty because of the "failure of Mr. Hamm to identify any of the defendants positively."

The Outfit never gave up on their plan to destroy Touhy, immediately framing him for another kidnapping, that of "Jake the Barber" Factor. That kidnapping would ultimately prove to be a hoax, but Touhy would serve decades in prison for it, until being exonerated by a federal judge. Finally freed in 1959, Touhy was assassinated on the steps of his home by gunmen who were never caught.

As for William Hamm, pestered by newsmen after the trial, he sent a message via Billy Dunn: "Tell the reporters I have nothing to say."

This drama could have had few more avid followers than Harry Sawyer. Harry knew that Jack Peifer had engineered the kidnapping, collecting part of the ransom in collaboration with Tom Brown. His wife Gladys would tell the FBI, "Harry was bothered because Brown had gotten $36,000 in the Hamm case, and Harry was getting the heat but none of the cash."

Both Harry and Gladys knew which gang members took part in the kidnapping. Harry may have guessed that the prime motive was not ransom money. He knew Jack Peifer had gained an edge over Leon Gleckman by kidnapping him and arranging for his release. It stood to reason that the Hamm kidnapping was Peifer's way of intimidating the family and making a shadowy claim on the brewery.

This interpretation was emphasized by the official end of Prohibition, which followed the Touhy verdict by a few weeks. Brewers were going to make money like never before, and it was going to be legal now. That threatened to marginalize men like Jack Peifer and Harry Sawyer. So it was time for Harry to make his own claim on the future. "The boys" were straggling back from another jaunt to Reno, looking for a new job to pull.

One of the FBI's most credible informers in St. Paul was Bess Green, common-law wife of a man who had helped both the Dillinger and Barker gangs pull off robberies. "Bessie Green states that Tom Brown of St. Paul Police Department is planning to run for sheriff of this county," FBI director J. Edgar Hoover learned by telegraph. "She states that Eddie Green, John Dillinger, John Hamilton, Homer Van Meter, Baby Face Nelson, Tommy Carroll and Tommy Gannon each contributed equal parts to make up 1500 dollars which was delivered personally in cash to Tom Filben here for Brown's campaign."

With Brown's star rising again, and the Barker gang eager for work, Harry began to plot a way to see Jack Peifer's hand and raise the stakes. Even if Brown didn't win as sheriff, he was in perfect position. He had been promoted to the kidnap investigation squad.

So in December, Harry began to foment a kidnapping of his own. Karpis and Barker showed up together one frosty day at the farm, and they all had a good laugh at the FBI's bumbling in the Touhy trial. But Karpis balked at another kidnapping, saying it would bring "too much heat."

Harry tried to convince the gang. His connections went deep, he said, and hadn't the Hamm snatch been quick and profitable?

From the gang's perspective, the Hamm kidnapping seemed a brilliant success. The ransom was quickly paid, laundered, and divided. The victim gave them no trouble and was unharmed. The intermediary, Billy Dunn, proved himself a reliable member of the underworld. Detective Tom Brown had kept them advised of every important turn in the investigation and helped them avoid a police ambush.

Daylight bank robberies often devolved into dangerous shootouts. Barker gangster Earl Christman had been slain in one robbery, Charles Fitzgerald wounded in another. Even when the gangsters got away, they often left dead cops, which brought intense heat. In the Hamm kidnapping, not a shot was fired. And now, like a gift from the gods of the underworld, the federal government prosecuted the wrong gang and then let the Hamm case go cold.

The Hamm kidnapping was the kind of success that leads men to overconfidence and disaster. Fred Barker, always game, wanted to make another snatch. Karpis fantasized about pulling one last job, then escaping to Australia.

Sawyer, Fred, and Karpis argued and drank all night, and by daybreak decided to leave it up to Ziegler. A college graduate, Ziegler was held in awe by his fellow gangsters. Fred and Karpis drove to Chicago, detouring to make the obligatory visit to Ma Barker. They treated Ma to a movie and then looked up Ziegler. The ransom in this snatch would be double, they told Shotgun George. $200,000! That appealed to Ziegler, who'd lost a fortune in the futures markets. "Yeah," he said, "I'd go on the damn thing."

So Harry Sawyer, in the haze of a quart-a-day booze habit, began to plot the crime that would destroy them all.

All, that is, except for Harry's friend at the police station.

22

"WITH OPEN ARMS"

The details were worked out in the steam-heated apartments in St. Paul's Grand Avenue district. It was deep winter, the weather frightful, the internal climate paranoid.

Alvin Karpis again served as detail man. He had stashed Dolores Delaney in a Chicago apartment and disappeared on "business." When they first met, he had told Dolores he was an auto salesman. He confessed to being a criminal after she saw his picture in a newspaper. "He told me that if I desired to leave him," Delaney told the FBI, "he would give me some money and I could go where I desired. However, because of my affection for him I refused to leave." They celebrated Christmas at a Chinese restaurant. Karpis promised to buy furniture and settle down.

They'd had an adventuresome fall. In September, the Barker gang erupted in another brazen robbery. They tried to rip off the Chicago

Federal Reserve, the result being one dead policeman, Doc Barker's pinky being nicked by a bullet, and the theft of worthless sacks of mail.

In the cool-out that followed, the gang motored to Reno. Karpis drove Delaney out there in his Dodge sedan. They went club-hopping with Freddie and Paula. The gang favored the Bank Club Casino, "a pretentious gambling establishment," according to Edna Murray.

Ever restless, Karpis drove Dolores to San Francisco, where they toured the underworld joints. He must have seen the new federal prison, Alcatraz, when taking the ferry across the bay, and we can only wonder whether it sent a shiver of foreboding through him. He and Dolores zigzagged south through the Sierra Nevada, gawking at the construction of the Hoover dam, then movie star gazing in Los Angeles.

In some ways Delaney was a naïve kid, but in gangster ways she was a punk, cynical beyond her years. J. Edgar Hoover, rarely generous toward women, described her as a "cheap, deluded, silly little moll." FBI informant Bess Green described her as a "real tiny" woman with a pale complexion, light brown hair, and brown eyes who used "quite a bit of makeup." Green disparaged Delaney as a "poor dumb little thing." But in letters to her family, Dolores wrote in a witty, intelligent voice.

While still a teenager, Delaney took the witness stand in the bank robbery trial of Clarence DeVol, brother of the infamous "Chopper." She helped him get an acquittal by providing an alibi.

But in Hollywood, she was a star-struck teenager. While Karpis kept to his room awaiting phone calls, Dolores roamed the streets hoping to see Fred Astaire, Gary Cooper, Greta Garbo, Jean Harlow, or maybe one of the Marx brothers. But how could you tell who the stars were, she complained, when everybody in L.A. was wearing sunglasses?

So much for California. By Christmas, Karpis and Fred began appearing at the Green Lantern and the Hollyhocks. Having used up the IDs of Stanley J. Smith and wife, Fred and Paula became the Bergstroms. Under that name they rented a swell apartment on St. Paul's Grand Avenue. Predictably enough, neighbors said the Bergstroms "did a lot of drinking" and had visitors at all hours. Paula pretended to be an Irish immigrant. Neighbors described her as "a sandy-haired 30-year-old Irish-woman with crossed eyes and a thick brogue."

Attending these St. Paul planning meetings were a couple of fellows from the Barkers' wilding days in Oklahoma. Harry Campbell was a dullard, a follower looking for a leader. Volney "Curly" Davis was overshadowed by his infamous girlfriend, Edna "the Kissing Bandit" Murray. Also rejoining the gang was "Lapland Willie" Weaver, who'd been living under St. Paul's protection racket. Davis and Weaver were desperate for cash and in debt to various gangsters.

The others at the meetings were the "heavies": Karpis, Fred, Doc, and Shotgun George. Harry Sawyer attended as scriptwriter. A couple of the actors suggested a different scenario: Hey, the target's family owns a bank, don't they? Why not just rob it? But Harry shot that suggestion down.

Harry's target was Edward Bremer, whose family was even wealthier than the Hamms. The Bremers dealt in two indispensable commodities: money and beer. The family's brewery and banks had survived an era that had been brutal to both businesses. "Brewers have been compelled or forced to go into politics and have as a consequence many shady political connections," noted FBI man Harold "Pop" Nathan. The Bremers admitted to dark dealings with the underworld that included money laundering.

Harry was friends with the scion, Edward Bremer. But Gladys Sawyer told the FBI that in 1933, her husband and Ed Bremer "got into a dispute over alcohol." Harry felt that Bremer owed him money. "I don't know what Harry's beef was," Karpis noted, "but he sure didn't like Bremer."

While all this was happening in the underworld, in the bright snowy overworld people were anticipating how quickly FDR would bring back legal booze. On January 20, speakeasies could apply to become legitimate taverns. Bootleggers formed liquor distribution companies and began advertising. Some of the businesses started by bootleggers are still selling liquor in the Twin Cities today.

In January of 1934, Tom Brown declared his candidacy for sheriff. The *St. Paul Daily News* pronounced him a top candidate, citing his "successful crime investigations over the past several years, including the kidnapping of Leon Gleckman."

Despite that endorsement, newsmen certainly had heard rumors that Brown had dark dealings. After all, the Green Lantern was a hangout for reporters too. But rumors were unfit for print, and Brown was a power not easily challenged.

Detectives Charles Tierney and Tom Brown, publicly at least, fancied themselves law enforcement innovators. They had formed "what is believed to be the first anti-kidnapping squad in a metro police force," according to the *St. Paul Daily News.*

Both Tierney and Brown claimed to be the leader of this two-man squad.

"With several millionaires about," the news article said, "St. Paul has been modeled into a steel-jawed trap for kidnappers."

The article said that "unpleasant surprises" awaited kidnappers in St. Paul. Wealthy men and their families had been given advice on "what to do from the time an abduction may become imminent."

Tierney was quoted as saying, "By bulldogging the details of every big kidnapping in the nation, our squad will acquaint itself with known kidnappers and their methods. When they hit St. Paul, we'll be ready for them with open arms."

He chose his metaphor well.

Perhaps Charles Tierney's intuition was trying to tell him something. His partner Tom Brown was indeed researching wealthy people, but not for the purpose of protecting them. Detective James Crumley told the FBI that Brown used the information he'd gathered as a cop to help target Bremer. Crumley said that many St. Paul cops "figured Tierney was in on it too" but later changed their minds. Tierney, his fellow officers concluded, was "on the square but did not act very intelligent in allowing Brown to pull these things over on him."

For Brown, it was a busy January. He was consulting with Harry Sawyer on how to set up Ed Bremer for the kidnapping. He was running for sheriff. He was advising the kidnappers on how to fend off the cops. And he was soliciting St. Paul's criminal population for campaign contributions. But he never attended a kidnap planning meeting. "Brown has apparently been smart enough to deal only through Harry Sawyer," concluded the FBI.

Federal agents would later determine that three kidnap planning meetings were held. Myrtle Eaton testified: "The men sat in the living room and talked. The women stayed in the kitchen. We could not hear their conversation."

The final meeting was held at Myrtle's place on the evening of Friday the thirteenth. As it ended, rumors of a prowler began circulating. In a neighborhood of apartment dwellers, these rumors received varying interpretations. To Fred Barker and Alvin Karpis, it seemed obvious that the prowler must be a cop spying on them.

Across the alley, a Mrs. Corwin returned to her apartment from a bridge match. Convinced she'd seen a prowler in the alley, she called her husband. Mr. Corwin was out at the airport, having fun with his buddy, Roy McCord, a Northwest Airlines radioman working second shift. These two were listening to radio traffic and watching planes land when the phone rang: It was Corwin's wife in a panic.

Prowler in the alley!

McCord held her on the line to calm her down while Corwin rushed home.

At midnight McCord clocked out, grabbed a .32 pistol and a pair of brass knuckles from his desk, and drove for Corwin's apartment. He wore his Northwest uniform: a peaked hat and a dark jacket with brass buttons.

At Corwin's apartment, McCord, who had a bit of the cowboy in him, persuaded Corwin and another man to look for this peeping pervert. Corwin had called the cops, but they had found no prowlers.

Well, the St. Paul police had long since earned the public's distrust. So the three friends drove around until they saw a car speeding down an

Myrtle Eaton's mug shot.

alley. It stopped. McCord pulled abreast of it, pistol and brass knuckles ready.

To Fred Barker and Alvin Karpis, McCord looked, in that dark wintry alley, like a uniformed cop. "Freddie was at the wheel," wrote Karpis. "I leaped out of the passenger side with a machine gun. I must have thrown twenty or thirty slugs into the 'cop car.'"

Karpis, who always imagined himself the center of the universe, neglected to mention that Fred did some of the shooting. Police found the car riddled with shotgun pellets and forty-six Tommy-gun slugs, including the six that tore into McCord's body. Corwin escaped with minor injuries, and their friend in the back seat was unharmed.

The next day, the newspapers went ballistic.

MACHINE GUN GANG HUNTED
LITTLE HOPE HELD FOR LIFE OF RADIOMAN

"Overlooking no clues, police were looking for a bandit who had held up a drugstore" just before the shooting, the *Daily News* said. The cops arrested Weste Grand, 24, on suspicion of the shooting. The man had been a suspect in a string of one-bandit drugstore holdups. How he morphed into a murderous superman able to fire both Tommy gun and shotgun simultaneously, the police never explained.

McCord was so badly injured that doctors offered little hope for his survival. Newspapers splashed pictures of his pregnant wife and their six children all over the front page. The gangsters' bullets "tore their murderous way through the hearts" of this family, said the *Daily News*. McCord was portrayed as a hardworking father who'd learned his radio skills at night school. The family had just moved from Fargo, North Dakota. The move was motivated by Roy McCord's grief over the death of a young son there, his wife told reporters. Mrs. McCord, new to the neighborhood, had no relatives or friends to rely on.

The newspapers played it for sentiment. "Daddy plays radio with us," reporters quoted the McCord children as saying. "Daddy takes us for airplane rides." Then the kids asked their mother, "Are you going to bring daddy home?"

McCord endured surgery after surgery. Doctors took days to pick the windshield fragments out of his skull. He came out of the hospital in a wheelchair. He was rolled back in for more surgery. McCord was still having shooting-related surgery thirty-two years later, in 1966.

St. Paul police couldn't locate the shooters. Some alert citizen gave them the license number of the shooters' car. Nope, the cops said, it didn't check out. The FBI later traced the license plate to Barker gangster Volney Davis. The *Daily News* pronounced it "disheartening" how the crime was "accepted by police and to some extent the public."

The shooting took place just outside Myrtle Eaton's apartment. Police certainly understood her connections to the underworld. Detective James Crumley, who knew Myrtle's number when he was feeling frisky, couldn't seem to remember it now. Police "interest in the case has ceased," the *Daily News* complained.

But one treacherous cop was on the job as usual. According to testimony from Edna Murray, Tom Brown visited her boyfriend Volney "Curly" Davis after the McCord shooting. He advised Curly that he was a "dumb yokel" to be living under his own name while planning a kidnapping. Brown also complained that the shooting of Roy McCord would make it harder to pull off the Bremer job. When he wasn't playing criminal consultant, Tom Brown was running his campaign for sheriff, promising voters a "clean, efficient and courteous" administration.

Meanwhile, Harry Sawyer called at Fred Barker's apartment. The message from both Harry and Brown was: "The shooting of that radio man has made this town hot. You'd better wait a while."

Nobody ever had much luck asking Fred Barker to be patient.

23

"WELL, I GOT EXCITED"

In 1934, Edward Bremer was 37 years old and president of his family's Commercial State Bank. A big rugged guy, six foot three and two hundred pounds, Ed had served in the navy in the Great War, earned a law degree, and then come home to help his father run the Jacob Schmidt Brewery. But Ed alienated so many brewery employees that Papa Adolph banned him from the works. Ed "is very much disliked, not only by his family, but generally," the FBI noted. "He has an uncontrollable temper, is very selfish and inconsiderate and has few friends." So Adolph stuck his son and heir in the glassy corner office of a downtown bank.

Around New Year's, Ed moved his wife, daughter, in-laws, and servants to a mansion overlooking the Mississippi, down the road from that infamous nightclub, the Hollyhocks. The move caused bad feelings in the family, because Ed had bought the mansion against his father's wishes. Father and son were growing distant and cold toward each other.

Ever since the Hamm kidnapping, Ed had been "very apprehensive" about being abducted. He was being advised on avoiding abduction by Tom Brown. Just as the Barker gang began planning the kidnapping, Ed Bremer, heeding Brown's advice, dismissed his bodyguard and allowed the St. Paul police to assume that duty.

On the morning of January 17, this temperamental millionaire worked into his overcoat and escorted his daughter Betty, 9, into his Lincoln. It was one of those boxy, dark sedans that seemed to be about half engine. He pressed the starter button and the big V-8 began to warm up.

It was mid-January, 17 degrees, and the streets of St. Paul were icy. Bremer drove a few miles to Summit School, dropped Betty off, and turned for his bank office downtown. "I stopped the car at Goodrich and Lexington and put the car in low gear," he later testified. The passenger door was suddenly flung open and "an arm with a gun in the hand was put into the car and a voice said: 'Don't move or I'll kill you.'"

Bremer stepped on the gas, but the Lincoln's engine stalled. Two cars roared up and boxed him in, front and behind. The maniac who'd pointed a pistol at him leaped into the car and began beating him. Now a second maniac leaped in, this time from the driver's side, and pounded Bremer with a pistol. "I was being beaten by both people . . . blood was streaming into my eyes."

Kidnapper number one, a tattooed punk, shoved Bremer to the floor of the car. Kidnapper number two slid into the driver's seat and began searching in panic for the starter button. Bremer hoped somebody would arrive to help him. The kidnappers kept slugging him, and one screamed, "Where's the starter button?" Bremer finally reached up from the floor and pushed it, and kidnapper number two, later identified as Lapland Willie Weaver, drove while the tattooed punk, Doc Barker, strapped taped goggles over Bremer's head. Bremer was now blind and bleeding on the floorboard of his own rumbling, speeding luxury automobile. His knee throbbed where one of the maniacs had slammed the car door on it.

There were two witnesses to the abduction, according to press accounts. Mrs. Cressens Dehmen saw the scuffle and reported that Bremer had been hit fifteen to twenty times. A milk-wagon driver said he gawked at the abduction from a block away, thinking it was a traffic accident.

Weaver drove the Lincoln toward Highland Golf Course, at the edge of town. He pulled up alongside two other cars. At that point "I was told I was kidnapped," Bremer recalled. Shotgun George Ziegler lifted Bremer's goggles just enough to get his signature on two ransom notes. Bremer gave his kidnappers the names of five men who might serve as ransom negotiators. Then the Lincoln was abandoned, and a two-car convoy headed for Chicago.

Alvin Karpis drove. Stuffed behind the back seat, Bremer howled in pain. Karpis said Bremer had caused his own trouble by struggling so hard.

"Well, I got excited," Bremer responded.

As the cars drove into the frozen landscape, the kidnappers fed him "half a chicken sandwich," and "after dark," he recalled, "I was allowed to sit up front." The tailing car was the refueling vehicle. They stopped at remote Wisconsin roadsides, and Doc Barker hopped out and poured gas from cans into the car Karpis was driving. Then Doc ditched the cans and funnel in the woods.

Much of the Bremer kidnapping worked on the Hamm pattern. Bremer was driven to the same suburb, Bensenville, Illinois. Ed Barthelmy, now the postmaster, was not game to have his house used as a hideout again, so Ziegler found Harold Alderton, a debt-ridden, unemployed railroad worker to take his place. Bremer was locked into Alderton's back bedroom and made to face the wall. The lone window had been boarded over. "I had numerous cuts on my head and bled a lot," Bremer later testified. "I asked them to cut the hair off, so no infection would set in, which they did." Bremer's nurse was William Weaver, the same man who had inflicted much of the damage. "They bandaged my head up, and eyes and ears." Bremer was fed "eggs and sausages, sausages and eggs" in a room that was "awfully cold" because the home's only stove was in the kitchen.

Shotgun George summoned Byron Bolton from Phoenix. Bolton's instructions were to "Go to Bensenville and see if there is anything I can do and ask the people there if there were any instructions for him."

Sometime past eleven that evening, Bolton knocked on the back door. Karpis answered. In the kitchen, Bolton saw the homeowner, Alderton, drinking beer with Doc Barker, Weaver, and Campbell. "Someone called from the bedroom and Weaver went in," Bolton later testified. "He led a man out of the bedroom to take him to the bathroom. The man had his head bandaged, with tape around his eyes. That man was Edward Bremer."

Doc Barker, Bolton reported, was cracking up the kidnappers by "talking like a Mexican" in the hopes of throwing off Bremer's notion of who had abducted him.

The gang had no special message for Shotgun George. So Ziegler headed back to St. Paul, where he would again be minister of communication, using Volney Davis as his messenger boy, typing ransom note after ransom note, and finally ditching his typewriter in the icy Mississippi.

24

"ONE MORE CHANCE"

Walter Magee arrived in St. Paul penniless in 1914. But when Prohibition arrived, he found that bootlegging paid better than honest work. He ran rum for the Tobin Saloon, a popular dive. He expanded his services to include pimping. According to the FBI, Mrs. Tobin, wife of the proprietor, became "somewhat enamored" of Magee and wanted her husband out of the way.

Well, more than somewhat enamored. She shot and killed Tobin and was sentenced to life at Stillwater Prison.

That worked out swell for Magee, whom federal agents characterized as a "rather shady character." With both Tobins out of the way, he took over their saloon. He attained enough status among bootleggers that he was a pallbearer at the 1928 funeral of the Irish godfather, Dapper Dan Hogan.

The 1929 crash broke a lot of people, including Walter Magee. He recovered by donning a chauffeur's cap and squiring the Bremer family around. Magee held a charm for females and became a favorite of Mrs. Adolph Bremer. She insisted Magee be the driver when she accompanied her men on hunting safaris to the wilds of Minnesota. "Adolph's wife took an interest in him," the FBI reported, "and reformed him and he is now straight."

Mrs. Bremer had since died but that did not diminish Magee's standing with the family. Adolph Bremer set up Magee in a construction company that primarily bid on government contracts. In October 1931, for example, Magee's company got a road contract for $473,204, the largest of twenty-three contracts in that round. After the election of FDR, Magee was awarded a big contract for dam building. The FBI would eventually conclude that Adolph Bremer was the power, and Magee merely the front man, for Magee Construction. Despite the construction company's "frequent disastrous losses," the FBI reported, "Magee enjoys the faith and friendship" of Adolph Bremer.

On January 17, 1934, at nine thirty in the morning, Magee "got a telephone message . . . telling me they had taken Ed Bremer and were holding him." Told to check underneath the steps of his office, he found a note declaring the abduction a "very desperate undertaking." The kidnappers demanded $200,000 ransom. The note instructed the Bremers to take out an ad in the *Minneapolis Tribune* when they had assembled the money. The ad was to say WE ARE READY, ALICE. Only much later would it be learned that "Mother Alice" was one of Kate Barker's nicknames.

"I called the chief of police," Magee said, meaning Tom Dahill. "He called back and asked me to meet an officer in the lobby of the Ryan Hotel." That officer was Tom Brown. "We immediately took a room at the hotel." They were joined for a strategy meeting by St. Paul detective Charles Tierney and FBI supervisor Werner Hanni.

At 1:00 PM Adolph Bremer and Walter Magee discovered Ed's Lincoln at the edge of the snowy Highland Golf Course. The cushions and floorboards were crusted with blood. Hoping to spare his boss's feelings, Magee took the Lincoln to a car wash, which removed Ed Bremer's blood but also the fingerprints of the Barker gang.

The Bremers ran the newspaper ad as instructed, but the first response to WE ARE READY, ALICE was a worrisome silence from the kidnappers.

Adolph Bremer and Magee again strategized in a hotel room with the FBI's Hanni, Chief Dahill, and Tom Brown. That bloody Lincoln had half-convinced Adolph that his son had been killed. Together with the policemen, he drafted a note demanding proof that Ed Bremer was alive. The note was never sent to the kidnappers, however.

Brown took Chief Dahill aside and urged him not to share information with the federal "glory hogs," detective Charles Tierney said. The FBI, having so recently bungled the Hamm case, seemed confused and perhaps awestruck by the Bremer kidnapping. One agent reported it was "the work of a professional outfit . . . one of the most perfect things that ever happened."

Hoover soon wrote Hanni that he was "entirely dissatisfied" with his work on the Bremer case. Hoover was infuriated because Hanni sent him the ransom note but failed to wrap it in cellophane, thus making it harder to obtain fingerprints. Hoover complained that he was getting better news from the press than from Hanni.

One reason may have been that details of the kidnapping were leaked to the local newspapers and the wire services carried them to the wider world. Reporters, photographers, and newsreel men descended upon St. Paul. As a result of all the news flashes, the FBI was swamped with bad tips. People claimed to have seen the kidnappers in Madison, Wisconsin; Lincoln, Illinois; Blairstown, New Jersey. It seemed that hundreds of people, hoping for a reward, cheap publicity, or a chunk of ransom money, were sure they had seen Ed Bremer. One deranged fellow in Brooklyn claimed to be holding him hostage. Another kook claimed Bremer was "being held in a lumber camp outside Montreal."

FBI agents were now the desperados. Under pressure from J. Edgar Hoover and FDR, they chased any lead. So did the press. Joseph Keenan, assistant U.S. attorney general for St. Paul, complained that "a hundred newspapermen and photographers are gathering in the city, liberally pursuing agents of the government and local police as well as surrounding the premises of Mr. Bremer." Keenan said he was being pestered by men from Paramount Newsreel and was trying to discourage them without alienating them.

Meanwhile, detectives Tom Brown and James Crumley both visited the Sawyer farm. Through Harry, they got a message to the kidnappers: the Bremers would pay no ransom unless they had proof that Ed was alive.

On the morning of January 20, Dr. Henry Nippert awoke to "a heavy noise." He assumed a milkman had dropped a bottle in the cold dawn. He rolled over and drifted back to dream land.

Dr. Nippert was a German immigrant, nearly 65 years old, and a physician to the Bremer family who lived on prosperous Summit Hill.

Dr. Nippert's wife had an awful cold. To keep from being disturbed in her restless sleep, she had silenced the bells of their bedside phone by stuffing tissues into them.

"I arose at 7:15 and while shaving, the telephone rang," Nippert recalled. The maid had answered the downstairs extension, which was ringing properly. "The [voice on the] telephone said to look under the front porch and don't be scared."

So he instructed his maid to check the front door. Its glass had been shattered by an empty bottle, and messages had been left in a "rather large envelope."

Dr. Henry Nippert's front door, broken by Bremer kidnappers delivering a message in a bottle.

One of those notes had been typed by Shotgun George Ziegler. It was meant for Walter Magee and chastised him for contacting the police:

YOU MUST BE PROUD OF YOURSELF BY NOW. IF BREMER DON'T GET BACK, HIS FAMILY HAS YOU TO THANK . . . WE'RE GOING TO GIVE YOU ONE MORE CHANCE, *THE LAST*. FIRST OF ALL, ALL COPPERS MUST BE PULLED OFF. SECOND, THE DOUGH MUST BE READY. THE MONEY MUST NOT BE HOT AS IT WILL BE EXAMINED BEFORE BREMER IS RELEASED. IF DAHILL IS SO HOT TO MEET US, YOU CAN SEND HIM OUT WITH THE DOUGH.

Also in the envelope was a note from Bremer to his wife and daughter, addressing them by their nicknames.

My dearest Patz and Hertzy.
Oh, I've been thinking of you so much, day and night . . . I can just see you waiting for me to come back. My dears, don't lose courage. I'll be holding you both in my arms before long and that is all that I want in this world is both of you.

Ed Bremer's heartfelt letters amounted to a response to the letter Magee and the police had drafted demanding "proof of life." The trouble was, Magee had never sent that letter to the kidnappers. There was another intriguing twist.

IF DAHILL IS SO HOT TO MEET US . . .

This seemed to refer to a police meeting at which Chief Dahill was showing off a rifle given to him by the FBI. He picked up that rifle, aimed it at the window, and said he wished he had the kidnappers in his sights. Somehow the kidnappers heard about that scene. Its only witnesses were Dahill himself and the two members of the kidnap squad: Charles Tierney and Tom Brown.

Who had told the kidnappers about it?

The kidnappers' notes had also included a direct threat: "You better stop listening to those assholes [the police] and *this time* do what *we* tell you. The money must be delivered tonight. With all the conniving, we still got the boy. Either you get him back tonight or the coppers get him back stiff."

The kidnappers instructed Magee to go to the Jefferson Lines bus station in St. Paul "at 8:20 P.M. *sharp*. Take the money and get on the bus leaving this station for Des Moines at 8:40 P.M. Register at the Fort Des Moines hotel."

Phillip Smith, head cashier at Otto Bremer's American National Bank, had prepared the ransom and locked it in the vault, twenty-five packages of $5 and $10 bills stuffed into two suitcases. But Magee couldn't comply with the kidnappers' instructions because "the time lock at the bank was set for 8 o'clock [in the morning] and we could not get the money."

"In this instance Tom Brown got word of this fact to the boys who were waiting at the pay-off spot," Edna Murray told the FBI. "They immediately abandoned their position."

Now Adolph Bremer called on his friend Floyd Olson, governor of Minnesota. Olson had been swept into office during a wave of populist anger. He had run on the platform that "every person is entitled to an opportunity to earn a living." Olson advocated the "abolition of capitalism for a system of public ownership."

That was his public position, anyway.

Sitting in his office was his friend, capitalism incarnate, Adolph Bremer, godfather of beer, money, and real estate.

Bremer told the governor that he had begun to worry that a $200,000 cash drain might cripple his business.

The kidnappers, he told the governor, were willing to give it another try, and their latest ransom note demanded that four stickers of the National Recovery Administration be used as signals that the ransom was ready. These stickers bore the symbol of the NRA, a dark blue eagle. The stickers were to be placed on windows at the Magee Construction Corporation when the ransom was ready.

Governor Olson suggested cutting the eagles in half to send a negotiating signal to the gang.

The next day, a Sunday and day five of the kidnapping, J. Edgar Hoover sent his troubleshooter Harold "Pop" Nathan to meet with the Bremers. Adolph floated the idea of offering the kidnappers $50,000 for his son. Pop Nathan said whatever Adolph decided to do, the FBI would stay in the background until Edward was delivered. Then they would expect the family's full cooperation in hunting the kidnappers.

Meanwhile, Shotgun George was busy on his typewriter, impatient with Adolph Bremer's stall tactics. On Monday he had Volney Davis leave a note at the home of a coal company executive. It warned Adolph Bremer to "pull off the cops, newspapers and radio" and added: "You can go fuck yourself now."

The details of the kidnapping, including the supposedly confidential ransom notes, were now making headlines. Adolph suspected the St. Paul cops were feeding the media. He called for another meeting with Pop Nathan and finally showed him all the ransom notes. Nathan sent them to Washington.

The *St. Paul Daily News,* in particular, seemed much too well informed, Pop Nathan decided. He called Chief Dahill to a meeting at a hotel room to talk about this and other matters. Dahill, whom the FBI had classified as "dumb," had pulled off a neat trick and now revealed it to Pop Nathan.

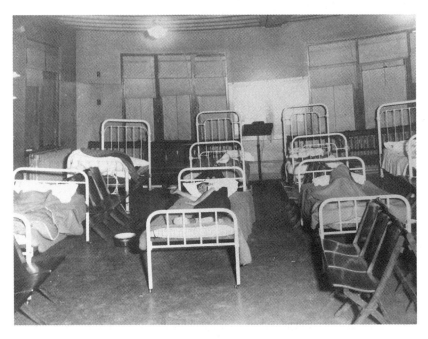

St. Paul policemen slept on cots at the station during the Bremer kidnapping, January 22, 1934.

Dahill had met with his two-man kidnap squad, Charles Tierney and Tom Brown. They were the only three people in the room. Dahill said that a milk bottle had been thrown through Dr. Nippert's door. It actually had been a Lavoris mouthwash bottle. Brown left the meeting while Dahill and Tierney stayed to work on strategy. A few hours later, the *Daily News* published an extra saying that the message had been contained in a milk bottle. Neither Dahill nor Tierney had left the room.

That proved that Tom Brown was secretly feeding the press. Brown's treachery was compounded by the fact that the *Daily News* was launching page-one assaults on Dahill's police department. But Dahill suspected Brown of a deeper betrayal. He told Pop Nathan, "It's my belief Brown eased the Hamm and Bremer kidnappings."

Adolph Bremer expressed "considerable surprise" when informed of the FBI's growing suspicion of Brown. He had been responsible for Tom Brown being made chief of police, he told the FBI, and "felt very badly that any suspicion could be raised against him." Walter Magee, also surprised, "narrated at length the political indebtedness of Tom Brown to Adolph Bremer."

So the FBI was learning how it had worked in St. Paul during Prohibition. Leon Gleckman bought off the politicians. Adolph Bremer brewed the illegal beer. And Tom Brown, fat with bribes, overrode the honest men on his police force. Brown had been appointed chief with the blessing of both Leon Gleckman and Adolph Bremer.

Active in Democratic Party politics, the Bremer family was bound to create enemies. One of them, Joseph Mulheran of Minneapolis, wrote U.S. attorney general Homer Cummings to opine that the Bremers had been "caught in a machine made by their own hand." He noted that the Bremers had been influential in electing Olson governor: "This, sir, is to my way of thinking the number one reason why Minnesota has been both a winter and summer resort for the mobs, gunmen, stock salesmen and what have you. The Bremer-Olson machine ain't what she used to be but she's still in good working order. Look up one Mr. Walter McGee [*sic*], Bremer's boy Friday. Look up 'Stillwater' [Penitentiary] releases and pardons."

A newspaper publisher from North Dakota wrote to the Justice Department: "Regarding the Hamm and Bremer kidnapping cases, there is talk that both [victims] belonged to an alcohol ring and . . . failed to make a satisfactory adjustment" with gangsters when Prohibition ended.

"This seems to be the general impression throughout Minnesota." The FBI heard from another source that many Minnesotans were skeptical about the kidnapping and presumed it was an "inside job" since Ed Bremer's bank was known to cater to racketeers.

Meanwhile, in Bensenville, Edward Bremer endured another day of his "living hell," hogtied in bed, fed greasy food, and being frog-marched to the bathroom. The gang had confiscated his rosary and so he prayed in the dark room, using his fingers to count the Hail Marys.

One of his guardians, Lapland Willie Weaver, "would come in many times and say, 'I know it is getting awfully tough, Ed, but grit your teeth. You have got to stick it out. It will be worse for you if you don't' . . . Several times [Weaver] asked me to join him for a highball."

Sometimes his guard was Alvin Karpis, and Ed tried to wheel and deal with Creepy. Ed said he was buddies with Jack Peifer and Harry Sawyer. He asked whether Karpis knew those guys. Karpis, ever cagey, said no.

"You just ask them about me and find out how many times I've handled hot bonds for them," Bremer said. "You'd have made more money by coming to me, kidnapping somebody else I'd told you about." He then named a St. Paul railroad heir and a banker as the best targets.

Apparently the gang did not trust the telephone, assuming, rightly in some cases, that the lines were tapped. They communicated via Shotgun George. He drove back and forth from St. Paul to Bensenville, an eight-hour drive on sometimes icy roads. On this particular night, Ziegler told the gang he had cruised past Walter Magee's construction company. Its windows were festooned with half-eagles. He interpreted this correctly as the family's effort to reduce the ransom and got that message back to the gang in Bensenville.

Karpis, chronically sick to his stomach, was getting depressed. There was no way they'd take half the money. Fred Barker began floating the idea that they'd have to kill Ed Bremer and run for it.

25

"MOST UNBEARABLE"

After the first week of the Bremer kidnapping, Tom Brown, under suspicion, was shut out of police strategy meetings. The kidnappers had gotten their last insider dope. From now on they'd have to rely on what they read in the papers and on rumors collected in St. Paul by Harry Sawyer and Shotgun George.

On January 25, Ziegler stuffed a note inside a coffee can and dispatched Volney Davis to drop it at the home of John Miller, a pool hall proprietor and Bremer family friend. Davis phoned Miller and said, "I put a Hills Bros. coffee can on your porch. There are some children playing out front and I wish you would run up immediately and pick it up and take it to Adolph Bremer."

The note directed the Bremers to locate a black bag in the Union Depot with further instructions. The kidnappers, optimistic that this would finally shake loose the ransom, sent Davis to buy three flashlights with extra bulbs and batteries at Grand & Silver, a St. Paul hardware store. Davis asked for red lenses for the flashlights, a request that made the transaction memorable to the clerk, Florence Humphrey. The lenses and flashlights were essential in the plan for the ransom drop.

St. Paul had been swirling with rumors, and now they reached a crescendo. A man named Harry Wunderlich accused Ed Bremer of conspiring with con men to swindle him in a horse-racing scam. The rumors grew wilder, and the supposed conspiracies darker, until the Bremers were suspected by some of engineering the kidnapping for financial gain. The Commercial State Bank's gangster connections were dissected in living rooms, taverns, and coffee houses and on street corners. The Associated Press and the city's newspapers threatened to publish these rumors unless the Bremers gave them something else to print. It amounted, said FBI agent William Rorer, to "blackmail."

So Adolph Bremer held a press conference in his capacious drawing room. He was a handsome, good-natured fellow, elegantly dressed and with short-cut white hair. The reporters jammed in there amid luxurious furniture, polished floors, and potted ferns.

The *Daily News* reported that with "tears in his eyes, his usual smile replaced by deep lines of worry," Adolph broke down when he tried to speak.

Magee, at Adolph's side, said, "You don't have to say anything, Mr. Bremer."

But Bremer had a message for the kidnappers. The Bremer houses were watched, the phones tapped, he said. Therefore, he and the kidnappers would have to foil the FBI by turning to another communications channel. He was determined not to pay and then find his son had been killed. He demanded another note in Ed's handwriting and gave the kidnappers a deadline of three days.

The next day, Lillian Dickman, a cashier at Bremer's bank, answered a knock on her door. There stood Volney Davis, whom Dickman described as "tall and thin with a sandy complexion." He handed her two notes, one written by Ed Bremer: "Pa, I'm relying on you, this is most unbearable. It's just a living hell."

As their final surprise emissary, the gang chose a priest close to the Bremers, Father John Deere. Volney Davis thrust a note into the priest's hand with instructions for the delivery of the money. Perhaps the gang was hoping for the intervention of the Almighty. Strangely enough, it worked.

On February 6, three weeks into the kidnapping, Walter Magee drove to a St. Paul intersection, looking for a Chevy coupe with Shell Oil signs on the door. Its side windows had been clouded by some chemical. Magee loaded the car with two suitcases containing almost twenty-five thousand $5 and $10 bills.

He drove the Chevy into the countryside and, as instructed, followed a bus heading for Rochester. Spying a group of red flashlight beams, he turned down a country road and drove until he saw five flashes of headlights, then set out the suitcases and drove off.

One day later, in that Bensenville room, Ed Bremer was given a new suit of clothes. The gang had read how the FBI recently had figured out how to lift prints from clothing. They stuffed Bremer into the back seat, where he crouched amid smelly refueling cans. In Wisconsin during an icy rainstorm, they pulled over and Doc Barker refueled the car.

Doc spilled gas on his gloves and took one of them off. He tossed the empty cans into a farmer's field and then the kidnappers drove toward Rochester, Minnesota. From Bremer's description, the gang may have been planning to execute him if it discovered that the ransom money was marked. "We stopped near a railroad track. I was told to get out of the car. Two men remained with me and walked me off the road and into a ditch, up against a fence alongside a railroad track." Another gangster drove off to "make a phone call to see if the money had been transferred satisfactorily, or whether it was marked." About twenty minutes later, the car returned, its driver satisfied that the money was unmarked.

The kidnappers drove Bremer to Rochester, instructing him to take the bus back to St. Paul. Karpis was glad to get rid of this prickly million-aire. "All right, Bremer," he said, "beat it."

"I took a train from Rochester," Bremer recalled, "then from Owatonna to St. Paul I traveled by bus. I got off the bus on Wabasha Street . . . and went to my father's house in a taxi." As a precaution, he had the cabbie pull over two blocks short of his father's mansion. It was 1:00 AM when he appeared, a limping phantom at the mansion's front door. He saw his sister Louise through the glass and tapped on it with his key.

She screamed.

26

"TO HELL WITH DUTY"

Every city has its mother road, the cow path that became a wagon trail, then a rutted dirt road, then the mail pike, then two lanes of asphalt, then a congested urban artery. St. Paul's mother road followed the trail from Fort Snelling to the cabins of Pig's Eye Parrant and other whiskey sellers, set up just outside the military reservation. The road was beaten by soldiers trekking in for fun and peddlers journeying to the fort for profit. Originally called Fort Road, it was renamed West Seventh Street by city fathers with a tin ear for history.

The grandest property on Fort Road is the disused, fifteen-acre Schmidt Brewery. In its beer-making years it was a steaming, bustling Bremer fiefdom of brick towers and cobblestone streets. Across Fort

Road from the brewery stands Adolph Bremer's mansion. It's a gritty, untenable site for a mansion now, but in its day, surrounded by orchards and gardens, it must have been lovely.

During the second week of February 1934, the streets around the Bremer mansion were clogged with the automobiles of police and news reporters. The press reported that Ed Bremer "slept today with government agents posted at every entrance to his home."

Federal agents blocked Tom Brown when he tried to walk into the mansion. In the eyes of the FBI he was no longer a cop but a suspect. Only after the repeated intercessions of detective Charles Tierney was Brown allowed into the house. County attorney Michael Kinkead kept showing up at the Bremer mansion too, unwelcome by both the FBI and Chief Dahill. The chief knew Kinkead was Brown's ally. Kinkead was "on intimate terms with the Bremers," the FBI said, and encouraged the family to offer minimal cooperation with federal agents. "The attitude of Kinkead and the Bremer family is not all it should be," noted FBI man Hugh Clegg.

Adolph Bremer had called a press conference, and now his parlor was a riot of jostling reporters, photographers, and newsreel men. Their

Adolph and Edward Bremer, dressed to give a news conference, February 1934.

focus was a man "bruised about the head" who could hardly walk on a gimpy, throbbing knee, an "intensely nervous" man who often "covered his face with his hands, and breathed in a whistle through his teeth as if in great pain." Edward Bremer, smoking Chesterfields and clad in a "lounging robe, patent leather slippers and a white shirt open at the neck," tried to answer reporters' questions but often broke down sobbing.

Dr. Nippert warned photographers that their flashes were disturbing to a man who had "been in a dark room for several weeks." He checked Ed Bremer's pulse. Watching from the sidelines, Adolph the patriarch leaked tears.

Ed Bremer recounted how the kidnappers had beat him until his eyes had filled with blood. How they had rammed his head under the dashboard. At the hideout, he said, his captors examined his head and "washed my cuts as best they could." But they also threatened to chain him to the bed if he gave them trouble. They spoke mostly in whispers, he said.

It made great copy. But Edward Bremer was telling the press much less than he knew, and he wasn't much more truthful with the FBI. On the day after his release, Bremer told the FBI that in twenty-two days of captivity he "never got a look at one of" his kidnappers. He told conflicting stories about how long he'd been blindfolded.

In truth, Ed Bremer had conversations with his kidnappers in Bensenville, sometimes face to face. But he told his father that the Bremers could not cooperate with the FBI out of fear of what the kidnappers might do to his wife and little Betty.

J. Edgar Hoover, obsessed with Dillinger, wanted to pin the Bremer kidnapping on him. He once again dispatched his troubleshooter, Harold "Pop" Nathan, to the Bremer mansion for a cozy with Adolph.

Nathan reported that Adolph was a gregarious fellow who "had built a large following" in St. Paul and in forty years of business had fired only one man. But Pop Nathan wasn't easily charmed. He told Adolph: your son's claim that he can't identify his kidnappers is "bunk."

Adolph said, "go easy on my son, give him a few days."

When Ed Bremer finally did grant Pop Nathan an interview, he kept insisting he never saw his captors' faces. When reminded of his duty to help find the kidnappers, Bremer replied, "To hell with duty."

Then the FBI got lucky.

On Sunday, February 10, Reuben Grossman, a farmer on an ice-fishing expedition near Portage, Wisconsin, happened upon four gas cans and a funnel. He took his curious discovery to the local sheriff, who contacted the FBI.

Meanwhile FBI man William Rorer, who had made his reputation by tracking down Machine Gun Kelly, had taken charge of the Bremer case. That afternoon he interviewed Ed Bremer. According to an FBI memo, Bremer was "filled with fear. On one occasion he cried and left the room. He stated that his daughter was threatened with death if he talked and he was not going to talk. He was antagonistic to all who sought to solve the case."

The FBI was unsympathetic. The day after he took over the case, Rorer issued a threat of his own. The agency drafted a statement intended to publicly chastise Ed Bremer for his non-cooperation. Agents showed it to Bremer. Suddenly Bremer's memory improved, and the Rorer interviews went on all week. Hoover, convinced that the key to cracking the case was finding the hideout, pressed his agents to sweat Bremer for details.

During these interviews, Bremer dropped hints about his family's involvement with the underworld and the corruption of the local cops. The gangsters were "not afraid of St. Paul Police, but are afraid of federal agents," Bremer said.

Bremer "knew plenty he would never tell about banks and politics that had caused the kidnapping," the FBI reported.

Then came a news flash from FBI headquarters in Washington. The gas cans found in Wisconsin bore the fingerprints of Doc Barker. Freed of their Dillinger obsession, the FBI began to see things more clearly. The Barkers . . . the Green Lantern . . . Harry Sawyer.

Under the assumption that the kidnappers had used the Green Lantern for central planning, police shut the tavern. Added to the unemployment rolls: a "crippled Frenchman" cook, a piano player named "Doc," and two "colored" employees, a porter and a cleaning woman.

The FBI focus on Sawyer raised questions about his long-rumored connection with St. Paul police. One agent promised a newspaper "disclosures that will knock the roof off this town."

27

THE HEAT

Never had the Barker gang felt this kind of heat. By the spring of 1934, their protectors, Tom Brown and Harry Sawyer, could no longer offer refuge in St. Paul. The Barkers weren't welcome, either, in Frank Nitti's Chicago. They couldn't retreat to Missouri, where Sheriff Kelly's gun-toting widow was eager to escort Fred and Karpis to the gallows. What kept the gang from splitting was $200,000 that was too hot to spend.

The day Bremer was released, the Barker brothers, Volney Davis, Shotgun George Ziegler, and Byron Bolton met at Ziegler's apartment. "Fred Barker and Volney Davis each carried a large suitbox," recalled Bolton. "Fred Barker said, 'Well, here is the money, we had a hard time getting it.'"

But they would have a harder time spending it. To track the ransom money, the FBI adopted a nascent form of computer technology. Using its own clerks and a few temporary hires, the agency had every serial number from the Bremer ransom bills recorded on punch cards. The machinery was made by the Tabulating Machine Company, founded in 1880 and fated to become part of IBM. Since the ransom amounted to 25,000 bills, the tabulation took a few days. The point was to produce an ordered list that bank tellers could consult. That list was sent to every bank in the nation.

The gang realized that the serial numbers had been recorded, but they were desperate for cash. When Shotgun George Ziegler exchanged $5,000 in Chicago, the news was all over the papers. Doc Barker then took $100,000 out to Reno, but his connections there would process no more than $10,000. Through aspiring gang member Willie Harrison, the Barkers approached a Toledo casino, but the money was too hot for them as well.

The kidnappers were reluctant to leave Chicago without dividing the ransom, but they couldn't stay either. By mid-March, the FBI publicly identified the Barkers and Karpis as suspects in the Bremer kidnapping, and their pictures started appearing in newspapers and on post office walls.

The pressure was so extreme that it drove Fred and Karpis to the most desperate act of their lives. Karpis packed up and told Dolores

Delaney he would be gone for a while. In truth, he wasn't going far. He and Fred had persuaded Doctor Joseph Moran, a drunken abortionist, to perform gruesome, painful plastic surgery meant to alter their appearance and remove their fingerprints.

The surgery was performed in a Chicago hotel room, and Fred and Karpis would be swathed in bandages for days. The surgery was absurdly crude: Moran wrapped their fingers in rubber bands, injected the fingertips with cocaine, and shaved flesh off. The pain was so excruciating that neither Karpis nor Fred left the hotel room for ten days.

During this time, Fred was visited by a Chicago crook named Oliver Berg. Fred wanted Berg's help in laundering the ransom. Berg couldn't get a deal done because Fred was in such pain, and even Moran's shots of morphine didn't help. During one of Berg's visits, Fred opened his hotel room window and threatened to jump out. Then he begged Berg to shoot him. Berg, perhaps hoping to enjoy a 12.5 percent laundry fee, declined.

Meanwhile Dolores Delaney, three months pregnant, shopped and caroused with the Barker crowd. She ate dinners with Shotgun George Ziegler and his wife Irene. She went drinking with Fred's girl, the abrasive Paula Harmon, whom she was beginning to loathe. She attended the wondrous World's Fair. She visited Ma Barker and enjoyed Ma's fried chicken, biscuits, and gravy. The next time she saw Fred at Ma's apartment was a shocker. "I noticed that Fred's hands were bandaged and asked him about Alvin, as I believed they had been in some accident."

Not to worry, said Fred, Alvin will be home soon, and get ready, because we're all leaving for Toledo. But not everybody would make it to Toledo.

Near midnight of March 20, Shotgun George Ziegler was leaving Minerva's, a restaurant in Cicero, Illinois. This was the Chicago suburb that was "owned" by Capone's Outfit. A car drove by, shotguns appeared in the windows, and after four blasts Ziegler lay dead on the sidewalk. He lived by the shotgun and died by it as well.

Dolores Delaney visited Ma Barker's apartment the next day and found Paula Harmon with Ma, reading newspaper accounts of Ziegler's assassination. Later that day, Ziegler's wife Irene drifted into Ma's apartment, and Delaney offered her sympathy money. She declined, saying Ma Barker had already given her what she needed.

Nobody was ever arrested in Ziegler's murder, but among the suspects would be the Barker gang. Shotgun George had been drinking in Chicago, boasting about his role in the Bremer job. Ziegler, however, also had enemies in the Chicago mob who may have arranged his murder.

If it was the Barkers who engineered the murder of Shotgun George, they had made a crucial mistake. The FBI swept through Ziegler's belongings, and Purvis wrote that the agency "got more information from Ziegler dead than we would have alive." The Chicago underworld's suspicion and resentment of the Barkers grew, Purvis said, until there was no safe place for them in town.

Most ominously for the Barkers, the death of Shotgun George severed their link to Byron Bolton. Ziegler's golfing buddy now owed the Barker gang no loyalty. Neither Karpis nor Fred seemed to recognize that the death of Shotgun George made Bolton a grave danger to their freedom.

28

"NO CRIMINALS HERE"

After the Bremer kidnapping, the *St. Paul Daily News* went into a frenzy. Behind its managing editor, Howard Kahn, the newspaper launched verbal assaults on the St. Paul police. These were not bland editorials buried inside, but screaming, boldface screeds on page one. Underneath end-of-the-world headlines it ran accusations PRINTED IN ALL CAPS. These verbal fireworks exploded regularly atop page one. The newspaper also printed excerpts from citizens' letters supporting its position.

On the surface, the *Daily News* was rabid for reform. But closer examination raises questions about the paper's motives. The focus of their attacks was Chief Tom Dahill, a man of relative integrity in a long line of corrupt police officials. The police department that the *Daily News* sought to embarrass had been largely built not by Dahill but by Tom Brown. It was Brown who ran the protection scheme that brought robbers, killers, and kidnappers to St. Paul. It was Dahill who tried to bust up the protection racket.

Tom Brown and James Crumley had money to pass around and so remained a powerful faction within the police force. Yet the *Daily News* never targeted Brown, Crumley, or their patron, Leon Gleckman. Later events were to show that Brown and Gleckman served as anonymous sources for insider information that the *Daily News* turned into splashy stories. The *Daily News* also publicly backed Brown's failed campaign for sheriff. Brown was friendly with *Daily News* managing editor Howard Kahn and city editor Fred Strong. Whether the newspaper was manipulated by Brown, or played along to obtain exclusives that built circulation, or had some hidden interest in common with his faction, is a question that can't be answered with the evidence at hand.

One of the newspaper's most sensational charges was directed at detective Charles Tierney, a Dahill ally. It was printed while Tierney was on the kidnap squad, investigating the Bremer case. The *Daily News* noted that Dillinger gangster Tommy Carroll was arrested in St. Paul on September 4, 1933, and released by Tierney on September 6. Carroll was one of the nation's most wanted men. After Tierney let him go, Carroll robbed a bank in Brainerd, Minnesota, and then killed a policeman in San Antonio, Texas.

The St. Paul street cops who arrested Carroll for drunkenness and weapons possession had done their jobs, the *Daily News* noted. But their honest efforts had been undermined by the old guard of corrupt detectives who'd learned their tricks during Prohibition. This, the *Daily News* said, destroyed police morale. It noted "hundreds" of cases where St. Paul cops laughed when citizens asked them to enforce the law.

To bolster its case, the newspaper quoted Val O'Farrel, "city of NY ace police detective." "St. Paul is the kidnapping set's playground," O'Farrel said. "Gangsters know they can get away with murder there. It is a notorious layoff spot where criminals have felt secure for years."

The corruption in the police department ran deep, and although Dahill tried, Brown's clique was tough to root out. Civil service protection and political favoritism limited Dahill's power. One "reform" in the post-Brown era was to put detective William McMullen in charge of a special crime squad, which supposedly would prove incorruptible. But McMullen was also a Brown crony, the FBI learned, and "friend of Harry Sawyer and a contact man between the police department and the underworld."

St. Paul's street cops didn't bother hiding their cynicism from news reporters. Posted on a highway and ordered to check every passing car after a bank robbery, cops and reporters alike retreated to a roadside café. There they drank beer, ate sandwiches, and played poker as cars zoomed by outside. One cop joked that, since they had only pistols and the bank robbers were armed with Tommy guns, the police would have to "hide in the weeds" if any gangsters drove up.

But the men who had done the most to encourage that corruption, Leon Gleckman and Tom Brown, got a pass from the *Daily News*. A skeptical columnist for the labor weekly the *Union Advocate* cited Kahn's "open friendship" with Gleckman. The columnist wrote that he would love to be privy to "some of the conversation that took place between Kahn and Leon Gleckman" when Brown was police chief.

It was probably no coincidence that the *Daily News* front-page editorials began in election season. Incumbent St. Paul mayor William Mahoney was a founder of a labor movement that many found threatening. His opponent, Mark Gehan, stood for the city's old guard.

By the mid-1930s, all three St. Paul daily newspapers were owned ultimately by the Ridder family. Newspapers were highly labor intensive and had every economic reason to oppose Mahoney, who campaigned for higher wages, shorter hours, and more advantageous collective bargaining rules. One especially sensitive issue for newspapers was the movement to toughen child labor laws, since publishers employed children in their distribution systems. Mahoney complained that because of this self-interest, all three St. Paul dailies were slanting the news against him and his party.

But Mahoney knew all about blaming crime on the incumbent mayor. During his campaign for office in 1932, he was editor of the *Union Advocate*. His newspaper plastered the legal troubles of Leon Gleckman all over page one. These articles blamed the city's corruption on the incumbent mayor's inability to thwart Gleckman's power. As soon as Mahoney won election, all mention of Gleckman and crime miraculously disappeared from the *Advocate*'s front page.

As a climax to the *Daily News* front-page crusade, Howard Kahn, its commander, demanded a grand jury investigation of the St. Paul police. This demand may have impressed readers, but the Brown-Gleckman faction had little to fear from a grand jury led by county attorney Michael Kinkead. As the prosecuting attorney, he would decide which charges were made and what evidence was presented. The *Daily News* campaign, in effect, supported the restoration of the Brown-Gleckman empire. The targets of the newspaper campaign, Mayor Mahoney and Chief Dahill, occupied the power spots coveted by Gleckman and Brown.

Meanwhile, Mahoney succumbed to incumbent syndrome, that form of denial that makes politicians declare that all is wonderful under their watch. Mahoney looked back at his promise to round up criminals and judged that he'd done a mighty fine job. In his fantasy world, there'd been no bank robberies or underworld murders during his term. He pointed to municipal court records showing thousands of cases processed during his administration. An opponent pointed out that these were mostly traffic citations.

Police commissioner John McDonald—perhaps sober, perhaps not—leaped to the mayor's defense, claiming that St. Paul's crooks had "killed each other off."

But St. Paul was in for a national embarrassment. On February 16, a week after Ed Bremer stumbled home, U.S. attorney general Homer Cummings singled out St. Paul as the "poison spot" of American crime.

Mayor Mahoney and Police Commissioner McDonald joined in a chorus of denial. "There are no criminals here," Mahoney said, and then contradicted himself. "They just come to enjoy our lakes."

The *Daily News* answered: "How a mayor who was elected on a platform of cleaning the gangsters and racketeers out of Saint Paul can be so blind . . . is one of the miracles of modern government."

The threat of a U.S. Senate investigation caused Mahoney to join the call for a grand jury probe. One of his rivals for office, county coroner Carl Ingerson, said that "gambling and crime are linked amazingly and in a reprehensible manner with the police department." Ingerson promised to bring twenty witnesses to the grand jury. Mayoral candidate Mark Gehan vowed to clean up what Mahoney could not. Mahoney edged into paranoia, claiming to see a "gigantic conspiracy" against him.

Gangsters had served a social purpose during Prohibition, since no liquor could have flowed without them. But with booze legal, all the Prohibition era's thugs, robbers, and schemers were an army with neither mission nor purpose. The citizens of St. Paul lost their tolerance for gangsters. People were complaining of joints and dives springing up in the neighborhoods. Affluent families so feared kidnapping that many employed watchmen at their homes day and night. Women's clubs, among others, were demanding reform. Candidate Gehan appeared at the YWCA and asked his audience to consider why there had been four major kidnappings in St. Paul while Minneapolis had suffered none. He blamed the police, especially "a few men in key positions."

The *Daily News* kept its crusade going. One day it reported that St. Paul cops were simply ignoring many crimes, including thefts that took place at police headquarters. The paper complained that even killings went uninvestigated and singled out the case of a murdered holdup man named Carl Sager.

The *Daily News* kept the shooting of Roy McCord on the front page. Readers were reminded that McCord, "a cripple," was in great pain. More than two months after the shooting, he was in and out of the hospital. Across page one they splashed the picture of his six young children, sitting obediently in a row on a couch, with an inset of his worried wife. McCord had run through his savings and hadn't had a paycheck in weeks. The *Daily News* dunned readers for help. Fundraisers were set up, including neighborhood dances. "It is a comfort to know the children will not go hungry," McCord was quoted as saying. Why, the *Daily News* asked, had St. Paul police failed to find McCord's shooter?

Detective William McMullen had been trumpeted as the answer to police corruption in St. Paul. He was sold to the naïve as a tough, experienced cop with integrity. Supposedly, he was going to clean up the mess Brown had made. But McMullen was a member of the Brown clique, according to Bess Green, and according to Gladys Sawyer, he had run messages from the police department out to the Sawyer farm.

In early March of 1934, McMullen was drinking downtown with his partner, Michael McGinnis. When they left the tavern, they saw a parked car with a Fort Snelling soldier in it, in the company of two girls. Something about that set McMullen off.

McMullen, a big guy at over two hundred pounds, pulled the 19-year-old, 135-pound soldier from the car. He flung the soldier, Emmond Webb, to the ground and started stomping him. The girls tried to interfere, and McMullen sent them sprawling to the sidewalk. Then as his partner McGinnis tried to stop him, McMullen jumped on Webb's legs, fracturing one of them.

Another soldier tried to help Webb, and McMullen tossed this kid through the plate-glass window of a café.

Six witnesses came forward. They added that McMullen, after the stomping, had threatened passersby. No police report was ever filed on this beating. Confronted by *Daily News* reporters, McMullen said, "I admit I had been drinking and had a bottle in my pocket. There is no regulation against carrying a bottle. It was not opened."

Chief Dahill, asked if he had read accounts of the beating, said, "I never read the *Daily News*. The story reported to me varies greatly" from the account in the newspapers.

Case closed.

So in the bizarre politics of the St. Paul police, Dahill was now a defender of McMullen, an ally of his enemy, Tom Brown.

Meanwhile, the grand jury called dozens of witnesses. Curiously, just then the St. Paul police began a roundup of criminals. It made a nice headline. But of the seventeen they nabbed, thirteen were quietly back on the streets the next day.

The grand jury heard that certain St. Paul clubs were held safe from police raids by a "Nightclub Protective Association." Included in that shadowy group were many police officers. They were "protecting" the casinos so they could raid them and rip off the cash.

Familiar names were called to testify: detective Charles Tierney, chief Tom Dahill, and nightclub owner Jack Peifer. One of the gambling dives in question, built into the Mississippi bluffs, was called Mystic Caverns. It was no mystic revelation when the jury discovered that Jack Peifer owned a piece of its action.

A partner in this illegal gambling club was a cop, lieutenant Jack Foster. His official duties were to conduct the police band, so he had plenty of time to oversee the roulette wheel. Individual cops on the St. Paul force kept the profits from designated slot machines at Mystic Caverns.

When St. Paul police heard rumors that bandits were about to rob the Mystic Caverns, cops surrounded the club in ambush. The bandits outsmarted them by staying home. Among the leaders of the frustrated ambush were two cops who knew how the game was played in St. Paul: Fred "Hitler" Raasch and "Big Tom" Brown.

One of the cops called before the grand jury was Carl Kalmen, who moonlighted as the bouncer at Mystic Caverns. He testified before the jury and was asked to come back for more. He failed to show up for his next patrol shift. Reporters called his wife to ask his whereabouts. "I don't know," she said and hung up. Chief Dahill gave the same response. Kalmen would reappear only after the grand jury disbanded.

Just before Easter, the grand jury issued seven indictments, all naming owners of nightclubs. Jack Peifer, godfather of St. Paul gambling, was miraculously unindicted. The jury also pronounced the police department innocent of any connection with gamblers.

The FBI would hear that county attorney Michael Kinkead, the official in charge of grand juries, was himself suspect. Detective James Crumley told the FBI that Kinkead "was the man from whom Tom Brown gets his support." Crumley said that Kinkead got a percentage out of a downtown money-laundering shop. Operated by a character named Frisco Dutch, it had fenced more than $350,000 worth of stolen bonds.

With Kinkead conducting, the grand jury sang a chorus of confidence in its hometown. "There's no justification," the lyrics went, "for charges that excess crime exists here." One historian concluded that corrupt officials "managed to 'reach' grand jurors and the result was a whitewash."

A fellow from Indiana, speeding toward St. Paul, was about to demonstrate just how wrong a grand jury could be.

29

"ONE TOUGH SWEDE"

That March, John Dillinger was making his famous escape from an Indiana prison, supposedly using a fake gun he'd fashioned out of a broom handle. The *St. Paul Pioneer Press* thrilled its readers with the headline: ARMY OF 20,000 HUNTS DILLINGER. The story noted that police expected Public Enemy Number One to fight to the death rather than be captured. His rumored destination: St. Paul.

Armed with machine guns, detectives from St. Paul were sent to guard the two bridges that connected the Twin Cities to Wisconsin. Their instructions were to check every car that crossed. This information, printed in the newspapers, was surely read by Dillinger's local connection, Pat Reilly. That, combined with the attitude of St. Paul cops, pretty much greased Dillinger's entrance to the promised land.

Dillinger's escape made him a media darling. Although the Barker-Karpis gang was more effective and dangerous, they lacked Dillinger's charisma and sense of audience. Alvin Karpis was too cold to be an idol. The Barker brothers were beady-eyed, illiterate pipsqueaks. But Dillinger! Here was a wise-cracking, gum-chewing, aw-shucks farm boy who tossed out one-liners as he boldly robbed banks. This guy sold newspapers. Here was a criminal Americans could root for.

Less than twenty-four hours after the Escape Heard Round the World, Dillinger arrived at the protected shores of the Twin Cities. A gang, including Baby Face Nelson, reformulated around him and addressed their cash flow problem by making armed withdrawals from banks. Dillinger had been out of jail for three days when Minnesota readers were blasted with the headline:

SIOUX FALLS BANK HELD UP; COP SHOT

"Using a car stolen in St. Paul . . . the six machine gun bandits lined up the police chief, a patrolman and 40 others at a Sioux Falls bank. The leader closely resembled John Dillinger." Women hostages had been taken to ensure the robbers' safe escape. Dillinger's gang slipped back to their Twin Cities hideouts and split the loot.

That "army of 20,000" who supposedly were looking for Dillinger might as well have been on leave. There were too many leads to follow. That March, Dillinger was allegedly spotted anywhere between Nova Scotia and Tijuana. Acting on a tip, St. Paul cops broke into the shuttered Green Lantern. In that musty tavern, they found two rifles that belonged to Dillinger stuffed into a golf bag. They also discovered a suitcase full of dynamite. But that was as close as they got to Dillinger glory.

They were closer than they knew. Dillinger, Baby Face Nelson, and Homer Van Meter were just down the road.

Van Meter was a buddy Dillinger had made in prison in Indiana. A tall, gangly goofball, an impressionist and a joker, a bank robber and cop killer, Van Meter had succumbed to the criminal fashion du jour and endured cosmetic surgery in order to blur his identity. He also had the surgeon grind the tattooed word HOPE off his arm.

Van Meter had been in and out of the Holy City for weeks. From Harry Sawyer, he purchased an insurance policy guaranteeing his freedom. As part of the deal, Van Meter donated $1,000 to Tom Brown's losing campaign for sheriff.

On March 14, Dillinger was wounded in a bank shootout. His St. Paul connection, Pat Reilly, got the bleeding bandit an appointment with Dr. Nels Mortensen. This man was Harry Sawyer's physician and had served as a reference for Fred Barker when he'd rented on Vernon Street. The doctor patched up Dillinger, who convalesced with his sweetheart Evelyn "Billie" Frechette in the Lincoln Court Apartments in St. Paul.

Billie would later recall her Dillinger days for the magazine *Startling Detective Adventures*.

"John kept pretty much inside [at Lincoln Court] and I did all the shopping and got out of doors occasionally for a motor ride or to see a motion picture. The gang came in for parties . . .

Evelyn "Billie" Frechette being escorted in May 1934 to her trial in the St. Paul Federal Courts Building (now the Landmark Center).

"We had a plan under which I was to answer the door should anyone knock. John . . . would stand in the living room to one side of the
door . . . If the visitors were police, I was to invite them in and then drop
to the floor in case there was shooting. The plot was, however, to avoid
shooting if possible and capture the officers, tying them up so a getaway
could be made."

At Lincoln Court, Dillinger had gotten a precious letter from his
sister and mother-figure, Audrey Hancock. It included pictures of himself as a boy. Touched by this, he wrote to tell her he'd been shot up
but she shouldn't worry. He was "one tough Swede" and "having a lot
of fun."

Of such stuff legends are made. Billie was a short, plump Indian
woman who'd never had much luck with men. "Billie's face was pock-
marked and her complexion was very bad," according to Bess Green.
Billie wrote that Dillinger was "the only man I've ever met who treated
me like a human being and gave me a square deal."

Rumors in St. Paul had Dillinger drinking in taverns and indulging his
love of the movies. At the St. Paul FBI office alone, agents fielded hundreds of phone calls from tipsters. One of them came from Daisy Coffey,
landlady of the Lincoln Court Apartments. "The FBI received lots of
tips of suspicious people," recalled FBI agent Richard Pranke. "In those
days we had very few FBI agents [in St. Paul]. Rufus Coulter . . . had been
given a routine lead, with no idea it was John Dillinger."

Mrs. Coffey had rented an apartment, cash up front, to a woman who
said she intended to move in with her husband. Soon, five people were
coming and going from that apartment. Those people were very quiet,
only used the back entrance, and kept the shades drawn. None seemed
to have a job. Most suspiciously, they had refused to allow the janitor to
enter to install a toilet paper holder.

Mrs. Coffey, unlike the grand jury and the mayor, believed that criminals did cluster in St. Paul.

So FBI agents Rosser "Rusty" Nalls and Rufus Coulter spent a
dull, cold Good Friday evening surveilling, from their car, the Lincoln
Court Apartments. The agents took down car license numbers. They
noticed that yes, the occupants of that apartment did draw the shades
early. They observed people moving around the apartment in a "normal
manner."

It wasn't a whole lot to go on.

As the agents shivered in their car, Public Enemy Number One was having a good time. Dillinger and Billie Frechette were carousing with Eddie and Bess Green.

Eddie and Bess were well connected. Eddie was an ironworker by day and a "jug marker" in his spare time. Gangs depended on local "jug markers" to select banks that were vulnerable to high-profit holdups. Eddie had worked on bank robberies for both the Dillinger and the Barker gangs. Bess was a nightclub manager who had gotten her start with Harry Sawyer at the Green Lantern. Together, the Greens knew every big-time gangster in the Midwest. When Dillinger and his gang sneaked into St. Paul, they depended on the Greens to set them up. It was Bess Green who'd rented the Lincoln Court apartment from Mrs. Coffey.

But Dillinger and Bess Green did not get along. She feared that associating with Dillinger would bring her husband down and her too.

"There appears to be some friction between this woman and Dillinger," the FBI later noted. "She dislikes this mob." Bess saw Dillinger and Billie Frechette as braggarts. Dillinger, in her view, was deliberately creating his own legend. In her opinion, Dillinger had merely bribed his way out of the Crown Point jail and "desired to exploit the toy pistol incident to his credit."

Dillinger had boasted to the Greens that he was able, despite his infamy, to attend movies. He and Billie said they'd just seen the film *Fashions of 1933*. Dillinger joked that this was a mistake, since it would give Billie expensive ideas. On Good Friday, as FBI agents watched their apartment's front door, Billie and Dillinger strolled out the back door and around the corner to a movie house to take in *Joe Palooka*.

As they waited in line for admission, two St. Paul cops pulled up in a squad car. They parked under the marquee so they could use its light to write the evening's reports. Dillinger and Billie acted so squirrelly that one cop got out of the car to ask if Dillinger was ill. He shook the cop off, paid his admission, and ducked into the movies. Dillinger marveled at his luck. He was like the Invisible Man.

On Saturday, the two FBI agents figured they might as well find out whether these tenants, who called themselves Mr. and Mrs. Carl Hellman, were legit. Coulter requested that his supervisor, William Rorer, ask Chief Dahill for backup. Dahill replied that he "cannot trust all his men" and could find only one reliable cop on duty, the 65-year-old detective Henry Cummings.

Agent Rufus Coulter was a tough, silent hombre, one of those recruited by Hoover to give his "college boys" some spine. Partly raised in an orphanage, he was a grammar school dropout who nevertheless worked his way through law school. He'd jumped to the FBI from the Little Rock police department.

Coulter approached the apartment door at Lincoln Court while his partner Nalls covered the front entrance. St. Paul detective Cummings stood behind Coulter, his only weapon a pearl-handled revolver. Coulter rang the bell.

Those three Dillinger hangers-on, the visitors the landlady had complained about, had left the apartment ten minutes before. They were bank robber John Hamilton and two women. Billie and Dillinger expected them to return shortly, so there was no immediate alarm when Billie heard the doorbell.

"John was in bed and I was puttering in the spare room when the doorbell rang," Billie recalled in *Startling Detective Adventures*.

She opened the door as far as the security chain would allow. There stood two cops wearing suits.

"'We would like to talk to Mr. Hellman,'" one of them said.

"Who?" Billie said, and then remembered Dillinger's latest alias.

"'May we come in and wait?'"

"'I'm not dressed,'" Billie recalled saying. "I shut the door in their faces and, heart fluttering, ran for the bedroom."

The cops had no warrant, so they waited in the hallway. Coulter slipped into the apartment superintendent's office and called Inspector Rorer downtown. Rorer scrambled two agents toward Lexington Avenue, but they arrived too late to help.

Inside the apartment, Billie panicked but Dillinger was cool. "Keep your shirt on," he told her. Dillinger and Billie managed to pack one suitcase, half clothes and half ammo. It was so heavy Billie could hardly lift it. Dillinger loaded his machine gun. They were stalling. Dillinger hoped Hamilton would return and give him a better chance in a shootout.

But it was the goofball Homer Van Meter who showed up, pulling to the snowy curb in his shiny green 1934 Ford Coupe. He breezed up to the third floor and headed for apartment 303.

Coulter challenged him.

I'm a soap salesman, Van Meter claimed.

Where are your samples? asked Coulter.

Van Meter said: Out in the car.

He turned to get them.

But he really wanted to give himself shooting room. Coulter followed him downstairs. When they got outside, Van Meter drew his pistol. "You see, asshole, you want this. Here it is."

He began shooting, and Coulter scrambled back into the building to give himself time to draw his weapon.

Dillinger rushed to his apartment window and blasted the street with his machine gun. Billie, trying to pack her clothing, saw Dillinger with "a smoking weapon in his hand and a grim smile on his face."

Before he left that window, a police bullet bounced off Dillinger's bulletproof vest. Then he burst out the front door and into the hallway, spraying machine gun fire in all directions. A bullet tore into his thigh. Billie led him down the stairs, toward the rear entrance, Dillinger bleeding all over the dirty snow in the parking lot. He swept the alley with machine gun fire as Billie backed their Hudson out of the garage. As she sped toward Bess Green's house, the wounded Dillinger scolded her: "Slow down, you'll attract attention."

Meanwhile, Van Meter ran down an alley.

Agent Nalls disabled Van Meter's car by shooting one tire flat. Van Meter hijacked a horse-drawn ash wagon and made a dusty getaway. Dillinger pal John Hamilton and his two women drove up just in time for the gun battle and decided on the safer option of getting the hell out of there.

All the shooting was over in thirty seconds. One neighbor called the cops, imagining somehow that a dog had been shot in the street. Lacking a car radio, agent Nalls ran to the corner drugstore to call for backup. It wasn't until agents tossed the apartment that they realized they'd been in a gunfight with Dillinger. They made a long inventory of what they found there. Included were:

One dark chinchilla men's overcoat.

A guide book to the bond market.

Two feet of dynamite fuse.

Dillinger's boyhood pictures.

"A great many bullets."

It was expensive being a gangster. The public enemies were always aspiring to lives they could never have. Shotgun George's North Woods resort, Harry Sawyer's farm, Dillinger and Billie's high-end wardrobe, Karpis's beach houses . . . all those expensive apartments left empty . . . all that beautiful clothing left behind . . . all those abandoned cars.

After the shooting, Dillinger and Billie Frechette showed up at the apartment of Eddie and Bess Green. "John was hurt, having been shot in the leg, although the wound was not serious," Bess Green told the FBI. The Greens arranged for Dillinger to be treated by a doctor. Bess was soon to become one of the FBI's most potent informers, giving them "certain names that might be put under observation."

The gods of irony arranged it so that Dillinger's escape hit the head-lines along with the news that the grand jury had found St. Paul to be gangster free. The next day was both April Fool's and Easter Sunday, and the St. Paul newspapers had plenty of ink to spill.

The *St. Paul Pioneer Press* editorialized that the Dillinger escape brought "shame and disgrace" to the city. The big black headlines in the *Daily News* screamed:

MACHINE GUNNERS ESCAPE;
NET SPREAD OVER MIDWEST

This was accompanied by pictures of St. Paul policemen examining bullet holes in a hallway and apartment. In a separate article, the Rev. Earnest Parosh, a neighbor of Dillinger's who had "dodged bullets," called for a cleanup of the city. "Gangs are now practically running our government," he told a reporter. The *Daily News* sarcastically noted in a front-page editorial that Dillinger "came here for the usual protection."

Chief Dahill, harping on his favorite theme, claimed that if only his cops had Tommy guns, his department would be transformed into an efficient crime-fighting unit. He did not mention to the press that of all the men on duty that day, there was only one he could trust.

J. Edgar Hoover berated his St. Paul agents for their "atrocious bung-ling." How could they have neglected to block the rear escape route at Lincoln Court? Hoover expressed his utter contempt for agents who needed help from the despised St. Paul force. He taunted his agents, suggesting that they lacked courage unless they had a "blue uniform" with them.

Police crowd the hallway at the Lexington Avenue apartment after the Dillinger shootout. The detective in the light-colored hat is Henry Cummings, who accompanied federal agent Rufus Coulter on the morning of the shootout.

Two boys, identified as Dick Blake (left) and Sam Sweet, show where they found bullet casings in the snow after the Lexington Avenue shootout.

His top agent in St. Paul, Werner Hanni, fired back that Hoover's phobia about using St. Paul cops was the real problem. If they'd only used more local help, Hanni wrote, Dillinger would have been trapped. That was enough backtalk for Hoover, who transferred Hanni to Omaha.

Landlady Coffey compounded the FBI's humiliation. She billed the agency $175.71 for gunfire damages. "The above total," she noted, "does not include wear and tear on furniture, carpets and rugs, nor the cleaning of same."

30

THE CLEANUP MAN

Wallace Jamie, boy wonder, was a criminologist, a rare thing for his day. This 24-year-old teetotaler and vegetarian had a University of Chicago education and a pedigree: His uncle was Eliot Ness. His father, Alexander Jamie, was chief investigator for the Secret Six, an anonymous group of Chicago businessmen who conspired to bring down Al Capone when the government could not. Alexander Jamie had hired his son Wallace to work on that investigation. It was a private enterprise model of crime-fighting that St. Paul would soon adopt.

St. Paul's civic fathers were beyond embarrassed. Two of the city's most eminent men had been kidnapped within a few months of each other. The *Daily News* blamed this squarely on St. Paul police. Now, with the Dillinger fiasco, which of the public enemies hadn't escaped from St. Paul?

Even before Dillinger's escape, St. Paul's business elite had been formulating a plan to investigate the police department. Richard C. Lilly, president of the First National Bank, persuaded nine other prominent men, including William Hamm, to donate $10,000 each to finance a sting. "Mr. Lilly advised that these persons were picked after due consideration," wrote an FBI agent, "and he made special mention of the fact that the Bremers would not be considered for this purpose under any circumstances."

The FBI memo added that "this organization did not desire to be uncovered, so they arranged to work through Mr. Kahn, editor of the *St. Paul Daily News*."

A few nights after Dillinger's escape from Lincoln Court, Lilly's group met with Howard Kahn. They persuaded him to campaign for reform both behind the scenes and in the pages of the *Daily News*. On May 16, 1934, Kahn and police commissioner Ned Warren hired Wallace Jamie to lead the probe, paying him $300 a month through the *Daily News* accounts. Jamie hunkered down with assistants and began an undercover probe that would consume him for the next year. His target was the St. Paul police department.

Meanwhile, the feds determined that Tom Filben had supplied Dillinger with getaway cars. Agents brought Filben in for questioning on a Friday morning. Filben's attorney, Thomas McMeekin, made a "very friendly" visit to FBI offices to discuss a writ of habeas corpus. McMeekin betrayed his client by agreeing to stall the writ until Saturday. "Mr. McMeekin confidentially informed me," wrote Hoover's trusted assistant, Hugh Clegg, "that this would permit Filben to remain available for questioning until Monday as it would be impossible for the judge to set the hearing on the petition before Monday." So McMeekin conspired with federal agents to set up his client to be interrogated all weekend.

But gangland pressure immediately got to McMeekin. "Friends of Filben were bringing tremendous pressure on [McMeekin] as they didn't know what [Filben] might have said and they wanted him released," Inspector Clegg wrote. McMeekin revisited the FBI office and told Clegg that he would be forced to file the writ on Friday afternoon, thus springing Filben.

Clegg had another trick in his bag. He made a backroom deal with federal judge Matthew Joyce so that Filben could be held over the weekend.

Clegg wrote: "Strictly confidentially—as I agreed with Judge Joyce that this would not be disclosed—I conferred briefly with him, explaining that it would be very convenient for the Bureau Agents to continue questioning Filben over the weekend, and as a result of our conversations Judge Joyce made arrangement so that he would not be in the Federal Building when the petition for the writ was filed."

The FBI exhausted their questioning of Filben around midnight on Sunday, but he was reluctant to leave. "He felt safer" at agency headquarters, Clegg wrote, because gangsters might be "laying for him." Filben's fears were a "source of considerable amusement" to agents because he "more or less insisted upon remaining in the office."

Despite all the forces arrayed against him, the glib and shrewd Filben gave the government nothing they could use.

Then the G-men got lucky.

The agents were pursuing Eddie Green based on a tip, which turned out to be false, that he had been Dillinger's accomplice in the Lincoln Court shootout. They trapped Green on the porch of a St. Paul house and shot him up without giving him a chance to surrender. The agents took Green to the hospital. Delirious, Eddie Green fed G-men all sorts of bad information, then died after a few days in the hospital.

The agents took his wife Bess into custody. In the newspapers, she was referred to as the "mystery red-head." They would not release her true identity, determined to hold her "in spite of the efforts of a local shyster to get her released."

Bess Green was spectacularly well informed about the doings of the St. Paul underworld. Agents pressured her by threatening to go public with all they knew about her, which would prove embarrassing for her teenage son. So Green gave federal agents the names of the Bremer kidnappers. She also said what many feds didn't want to hear: that Roger Touhy was innocent of the Hamm abduction and that the Barkers had pulled that one off too. The feds meshed her information with evidence obtained from Shotgun George's belongings and the gas cans with Doc Barker's fingerprints. Finally they began to focus on the Barker-Karpis gang as the perpetrators of both the Hamm and Bremer kidnappings. They were assured by Bess Green that Harry Sawyer was their godfather.

So in early April 1934, federal agents descended on the Sawyers' farm. But Harry and Gladys had been tipped off about the raid by William McMullen, the St. Paul detective who was a Brown operative. G-men cornered Betty Baerwold, the maid, but she didn't know where Harry was. A few days later, Harry sneaked back to the farm, packed his Plymouth coupe, gathered Gladys and Francine, and drove west in a hurry. In the assessment of Alvin Karpis, leaving St. Paul was Harry's worst mistake.

Criminals on the run will often touch home, and for Harry this was Lincoln, Nebraska. There lived the respectable Sandlovich family. One of Harry's brothers was a car dealer. Harry traded for a new car and drove for Reno.

There Harry ducked into one gambling dive after another, hoping to find Fred or Karpis. Harry, the fixer who believed he could fix anything, was after his share of the Bremer ransom. But neither Karpis nor Fred could be found in Reno. So Harry embarked on a wishful-thinking tour to a dusty, nascent city in the desert.

In the 1930s, Reno was the big Nevada city and Las Vegas just a gleam in the Mafia's eye. Harry scouted the godforsaken landscape for a joint he could run. He clung to the notion that he could reprise the Green Lantern's glory days. He later realized that this pattern helped his pursuers find him and said if he hadn't been drinking a quart of booze a day, he wouldn't have made this mistake in judgment.

Gladys Sawyer, sick with some unspecified illness, returned to St. Paul in May to see her doctor. She also looked up Jack Peifer and inquired about the Barker gang. Harry was desperate for cash and needed to find them, she told Jack. Peifer, who may have been worried about his own fate, said he hadn't seen any of them.

Shortly after Gladys returned to Las Vegas, Harry got a letter from Karpis, who was in Ohio. The gang was still trying to launder the Bremer ransom. Harry was invited to join them on the shores of Lake Erie.

Karpis was a changed man. Doctor Moran had rearranged his face and shaved his fingertips. When Karpis arrived at his Toledo hideout, his fingers were bandaged and his face, lopsided now, bore a livid scar below the right ear. He and Fred were "almost helpless," Dolores Delaney said, and depended on tender mercies delivered by her and Paula Harmon.

But Karpis, the thinker, the worrier, was made nervous keeping company with other wanted men in Toledo. He was spooked by how much everyone was drinking. "Toledo turned out to be an unhappy town for us," he would recall. "We fell into a lot of nasty bickering. We were all frustrated . . . We had the cash but we couldn't spend it."

So he moved himself and Delaney to Cleveland. From there he dispatched Dolores to Chicago to check on Ma Barker. Karpis denied having feelings for the cranky old lady but may have worried about what she might say in the hands of the FBI. Delaney became convinced she was being followed by cops and returned to Cleveland declaring that she'd be an errand girl no longer.

Harry Sawyer finally caught up to Karpis in Cleveland. Harry, Gladys, and little Francine moved in with Karpis and Delaney. Harry was drinking heavily and growing more paranoid. Delaney said he was "looking out his apartment window at airplanes, afraid that 'coppers' might be looking down at him."

Toledo was the last stop for Doctor Moran, who had followed his notorious patients to the Ohio lakefront. Moran had become infatuated with his own infamy as doctor to the public enemies. And if you can't boast about your infamy, what good is it?

The FBI learned that Moran had gotten drunk with Karpis and Fred at a casino one night and boasted: "I have you guys in the palm of my hands." This led his patients to invite him on a Lake Erie fishing trip, from which he would never return. When asked about Moran's fate, Doc Barker replied, "The fishes have probably et him up by now."

31

DEATH OF A COMEDIAN

In April 1934, Melvin Purvis and the FBI suffered another humiliation: the raid on the Dillinger gang at Little Bohemia, which resulted in the shooting of three innocent civilians, one of whom died, and the killing of federal agent W. Carter Baum at the hands of Baby Face Nelson.

Not only did Dillinger get lucky at Little Bohemia, so did his little buddy Pat Reilly, the Green Lantern's bartender. Pat Reilly was born to be an errand boy. A skinny guy with chronic bad breath and a mouthful of rotten teeth, he'd been a batboy for the St. Paul Saints. He performed an auxiliary function for local gangsters, just as he had for baseball players. He tended Harry Sawyer's bar, introduced his teenage sister-in-law Dolores to Alvin Karpis, and regularly found girlfriends, doctors, and apartments for visiting gangsters. Reilly had been partying with the Dillinger gang at Little Bohemia. He was sent to St. Paul on an errand and returned just in time to watch FBI fireworks from the driveway.

Purvis and his agents would get their next shot at Dillinger in Chicago in July, killing him in an alley near the Biograph Theater, creating a legend that, more than seven decades later, still reverberates in popular culture.

Dillinger's death moved the Barker-Karpis gang to the top of the FBI's target list. But it was Homer Van Meter who felt the most immediate

Cops inside Little Bohemia after the shootout.

impact of Dillinger's demise. In the summer of 1934, sensational Dillinger stories were being wired around the world. Van Meter's association
with Dillinger had made him too "hot," and none of the St. Paul underworld wanted him around. Yet he couldn't seem to stay in hiding. It
seemed Van Meter wanted to be a comedian like his idol Eddie Cantor,
and so needed an audience. He showed up, joking and backslapping, at
the homes of his underworld friends, at taverns and gambling joints.
FBI informant Bess Green said Van Meter was a "nut" and that he "must
be everywhere."

He haunted the bowling alleys of the German-American Club, rolling
frames, then sticking around to watch tournaments. He frequented
McCormack's Town Talk Sandwich Shop, which, being adjacent to the
shuttered Green Lantern, was full of cops and crooks. Compulsively
roaming downtown, he stopped at the Central Drug Store for beer and
was remembered as a "perfect gentleman."

Pat Reilly later told the FBI that Van Meter had been marked for
death by the St. Paul underworld because he would not stay in hiding.
The underworld tolerated Van Meter while Dillinger was alive, but by
August 1934, "Van" had lost his protector.

On the last day of his life, August 23, 1934, Homer Van Meter was doing the very thing that most irritated the St. Paul underworld: making the rounds. He visited Jack Peifer out at the Hollyhocks. He drove by Harry Sawyer's on the chance that "the sea lion" had sneaked home. Harry was keeping $9,000 for Van Meter in his gangster savings and loan, but he'd been on the lam in Nevada for months.

For much of the day, Van Meter was accompanied by girlfriend Maria "Mickey" Conforti. Then just before four o'clock he told her to buzz off. Van Meter "had an appointment with some person at 4:00 P.M. and refused to allow her to accompany him," she told the FBI. He drove to the St. Paul Auto Company to keep that appointment.

His last.

St. Paul police told contradictory stories about Van Meter's last day. Chief Frank Cullen told the *Minneapolis Journal* that Van Meter had been spotted "on his way to a date" with a beer parlor waitress. The woman's friends had tipped off police, he claimed. That waitress was Opal Milligan, and police arrested her on vague charges so she was not available to contradict the story they were feeding the press.

But Chief Cullen's story was only one of many that would emerge.

Detective Tom Brown fed the newspapers a long-winded account that began three weeks prior. Brown said he and Chief Cullen were "joking" with county attorney Michael Kinkead about capturing Van Meter. According to Brown, this joke started the cops on a search for Van Meter and Baby Face Nelson, who were rumored to be cabin camping outside the city.

"At the same time," Brown said, "we were working along another line of investigation. We knew from experience that when any of the Dillinger mob wanted a new car, he always purchased it 'right' as members of this gang had no use for hot cars, and when one of them purchased it in St. Paul he always went to certain auto dealers."

Brown, master of the half-truth, failed to mention that it was his fishing buddy, Tom Filben, who provided the gangsters with cars. He also neglected to mention the friendly chats he'd had with Baby Face Nelson in the Green Lantern parking lot and the campaign contribution he got from Van Meter.

According to Brown, the clever cops of St. Paul cooked up a scheme using Chief Cullen's nifty new auto as Van Meter bait. How exactly they lured Van Meter to the dealership at the corner of University and Marion was left to the newspaper reader's imagination. When Van Meter strolled in to consider a new car purchase, the four plainclothesmen listened from another room, Brown said.

The salesman, according to Brown, pretended that Cullen's car belonged to the auto agency and was for sale: "It's just the thing you want," he told Van Meter. "It's fast, sturdy and nice looking."

"Well, it looks all right to me," Van Meter supposedly said. "How much would you allow me on my old car? You know, I can make Rush Lake in an hour in my old car."

Bring in your jalopy, the salesman said, and I'll give you a price on it.

When Van Meter headed for the front door, the cops split up. Brown and Chief Cullen confronted Van Meter, while the other two cops slipped behind him.

"I was about 35 feet from the front door when the gangster emerged," Brown said. "I had my [sawed-off] shotgun up and pointed at him."

"'Hands up,' I shouted. 'We're police officers.'"

Then, Brown said, "Van Meter whipped out a pistol and fired at me."

Van Meter "dashed across University Avenue . . . Cullen and I dashed after him," Brown said. "We had been unable to shoot because at one time a woman came in direct line of fire, and automobiles were passing between the fleeing suspect and our gun range."

Brown said he heard the bullets whizzing past him as "every few seconds, Van Meter would turn and shoot at us."

Van Meter, like Dillinger, had the misfortune to duck down a dead-end alley.

"When he was in plain sight again," Brown said, "I let go my first blast at him with the sawed off shotgun. Van Meter, facing us, was hit, just as he was poised to fire at us again. As the slugs tore into his body, he jumped at least two feet in the air. I kept pumping my shotgun at him as fast as I could and I realized later that Cullen alongside of me was doing the same. [Fellow cops] Dittrich and McMahon were about to bring their machine guns into play when the second and third blasts from our shotgun finally brought the gangster down."

Most readers of this tale would not have realized that all four shooters were members of Brown's corrupt clique.

"He was already dead when we came to him," Brown told the press. "The shotgun slugs hit him in the chest, face and head. His fingers on both hands were shot off."

As Van Meter lay in the alley, one of the cops fetched his straw hat and tilted it over his face. A crowd gathered. Souvenir hunters began digging bullets and buckshot out of the alley's garages and fences. A few days later, some enterprising rube tried to sell what he claimed was Van Meter's tooth for $1,000.

It was tabloid fodder, complete with local heroes, and the press swallowed it whole. The *St. Paul Daily News* printed a picture of the four plainclothes cops, Big Tom towering above the rest. The paper praised "the best marksmen in the police department."

But Brown and Chief Cullen were seasoned street cops. Brown had already killed three men while on duty. According to Brown's own account, he and Cullen had Van Meter covered when they confronted him.

"I had my shotgun up and pointed at him."

It was just after five o'clock on an August day, and clear daylight. Van Meter was twelve paces away. Under these conditions, is it credible that four well-armed veteran cops allowed a Dillinger gangster to reach for his pistol, bring it out, and fire? At least two of those cops had him covered, and yet neither got off a shot?

Brown loved to portray himself as hero-gentleman, and so said that when Van Meter crossed the street, he refrained from firing because a woman was in the line of fire.

That woman was Mrs. Andrew Stedje.

"I heard a couple of shots across the street," she said. "I turned and saw a man running across University Avenue, carrying a straw hat in his hand. He passed right in front of me . . . then two men with sawed off shotguns who had followed him across the street rushed past me too. They were in regular clothes, so I figured they must be deputy sheriffs.

"The first man, I didn't know it was Van Meter then . . . turned left into the alley. The other two men followed. My two young children were playing around the neighborhood and I was afraid they might be here, so I followed too. Just as [Brown and Cullen] got to the entrance of the alley, they began shooting. I couldn't say how many times. Then I saw [Van Meter] down on one knee in the open space of the alley. I couldn't tell whether he had a gun or not, I was so excited.

"[Brown and Cullen] shot a couple more times and then [Van Meter] crumpled up and his hat rolled away. While he was lying there the two men fired several more shots at him. He didn't move when the two men who killed him bent over him."

Mrs. Stedje added: "[Van Meter] was well-dressed. He had on black and white shoes, a dark blue suit, a white shirt and was carrying a straw hat. It's funny, but I noticed all that when he ran past me."

Perhaps Mrs. Stedje, who after all was not a professional observer, can be forgiven for failing to notice that Van Meter had a gun and was firing it as he passed her. Perhaps she was distracted by the straw hat Van Meter was carrying. Or the color of his shoes.

Mrs. Stedje's description of Van Meter's attire matches exactly with the police report. Despite those astute observations, she somehow failed to notice Van Meter's gun, or the flashes from its barrel, or the noise of its gunfire as he ran past her shooting at the cops. According to Brown, Van Meter was getting off a round "every few seconds," but all that supposed gunfire somehow went unnoticed by Mrs. Stedje.

But she did notice that straw hat.

A witness identified as D. Peterson told the press he had to brake to avoid running over Van Meter: "He ran in front of me and held up his hand and I had to stop to keep from hitting him."

Well, if Van Meter clutched a straw hat in one hand, as Mrs. Stedje said, and a gun in the other, as Tom Brown said, which hand was he holding up as a stop sign to driver Peterson? Perhaps Peterson, like Mrs. Stedje, simply missed seeing the gun?

Or maybe not. "Then I saw the plainclothesmen step out of their car," Peterson told reporters, "and I thought it was a holdup when I saw their guns."

So Peterson *was* capable of recognizing a gun. And according to him, Van Meter's killers emerged from an auto and not the showroom.

Another witness who refused to be identified in print gave reporters yet another angle. He said that just before the shooting, two men ran across University Avenue, with Van Meter just behind them. The two men jumped in a car and zoomed away "as if abandoning him." At that point, Van Meter changed direction and ran across Mrs. Stedje's path.

That story suggests that Van Meter was driven to his final appointment by setup men. When reporters called this witness for more details, he "refused to amplify his story, asserting that he had been told by police to maintain his silence."

St. Paul waitress Opal Milligan informed the FBI that an unnamed policeman told her that Harry Sawyer engineered the ambush. "Harry Sawyer had several thousand dollars of Homer Van Meter's money," and Van Meter was in town to collect it, she said. Van Meter got in a car and "went out riding with Sawyer and two or three other individuals." Sawyer "previously had called the St. Paul Police" and advised them that they'd be at the corner of University and Marion at a certain time. "Van Meter left the car and walked a short distance away and then noticed the car of police officers." Van Meter turned back for the car, but the men who dropped him off pulled a gun on him and drove off, "whereupon Van Meter wheeled and started running."

There's one potential problem with Opal Milligan's story. In August of 1934, Harry Sawyer was in transit from Las Vegas to Cleveland. It's possible that Harry passed through St. Paul around the time that Van Meter was killed. Certainly his wife Gladys visited St. Paul during their months in exile. But there is no corroboration in the FBI files of Milligan's claim that Harry was directly involved.

FBI informant Frank Reilly presented agents with yet another angle. He said a crook named Tommy Gannon "delivered Van Meter [to the police ambush] in return for a promise he would be let go on some burglaries."

Maria Conforti also thought the setup man was Tommy Gannon, who "was picked out by the cops and offered money if he would rat out Homer Van Meter."

Van Meter had been carrying $18,000 that day, Frank Reilly said, because he wanted to bail out of the criminal life and was hoping to buy a farm. Reilly said that "if the ambush failed, [Van Meter] was going to be taken to a saloon, gotten drunk and rolled for his cash."

A few days after the shooting, the cops told yet another contradictory story, but no reporters challenged it, at least not in print. Police told reporters that they got a "tip" about Van Meter at 5:00 PM and the four cops "left the Public Service building immediately in the chief's car, carrying two shotguns and two machine guns."

If true, there was no time for Brown's story of luring Van Meter with the chief's car. Brown's purpose in relating that concoction was apparently to make himself seem clever in the newspapers. In a conference later with the FBI, Brown and Cullen told yet another version of the story, saying they had been cruising around for ten minutes and happened to notice Van Meter on the street. Why four heavily armed cops were cruising in one car, he did not explain.

"Approaching University Avenue on Marion Street," police told reporters, the four cops "recognized Van Meter strolling toward the corner. The four officers left their machine and headed toward the corner on foot, keeping close to the buildings so the gunman would not see them until they reached the corner. They shouted, Homer Van Meter whirled and fired twice."

Mrs. Stedje, though, did not report any shouting. Nor did she notice any gunfire after Van Meter passed her, except the shooting that came from the cops. Mrs. Stedje was a mother worried about the safety of her children. It seems highly likely she would have noticed Van Meter's gunfire.

In any event, an investigation would conclude that Van Meter's pistol had fired only two bullets.

FBI agent G. L. Hurley interviewed a manager at the St. Paul Auto Company, whom he never named. The manager said the St. Paul cops had been watching his business for ten days before the Van Meter shooting. "On the day in question," Hurley wrote, plainclothes "officers had a car secreted in the rear of the auto company . . . a Chevy stopped about 20 feet from the garage. Van Meter alighted from it and . . . police officers rushed from the rear entrance of the garage and commanded Van Meter to put his hands up." The manager characterized the Chevy's driver as a "stool pigeon" who had "put Van Meter on the spot."

The cops "allowed the Chevy to get away and did not fire [at Van Meter] while the driver of the Chevrolet was in the line of fire." The manager also told the FBI that one of his salesmen "set up Van Meter and knew more than he would say. Van Meter had an appointment with him to buy a car."

"The whole episode," the manager concluded, "had been put on more or less as a show for the police department."

Hearing that, the FBI sent in their tough guy, Rufus Coulter. He talked with H. H. McGill, another manager at the auto company. McGill said Brown had been hanging around the garage since 12:30 PM on the day of

Van Meter's death. About 5:00 PM, Van Meter drove up in a Chevy and walked into the dealership. He "appeared to be nervous" and "kept his hand in his suit coat pocket as if on a gun." Van Meter kicked a few tires in the showroom.

Brown and his squad were hiding in a back room, McGill said. Brown had described Van Meter and asked McGill to come back and tell him when Van Meter walked in. But at first, McGill didn't recognize Van Meter as matching Brown's description. When he figured it out, he slipped back and notified the cops. They left the building and got into a squad car at Marion and University.

When Van Meter realized he was being set up, McGill said, "he took off his hat and started running. The man in the Chevy moved over into the driver's seat and zoomed away. Homer Van Meter ran across the street and a Hudson had to brake in order to avoid hitting him."

McGill was friends with detective Charles Tierney and was angry at the St. Paul cops for "arranging this scene in front of his place of business." St. Paul cops eventually admitted to the FBI that they had been staking out that car dealership for a week.

However this jigsaw puzzle goes together, the one certainty is that Tom Brown repeatedly lied when recounting the death of Homer Van Meter.

Although Brown said he and Cullen fired to knock Van Meter down and that he was "dead once we got to him," Mrs. Stedje saw something else. The cops stood over Van Meter's crumpled form, blasting him. At this point, Brown said Van Meter "had a gun in his hand." But could Van Meter have been holding a gun? Weren't his fingers shot off? Or did the cops blast away to make sure he was dead?

The cops on the scene determined that Van Meter had about $8,000 on him. His girlfriend Maria Conforti said that Van Meter was carrying at least that much money when he left her an hour before the shooting. Yet after the autopsy, which Brown attended, only $1,400 was taken to the police property room.

Former chief Tom Dahill told the FBI he believed that the coroner, county attorney Michael Kinkead, and Tom Brown split Van Meter's money.

At the time of the Van Meter shooting, Brown's situation was shaky. He'd failed in his run for sheriff. He was hated and feared by many of his fellow cops. The FBI was questioning people about his role in the Hamm and Bremer kidnappings. Most frightening of all, Harry Sawyer was on the run somewhere, and if Harry talked, Brown was headed for Alcatraz.

Brown could not have failed to notice that the killing of John Dillinger made the FBI's Melvin Purvis a darling of the newsreels. Brown and Cullen cooked up hero stories after Van Meter's killing and planted them in the newspapers. By their account, Van Meter had been betrayed by a woman friend. Obviously the hope was to echo the national sensation over Dillinger's "lady in red." Brown had a powerful motive for rehabilitating his image. If he could fulfill his ambition to become sheriff, he could team up with Kinkead and run Ramsey County.

Van Meter had for a while been an asset to Brown, paying protection money and contributing to his campaign for sheriff. But with Dillinger dead, Van Meter would no longer be generating cash and would be of little use to the Brown clique. Not only did officials steal much of the money Van Meter had on him, the cops kept his auto and turned it into a police squad car.

Maria Conforti, Opal Milligan, Frank Reilly, Pat Reilly, Tom Dahill, two managers at the St. Paul Auto Company, and the FBI all subscribed to the theory that Van Meter was set up for his appointment with death. The corroborated points suggest that on the pretext of buying a car, Van Meter was delivered to the St. Paul Auto Company. The four cops hid in the back room until informed by the manager that Van Meter had walked in. The cops then slipped into Chief Cullen's car to hide the fact that they'd been waiting in ambush. The gangster who set up Van Meter, probably Tommy Gannon, zoomed away as the cops emerged from Cullen's car. Van Meter realized he had been "put on the spot" and ran, firing twice in the alley before being shot. Brown and Cullen blasted him while he was down, making certain he would not survive to tell his side of the story.

Normally, if the chief of police leads a raid on a wanted man, he takes public credit for it. Not this time. Chief Cullen backed off, saying he "did not want to appear to be boasting."

"A genuine Irishman even to his corn cob pipe," one journalist wrote, "Frank Cullen puffed clouds of acrid smoke . . . as reporters pressed him for details. With a twinkle in his eye he said, 'We had to do some straight shooting.' But he could not be persuaded to talk much."

It was detective Tom Brown, the chief's supposed subordinate, who gave the interviews and took the glory. The death of Van Meter was national news. Photos of Brown and his fellow shooters ran on all the wires. The story evolved and soon Brown was credited with firing the fatal shot. Both Brown and Chief Cullen had shotguns, so there was no way to tell who fired the fatal shot. No matter. Brown was the designated hero.

Mayor Mark Gehan wired congratulations from the road. He was traveling on a promotional trip with the St. Paul Booster Club. "Such display of courage and loyalty to duty should convince even the most skeptical," he wrote, "that St. Paul is sincere in its desire to sustain the reputation it has always had as a clean and law abiding town."

Yes sir!

The local newspapers joined in this orgy of hypocrisy.

The *Pioneer Press* congratulated itself for its campaign to arm St. Paul cops with Tommy guns. The weapons had "proved their worth in the Homer Van Meter case," the editors wrote, failing to mention that the Tommy guns had not been fired. The newspaper went on to intone that the shooting of Van Meter "proclaims the sincerity of police reform."

And who better to lead that reform than the resurrected Big Tom Brown?

32

THAT TROUBLE IN CLEVELAND

In the late summer of 1934, Harry Sawyer flew from Cleveland to Miami to Havana with two other men and suitcases full of ransom money. One of the men was a thug, a fanatical golfer and saloonkeeper named Willie Harrison, whom the gang had recently taken on "as a stooge." The other was the smooth and probably crazy Detroit con man Cassius "Cash" McDonald.

The Bremer ransom money had gotten wet when the gang had buried it, encased in a Gladstone bag at Karpis's hideout in Cleveland. Fred and

Karpis rigged a room with electric fans to dry the money before it rotted. The cash now had a strange, crinkled look.

McDonald, once a wealthy gambler and now desperate for money, had assured the gang the ransom cash could be moved through Havana to Mexico City and Venezuela. Harry and friends flew the crinkly cash to Cuba on September 1. While they were enjoying Havana's notorious nightlife, Gladys Sawyer was getting into big trouble in Cleveland.

Gladys, with 5-year-old Francine tagging along, went out drinking at the swank Bronze Room at the Cleveland Hotel. Gladys, 38 at the time, was a "notorious drunk who was frequently treated for overintoxication," according to an FBI informant. In Cleveland her drinking buddies were Paula Harmon and Wynona Burdette. Wynona, a 19-year-old parolee, aspired to be a radio singer but settled for being a girlfriend of Alvin Karpis's dumb but ruggedly handsome pal Harry Campbell.

The gang's women were having problems of their own. Wynona had surgery for "female trouble" in Ohio, and the complications kept her in the hospital for two weeks. Edna Murray's troubles were worse. She'd been in two serious car crashes with Volney Davis, then discovered she had breast cancer. When she sought treatment, the surgeon refused to operate unless she presented her medical charts. But Edna was a prison escapee. Rather than reveal her identity, she went away untreated.

Perhaps the desperado life was oppressing these women, because they got outrageously drunk. Paula turned loud and obnoxious. Gladys vomited on the elegant marble floor. The cops were called, among them policewoman Mildred Wilcox.

The gangsters' women would not quiet down. In that opulent hotel lobby, they back-talked the cop. Paula tried to bribe Wilcox, offering a diamond bracelet.

The three women and little Francine were hauled off to jail.

Mildred Wilcox began to suspect that the women in custody weren't just drunken housewives. They had an awful lot of money and flashy jewelry. Earlier in the day, the Cleveland cops had heard Baby Face Nelson rumors. Wilcox suspected a connection, although Nelson's supposed sighting in Cleveland never proved out.

Nevertheless, the gang's women nearly got away. One Cleveland cop offered to spring them in return for $500, Gladys told the FBI, and she was willing to pay. But before that could be arranged, Wilcox sat Francine, bright and precocious, in a chair in the squad room.

What does your daddy do for a living?

He runs a joint, Francine said.

Her daddy's friends never worked and had lots of money, she said. They also knew fun tricks, such as how to switch license plates on their cars. Wilcox called her supervisor, captain Frank Story, who called the FBI. Francine told the G-men more charming stories.

So Paula, Gladys, and Wynona were whisked off to the Chicago FBI office, and confessions were sweated out of them. Paula Harmon cracked under the pressure. She wrestled with agents, shouted them down, bit them, spit at them. Her descent into madness was so steep that the FBI concluded she would be useless as a witness. After weeks of interrogation, they spit her out of the Chicago office, and she slinked home to Texas.

"At the time of my arrest in Cleveland," Gladys Sawyer admitted to the FBI, "I had concealed on my person three $500 bills and seven $100 bills, one solitaire diamond ring, one double solitaire diamond ring, one pair of diamond ear screws and one unmounted diamond. I turned the money and jewelry over to Cleveland attorney M. Stanton and said: 'Try to reach Harry Sawyer and his gang and tell them to get out of town.'"

The lawyer kept the money and jewelry, Gladys said, but whether he got word to Harry is unknown. The day after Gladys's arrest, police raided the Sawyer apartment in Cleveland but missed the gang by a few hours.

The FBI let Wynona Burdette and Gladys Sawyer go. Common sense suggests they would have assigned agents to follow the women, but they did not. Francine was returned to St. Paul as a ward of the state and put into hiding. "Gangland would turn over every stone in an attempt to find her if they believed the child would tell federal authorities the secrets of the underworld," said Minnesota child welfare official Gertrude Cammack.

On September 14, Harry Sawyer and Cash McDonald returned from Cuba. The gang gathered at McDonald's Grosse Pointe, Michigan, home to split $66,000 of the laundered ransom. McDonald watched as Karpis the accountant tallied it.

"Are you sure now," Karpis asked McDonald, "that [the ransom] money is going to show up, as you said, in Caracas and Mexico City?"

"Yes, there's no question about that," McDonald said.

Edna Murray later testified that around that time she met Doc Barker outside a barbecue restaurant, and he said the gang would keep Tom Brown's share. "I guess you saw," Doc said, "where that dirty bastard killed Van Meter."

The next day, Karpis and Fred drove to Chicago. The gang had a certain internal honor, often paying shares to widows and to friends in trouble. They looked up Byron Bolton and paid him two ransom shares. One was for him and the other for Shotgun George's widow.

Then at Fred's insistence, they visited Ma's Chicago apartment. Dolores Delaney was keeping Ma company. Tough, spunky Dolores got along with Ma, who mostly hated the gang's girlfriends. Perhaps Dolores, barely more than a high school girl and full of naïve bravado, was the daughter Ma never had.

Karpis ordered Dolores to pack up and told Fred they could be in touch through the El Comodoro, a hotel that catered to crooks and gamblers in Miami. Dolores was pregnant again, and this time, she'd insisted, she was going to give birth. Karpis had a swell idea for a place to await the birth of his first child.

In the fall of 1934, the hunt for the Bremer kidnappers and just about everything else was blasted off America's front pages by the arrest of Bruno Hauptmann for the murder of the Lindbergh baby. Perhaps Karpis sensed that his own fate would soon play out on page one. He had long fantasized about an escape to Australia.

But for now, Cuba would have to do. On the drive toward Key West, he and Delaney were stopped by a Florida cop for speeding but let off with a warning. When they reached Key West, Delaney was again the wide-eyed teenager, in awe of this tropical bohemia. When they boarded the SS *Cuba* for the six-hour journey to Havana, Karpis was acting out his fantasy of escape.

Havana *sí*, FBI *no*.

But Cuba was in violent convulsion. Batista had just taken over. There were street riots, explosions all over town, and snipers on rooftops. Even for an armed gangster, Havana wasn't safe.

So Karpis and Delaney split for the beach resort at Veradero, where wealthy Americans and Canadians lived. Karpis bought a new Ford for

$1,074 cash. He rented a fabulous six-room beach cottage. He hired servants. The couple's neighbors were the Du Ponts and other American elites. Dolores, seven months pregnant, brought along her miniature bulldog, Wimpy. Apparently she wanted a home life, complete with dogs and children, but if so she had picked the wrong man.

Karpis, for a few weeks, achieved the gangster fantasy. Here was an idyll of warm ocean waves, moonlight, and palm trees. Ma Barker, overcome with envy, flew down for a visit, three days of beachcombing and fishing. Ma declared that she, too, wanted to live in Cuba. History does not record whether this declaration caused Delaney and Karpis to shiver in horror. But fate, bumbling along in its inevitable way, was catching up to Karpis. One day he drove his new Ford into Havana, visited his bank, and was alarmed when the teller handed him a crinkled bill. He didn't need to check its serial number to know this was ransom money. McDonald had lied when he promised that the hot cash would end up in Caracas. With the ransom showing up in Havana, Karpis reasoned, the FBI couldn't be far behind. He grabbed Delaney, she snatched up Wimpy, and they boarded a steamer for Florida. The high point of Karpis's life, this Cuba interlude had lasted barely six weeks.

In Miami, he and Dolores stayed at the El Comodoro. Fred visited, bringing a "great quantity of baby clothes" for Dolores and carrying a string of fish he'd caught in Lake Weir. Karpis and Delaney enjoyed a fish dinner with Fred, Harry Campbell, and Wynona Burdette. Fred invited everyone up to Lake Weir.

"That evening," Delaney said, "I became very ill and believed the baby was about to be born." Karpis confined her to the hotel room, bought her a "radio to keep her company," and spent his time carousing and fishing. He arranged for a doctor and a nurse to attend Dolores. His child was going to be born in a gangland hotel room and then . . . and then . . . ?

Karpis was running low on options.

33

THE SHOOTOUTS

By January 1935, Fred and Ma Barker were enjoying life at a lakefront home on Lake Weir, Florida. The house was gracious, surrounded by a low stone wall and grapefruit, orange, and lemon trees. Ma Barker employed a maid and a gardener. "Ma had mellowed out," Alvin Karpis remembered, and shed some of her animosity toward the gang's women. The Barker fellows and their visitors hunted deer, fished, shopped, and drank. Fred, your friendly neighborhood psycho killer, spent big and mixed sociably with the locals. Having lost Harry Sawyer and Tom Brown as informers, the gang was reduced to reading about the FBI's hunt for them in the Chicago newspapers that arrived daily in the mail.

Karpis visited the Barkers at Lake Weir but decided there was too much drinking going on. Doc was loaded all the time, and Karpis had a suspicion of heavy drinkers. Certainly Karpis remembered the Swift payroll heist, where Doc blasted a cop dead for no apparent reason. At Lake Weir, Doc and Fred had already riled the locals by shooting at ducks with a machine gun. That was just the kind of thing, Karpis knew, that would get back to the sheriff.

Anxious Alvin also was spooked by the presence of Harry Campbell's girlfriend Wynona Burdette. She'd been sequestered by the FBI for weeks after her arrest at the Cleveland Hotel, and Karpis believed the G-men would be tailing her. Or who knew? Perhaps they had turned her into an informer. The Lake Weir cottage just had too many negatives. So after a visit in January of 1935, he left, never to return.

Doc Barker lobbied the gang to pull a payroll heist he'd designed, but when his plan was rejected, he drifted back to Chicago. There, the FBI was closing in on his gang. The agency's latest information came from Irene Goetz, Shotgun George's widow, who had cracked up after his murder. The FBI visited her in a Chicago sanatorium. With her help, they added Ziegler's pal Byron Bolton to their list of suspects.

On January 8, an FBI team trapped Doc Barker on a Chicago street. Doc, unarmed, tried to run but slipped on the icy sidewalk. Agents found in Doc's apartment the machine gun that had killed two cops, one in the South St. Paul payroll robbery and another in the flubbed robbery in Chicago.

When the FBI arrested Byron Bolton, they figured him for a minor-leaguer, a mere accomplice to Shotgun George. Tough guy Doc Barker wouldn't tell the agents a thing. But Bolton began talking.

Bolton, a family man, was in precarious health and had never shaken the tuberculosis he had contracted in the navy. He desperately wanted to shorten the inevitable prison sentence. He owed no loyalty to the Barker gang now that he wasn't linked to them through Shotgun George.

At the time of his arrest, Bolton was 42 years old. As a young man, he apprenticed to a carpenter, then served in the navy in World War I. He married and, to support his two children, opened a restaurant in Illinois. It was bankrupted by the shutdown of the town's main employer, a coal mine. He tried to cure his tuberculosis in New Mexico's climate, receiving a monthly veterans disability check and occasionally working in gambling joints. After recovering his health somewhat, Bolton moved his family back to Chicago, where he worked as a car salesman. Then he met George Ziegler, who at first passed himself off as just another rich bootlegger.

They became golfing buddies. When the auto dealership that employed Bolton went bust, Ziegler took him and his family in. Ziegler seemed to have a genuine affection and protective instinct for Bolton.

In 1929, Shotgun George recruited Bolton to be a lookout for what turned into the St. Valentine's Day Massacre. That was a fiasco of the first magnitude, since it failed to eliminate Bugs Moran but brought heat on the Capone Outfit. Capone blamed Bolton in part, and issued hit orders. Ziegler "felt morally responsible for his predicament," according to a Chicago gangster's widow. So Ziegler sent Bolton up north to save him from Capone's gunmen. Bolton spent months fixing up Ziegler's property in the Wisconsin woods. Upon his return to Chicago, Bolton discovered that his patron had pulled off a robbery in which a cop had been killed.

Because he was in hiding, Bolton failed to appear for a disability physical and so lost his veterans payments. Shotgun George, a fellow veteran, felt this was his fault and sent Bolton money every week. By spring of 1933, when the Hamm kidnapping was being planned, Bolton had recovered enough of his health to give golf lessons in the Chicago suburbs.

And now, two kidnappings later, Bolton was sitting in a barren room at the FBI's Chicago headquarters. What the agents wanted to know most desperately was where could they find Fred Barker and Alvin Karpis.

Bolton had visited the Barkers' Florida cottage and told agents it was somewhere on a lake in northern Florida. The lake contained a famous alligator named Old Joe, but that was all Bolton knew.

The bureau kept Doc's arrest out of the newspapers. Pop Nathan denied that Doc Barker even existed, and agents invented a code name for him: Number Five. But the FBI knew their secret wouldn't be safe for long. Once Doc's arrest hit the papers, Fred, Ma, and Karpis would bolt. Agents scrambled to work the geography angle, but it took them days to find an obvious clue: a map in Doc's apartment had a circle drawn around Ocala and Lake Weir, Florida.

There were many lakes in the area. Every one, the agents were frustrated to discover, seemed to contain a legendary alligator named Old Joe. Finally a tip from the Lake Weir postmaster narrowed their search to a two-story lakefront house with a fishing dock. Agents gathered in Lake Weir. One of them actually chatted with Fred Barker on the fishing dock. The FBI that night assembled a fourteen-man strike force and surrounded the cottage. At dawn on January 16, the raiders made their move. Agent Earl Connelley called from the front yard.

Ma Barker opened the front door.

Connelley asked for Fred.

Ma said: Who wants him?

She shut the door. All went quiet. Agents called for them both to come out peaceably. They fired tear gas at the windows but couldn't land a shot inside. Fred answered by firing a Tommy gun from an upstairs window. During lulls in a long, furious battle, agents would call for the Barkers to surrender. Fred ran from room to room firing his Tommy gun out the windows. Since many FBI agents said that the firing came from two distinct places, it seems likely that Ma Barker had joined her son in mortal combat. The woods and orange groves behind the agents filled with spectators. After four hours, 3,000 rounds of ammo, and many canisters of tear gas, the Lake Weir house finally went silent.

FBI agents recruited the Barkers' caretaker, a black man named Willie Woodberry, to do something they were afraid to do. They persuaded him to approach the house, knock, then push in the door.

Woodberry called out: "They're all dead."

In Miami, Alvin Karpis and his sidekick Harry Campbell were out on the ocean, fishing for mackerel. Their girls, Dolores and Wynona, heard the chilling news on the radio that "the Bremer kidnappers" had been slain. When the boys got back from the charter boat, they took in the news, packed up, and blew town. Wynona and Dolores were put on a train. Karpis was afraid that Dolores, who was known publicly to be hugely pregnant, would be easily identified. So Karpis and Campbell drove, and they were all to meet in Atlantic City. Would Dolores make it? Her nurse in Florida was alarmed. She might deliver that baby on the train.

Karpis had arranged for the train to be met in Atlantic City by a sometime musician named Duke Randall, whose last employer was a Florida greyhound track. Randall may have been surprised to see that the Public Enemy's paramour was a tiny, pregnant teenager. He showed her a gun, vowed to protect her, and inquired whether he might join the Karpis gang. Delaney, unimpressed by his tough-guy act, said she had gotten out of many tight spots and wasn't afraid.

She should have been. She and Wynona ate dinner and went to bed, to be awoken just after 2:00 AM by the arrival of Karpis and Campbell. The men weren't there long before a beat cop spotted their car, which had been listed on a police Teletype bulletin. The Atlantic City cops bumbled into the hotel, and a gun battle ensued. As so often happened, the gangsters had the firepower and got off most of the shots. One of the bullets hit Dolores in the calf, passing through the flesh and then out again. She limped out of the building, hoping to meet the boys in the alley.

Karpis and Campbell jumped into their car, Campbell clothed only in underwear. They circled the hotel once and then zoomed away, leaving Wynona behind, along with Dolores, pregnant and bleeding.

Twenty police cars pursued Karpis and Campbell through Atlantic City, "with every traffic light in the city flashing off and on," the signal of a full-scale police emergency. Atlantic City is a narrow island, and twice Karpis and Campbell wheeled down a dead-end street, turned around at the boardwalk, and shot their way past the converging squad cars.

A few weeks later, Delaney gave birth to Karpis's son in a prison hospital. Nineteen years old, wounded and deserted, and facing years in prison, Delaney wrote a letter to her mom in St. Paul, begging her to take baby Raymond. "You know how I love that name."

She added, "My leg is getting along pretty good, although I can't walk on it yet. The bullet went clear through the leg, right between the knee and ankle."

To her sister she wrote: "Can you picture me as a proud mother? Listen Babe, if I'm sent up, can you and mom take care of the baby? It's not going to be any fun leaving it while it's so little, but you will take care of it won't you? Gee, I'm tickled to death [about the birth of the baby]. I wish I could see him. But my baby positively will never go inside a jail no matter what happens to me."

Neither Delaney's sister nor her mom volunteered to take the baby, who was raised by Karpis's humble, good-hearted parents. Karpis would meet his son twenty-three years later at Alcatraz but would never see Delaney again.

34

"BOLTON? WHO'S BOLTON?"

During Easter week of 1935, St. Paul was again bristling with Tommy guns, but these belonged to G-men. Federal agents, news reporters, prison inmates, lawyers, gawkers, and witnesses descended on the city as ten defendants went on trial for the kidnapping of Edward Bremer. For the victim, it was a frightening time. Star defendant Doc Barker had warned him that "I have plenty of contacts out there who would get you." Bremer's bank was just across the street from the federal courthouse. A report reached the FBI of a plot by Curly Davis and Alvin Karpis to assassinate Bremer as he walked to his downtown lunch spot.

FBI agents found the relationship between Ed Bremer and his kidnappers curious. Inspector Hugh Clegg wrote Hoover of a campaign being quietly waged by Ed Bremer. He visited agent John Brennan at the FBI's office on behalf of his kidnapper, Harry Sawyer. This happened in the summer of 1934, when Harry had been on the lam for two months. Harry owned real estate and personal property in and around St. Paul, Ed Bremer explained to the FBI. Would it be okay if Harry came back to dispose of it? Or would he be arrested?

A flabbergasted Agent Brennan coyly answered that there were no official warrants out for Harry's arrest. Ed Bremer then visited U.S. attorney George Sullivan at his St. Paul office, where he made "similar inquiries." He was told that the federal government might like to ask Harry a few questions. Bremer allowed that maybe he would get word to Harry that it was okay to return to St. Paul.

A few days later, Ed Bremer returned to the FBI offices with his "life-long friend" Andy Rothmeyer. This saloonkeeper had been Myrtle Eaton's sugar daddy, paying the rent and buying expensive furniture for her apartment. This was the apartment where the Bremer kidnap planning sessions had been held, while Myrtle was jilting Rothmeyer and taking up with one of the kidnappers, Lapland Willie Weaver. The FBI was hunting both Myrtle and Willie. Rothmeyer asked the feds: Could he go into Myrtle's apartment and get his furniture without being shot by the FBI? He said he wanted to put it in storage for Myrtle.

"Thus," Clegg wrote to Washington, "we have a strange alliance between the victim" and the kidnappers.

As the first Bremer trial began, defendants were brought from the jail via an ungainly armored car rented from a detective agency. Doc Barker and Byron Bolton were the only primary members of the kidnap gang on trial. Fred Barker and Shotgun George Ziegler were dead, and Karpis, Fitzgerald, and Lapland Willie Weaver were on the run. The rest of the defendants were accessories in one form or another, accused of harboring or ransom laundering. The trial marked a new government strategy for prosecuting kidnappings. Everyone connected to the crime, no matter how vaguely, would face the law.

Before the trial began, two defendants pleaded guilty. One was a minor-leaguer, J. J. "Jimmy" Wilson, assistant to gangster-doctor Joseph Moran. The FBI still didn't know whether Moran was dead but had evidence that he'd laundered some of the Bremer cash and that Wilson helped him. The other guilty plea came from Byron Bolton. His sentence was deferred. For the next eighteen months, Bolton would be the federal government's favorite witness as they tried to clean up the mess St. Paul had made.

Edward Bremer played dumb when newsmen asked for a reaction to Bolton's guilty plea. "Bolton, who's Bolton?" Bremer said. "I don't know who he is."

Arthur "Doc" Barker, in a
rare undated photo from the
Pioneer Press archives.

Bremer played the same game when he took the witness stand. He identified Harold Alderton, owner of the home where he'd been captive, and Elmer Farmer, who'd set up the house rental. But he stopped there. Bremer, fighting a severe cold, seemed composed on the stand but never glanced at Doc Barker.

Doc "never took his eyes off the witness," a reporter wrote.

During testimony, Bremer invented a cockamamie tale to make the gang seem honorable. He told the court that once the ransom was paid, the Barkers got an offer from another gang, who wanted to hold him to extract yet more money from the family. The good fellas of the Barker gang rejected that dishonorable offer, Bremer testified.

Ed Bremer's father was anything but composed. A handsome, distin-guished man, Adolph Bremer sobbed convulsively on the stand, "tears streaming down his aged face." Adolph sobbed when he talked of Father Deere, "an old, old friend of our family," who was used as a ransom mes-senger. He broke down again while recounting the night his son stum-bled into his mansion after twenty-two days as captive. Ed was in "poor condition and looked very sick. Very bad. He was so nervous he couldn't go to bed."

While his father was sobbing, his son whispered to a reporter, "He has a weak heart and I'm afraid he may collapse."

Maybe he had a weak heart. Or maybe he had a guilty conscience.

Adolph's underworld connections had come back to harm his family. The kidnapping had made an emotional wreck of his son. The gangsters whose business he'd once cultivated were now perceived as a threat even to his innocent granddaughter. Among the feared gangsters still at large was Weaver, the Green Lantern habitué Adolph had arranged to free via police bribery. That bribe had been paid to protect Adolph's illegal beer distributor, Harry Sawyer. Now Harry had been revealed as a planner of Ed's kidnapping and Adolph's misery.

Behind the scenes, the FBI was preparing Byron Bolton to be their devastating star witness. G-men tried to deny he existed. Then they seeded the press with a story that Bolton would change his plea, stop cooperating, and stand trial. In fact, the feds were preparing Bolton to link Harry Sawyer to the Bremer kidnapping.

During the trial, the FBI's identification of Sawyer as a prime suspect blasted its way into the morning headlines. But this added drama was hidden from the sequestered jury. On Good Friday, April 19, judge Matthew Joyce gave jurors the option of a half-day holiday. They declined. That afternoon they heard a witness who linked Alvin Karpis to the kidnapping. She was Florence Humphrey, a clerk in a downtown hardware store who believed she had sold three flashlights to Karpis. Those flashlights had been used to "light the way" to the ransom drop and were now offered in evidence.

Ed Bremer, sneezing with a cold, was barred from the courtroom by a cop. "Say, listen," Bremer protested, "if it wasn't for me, there wouldn't be any trial."

Over Easter weekend the FBI put it all together: the Roy McCord shooting; the Barker gang; the link between Harry Sawyer and the Barkers; the Barker gang and the Hamm kidnapping; the suspicious escape of the Barkers from 204 Vernon. When they reeled in this line of thinking, it led to two new suspects: Jack Peifer and Tom Brown. Agents chased leads on both of them. The Hamm investigation, frozen since the Touhy fiasco, was hot again.

After the Easter break, the FBI put on the stand Reuben Grossman, a farmer from Portage, Wisconsin. He recounted how, the previous winter, on the way home from ice fishing, he picked up four gasoline cans that had been discarded in the snow, along with a funnel. He put them on a shelf in his garage. Being a frugal fellow, he puzzled over why they had been tossed away. Four days later, his suspicions growing, he called the Portage sheriff. Soon farmer Grossman got a surprise visit from FBI agent Sam McKee.

Now police experts testified that those cans bore the fingerprints of Doc Barker. This was nail-in-the-coffin testimony, utilizing a new technology, and the defendants seemed absorbed in it, except for Edna Murray. At one point, she fished a letter out of her purse and read it. The Kissing Bandit, on trial for having gazed upon the ransom money, wore a sealskin jacket, appropriate to the Easter fashion season.

Doc Barker rocked in his chair as his attorneys fought in vain to exclude the evidence. The trial bogged down for days as the government tried to rope in the Chicago crooks who had attempted to launder the ransom. The most creative liar among them claimed that, as he drove along a Chicago viaduct, the money had mysteriously been thrown into his car through an open window.

Betty Baerwold, by now a hotel maid, testified that in 1933 and 1934 she was a housekeeper at the Sawyer farm. She swore she had seen Fred Barker and Lapland Willie there. She wasn't so fond of Harry and Gladys, claiming she'd quit them because they wouldn't let her off for church on Sundays.

Then Wynona Burdette, only 21 and in prison, her hopes for a radio career crushed, got in front of a microphone at last. She said that before and during the Bremer kidnapping, the Barker gang moved around St. Paul with impunity. They traveled to Reno; they returned to visit Harry Sawyer. She placed almost every member of the gang in St. Paul on the day of the kidnapping. Her hand shaking, she "timidly pointed" at Doc. His lawyers did not attempt a cross-examination.

Prosecutors were building a case against Harry Sawyer. But where was he?

On the Gulf Coast, in Pass Christian, Mississippi, running a "shabby gambling house" on that city's seawall. His clientele were African American men. "White men have to run those places in the South," Gladys

In May 1935, Wynona
Burdette, radio singer and
girlfriend of Barker gangster
Harry Campbell, was brought
from a federal prison in
Michigan to testify at
Doc Barker's trial.

later explained. "The colored race are not allowed to run them for themselves."

Harry paid protection money for the right to run this club. But no matter how much he greased the local wheels, a Yankee running a club in the "colored section" would not escape notice for long. Just as prosecutors in St. Paul were about to bring on their bombshell witness Byron Bolton, they were upstaged by the New Orleans FBI. Following tips from local cops, they walked into Harry's dive, and he surrendered without a fight.

End-of-the-world headlines ensued.

FEAR SAWYER WILL TALK

The *Daily News* wrote: "A trembling underworld nervously awaits" the arrival of Harry Sawyer. How much would he tell the feds?

"I haven't a chance in the world to make bond," Harry admitted. A *Daily News* reporter speculated Harry might help solve the mystery of the Homer Van Meter shooting. Did Harry set him up to avoid paying money he owed Van Meter?

That question, and many others, meant trouble for Tom Brown.

Doc Barker apparently had not dealt directly with Tom Brown. Shotgun George, whom Brown had met when setting up the Hamm kidnapping, had been silenced in Chicago. Fred Barker was dead, and Brown had never made any deals directly with Alvin Karpis. Byron Bolton knew plenty about Brown, but it was all hearsay. There were only three people whose testimony might put Brown in prison: his fellow detective James Crumley, Jack Peifer, and most dangerous of all, Harry Sawyer.

On May 6, two days after his capture, newspapers printed pictures of Harry being led to his cell in the St. Paul jail, handkerchief held over his face. If Brown's behavior pattern held true, he was scrambling around town to limit the damage.

When the trial resumed, Bolton took the stand. Looking worried and testifying in a voice that was "hardly audible," he identified Harry Sawyer

Harry Sawyer, cuffed and escorted down the stairs at the county jail, 1935.

as the "finger man." He told how Sawyer rejected Shotgun George's suggestion that the gang simply rob Bremer's bank. He described how Fred Barker and Curly Davis had brought the money to Chicago to be divided up.

Bolton, in ninety-five minutes of testimony, told the jury essentially what he had told the FBI: that he declined to participate directly in the Bremer kidnapping but did visit the house where the victim was held. He said he had seen Sawyer and Shotgun George together in Chicago in late January, while Bremer was still being held. Shotgun George, Bolton said, had complained that Harry was bungling his end of the deal, which was to find the kidnappers a safe house and to keep off the "heat."

After the ransom was paid, Curly Davis and Fred Barker each lugged a cardboard box tied with cord up the stairs to a Chicago apartment, dumped them on a davenport, and opened them to reveal the ransom money. Then they changed from hunting clothes to business suits before dividing up the money, Bolton said. All the while, the prime defendant, Doc Barker, stared at Bolton from the defense table. A brief cross-examination sought to damage Bolton's character but did not attack his story. Doc Barker never testified in his own defense. On May 17, he was found guilty and sentenced to life.

An "as told to" story signed by Edna Murray appeared in the next day's newspaper, calling Bolton a "sneak and a liar." Murray's story was an attempt to exonerate her lover, Volney Davis, whom she called "a gambler, not a kidnapper." Ultimately, however, Davis would confess to a role in the kidnapping.

The Bremer kidnapping trial lit a fire for the other kidnapping victim, William Hamm. His case had long been clouded by the misguided prosecution of the Touhy gang. Police chief Tom Dahill and his friend detective Charles Tierney clung to their belief that, somehow, Touhy's boys had engineered the Hamm snatch. Hamm suspected friends or perhaps even family had set him up.

Byron Bolton's testimony was a revelation, and Hamm came to believe it held the key to his case. In May 1935, Hamm arranged with the St. Paul police to interview Bolton in the Ramsey County Jail. He was accompanied by two detectives: Charles Tierney and Tom Brown.

It's amazing to think that the government let Tom Brown anywhere near a witness as important as Byron Bolton. But they did, and Bolton told Brown, Hamm, and Tierney essentially nothing. He was trading his testimony to the FBI in return for a light sentence, and these three St. Paul characters could do nothing for him, except bring trouble.

Charles Tierney was a quicksilver character. Even in the light of history, it is hard to know what game he was playing. Tierney had sometimes been a true O'Connor System cop, letting criminals go in return for a bribe. Now he seemed to be on the side of reformers. He and Chief Dahill were buddies. He and Brown had been partners. Dahill and Brown hated each other, so where did that leave Tierney?

Certainly Tierney reported this jailhouse visit to his chief, because Dahill sought federal permission to interview Bolton privately. Bolton told Chief Dahill he'd heard from Ziegler that the Hamm kidnapping

Bremer jurors lunch at the Hotel St. Paul after their dismissal on May 18, 1935. Clockwise from left: George Geiter of Racine, Harry Jones of Austin, Frank Beatty of Lake City, Earl Bateman of Plainview, Ben Buchminster of Lake City, Robert Barkhuff of Austin, William Scherf of Frontenac, Hubert Frank of Caledonia, Mrs. Alice C. Hall of St. Paul, Miss Mary McQuade of St. Paul, and Miss J. Maude Brown of St. Paul.

had been set up by a crooked cop named Brown. Curiously, Bolton also lied to Dahill, saying he did not know much about Peifer's role. He may have been instructed by the FBI to withhold that information until Peifer was put on trial. Or perhaps he was afraid that Peifer could harm him, even in the Ramsey County Jail. Or perhaps he had learned, as had many others, to distrust the St. Paul police.

For a long time, Chief Dahill seemed unwilling or unable to realize the true depths of Tom Brown's treachery. He once considered Brown an able officer whose underworld contacts were an asset. But lately Dahill began to see Brown's invisible hand behind a lot of things. He told the FBI that Brown and his clique were trying to undermine his authority. Sometimes, he said, they "had crimes committed in order to embarrass" the department. Digging for dirt on Tom Brown had "become an obsession" with the chief, the FBI noted. Dahill "keeps pestering the bureau" to develop new evidence against Brown. The FBI said that "Dahill and Brown are bitter enemies" and added that "Tierney is a close friend of Dahill's, so his sympathy would naturally lie there."

Frustrated and certain that Bolton was withholding information, William Hamm asked the FBI to tell him whom they suspected as mastermind of his kidnapping. They replied with the investigator's mantra: no comment.

35

THE RECORDING ARTIST

In early 1935, young Wallace Jamie began hanging around the police station. He posed as a college boy studying crime statistics. "He drew a bunch of diagrams, circles and graphs," said his paymaster, newspaper editor Howard Kahn. "The cops laughed at him behind his back," but as it turned out, Jamie "was an exceptionally intelligent young man working with dumb cops."

A few months after Jamie set up the wiretap, detective James Crumley discovered it. His phone line led not to the police switchboard but to another room. Hidden in there were operators who would switch on recording equipment when they heard an incriminating conversation.

Wallace Jamie examines a transcript of the wiretaps during the Civil Service
Appeals Board hearing for James Crumley and Fred Raasch, August 20, 1935.

They heard 2,500 of them. The conversations filled more than three
hundred Pamograph discs, which resemble vinyl record albums but are
made of aluminum. Crumley tipped off his fellow cops, but it was too
late. Twenty-one St. Paul cops were indicted. Sensational details leaked
to the newspapers.

In one typical conversation, recorded on March 5, 1935, bookie Harry
Reed answered the phone.

"Hello?"

Detective James Crumley: "Close up that horse book."

Reed: "All right."

Crumley: "No bets, see?"

Reed then phoned detective Charles Tierney, who had done honest
work on the Bremer and Hamm kidnappings but apparently was not
above helping a bookie whose bribes were supplementing police pay.
Reed said:

"This is Harry. Is the chief [Michael Culligan] there?"

Tierney: "Yeah, he's around. I'm waiting for him myself."

Reed: "Do you know if the place is going to be made tonight?"

Tierney: "There's a party waiting to see him about that right now. He's a big fellow. He counts for something with the chief. As far as the chief is concerned, it's all right to run. The heat comes from the other end of the building."

Reed: "You mean Warren?"

They were talking about Ned Warren, the police commissioner.

Tierney: "I know [Chief] Culligan is all burned up about that front office action. I know he wants that spot to run, see." By this he meant Warren was interfering with the chief's desire to let these particular bookies take bets.

Reed responded: "Well, I know who can take care of" Warren.

Is Reed asking whether Warren can be intimidated? Tierney suggests a milder approach: "The thing to do is take the goddamn fool out and put him where he has nothing to do with this stuff."

But Reed's horse book can't escape police harassment. On April 12, after getting another warning, Reed calls police chief Michael Culligan.

"Ah, say, did you have any idea how long they're going to be down, Mike?"

Culligan: "Quite a while."

Reed: "Oh, I didn't bother the Ryan Hotel down there, because that's a businessman's [poker] game . . . Or do you want me to call them too?"

Culligan: "Oh . . ."

Reed: "Because that's all a private game down there, see."

Culligan: "Oh, I think that's all right. What the hell."

Reed complains that his competitor, the Royal Cigar Store, is allowed to take horse-racing bets. "I don't want to be no stool pigeon or nothing, but what's good for one is good for all."

Culligan promises to shut the Royal: "All right, I'll have somebody over there."

Reed, sensing that the chief is not telling all, calls Crumley.

"Say listen Jim. Did anybody down at the Royal get permission for anybody to open, to run their horse book?"

Crumley: "Oh I don't know anything about 'em."

Reed: "I was wondering why the hell we should be closed and they should be open."

Crumley: "I don't know nothing about it, Harry."

Reed: "I just wanted to get a little cooperation because it hurts if one can't go and the others go. You know, it just hurts us, that's all it does. I don't give a damn if they make a million dollars there, Jim."

Crumley: "All right, partner."

The next day, the conversation between bookie and chief resumes.

Reed: "Goddamn it, it's murder down here, it's . . ."

Culligan: "Well, hell. Say, this is Holy Week."

Reed: "Holy? Hell! Everything is holy. I wonder how long. It won't be long, though?"

Culligan: "I'll advise you one of these days."

Two days later, the message penetrates Reed's thick skull. He calls the chief.

"Can I stop by for a few minutes?"

Culligan: "I'm just going out, Harry."

Reed: "Well, I wanted to ask you something. And then I got a little something here. What time'll you be back and then I'll be up there."

Reed has finally realized he's the sucker in a police shakedown. All the cops really want is more money.

The recordings also incriminate another longtime cop. Detective Fred Raasch, who led the delayed raids on the Barkers back in 1932, was heard to call the Riverview Commercial Club, which had many high-powered members.

"Take the slot machines down. This is Freddy Raasch. There's a couple of guys coming over. Stick 'em in the vault."

"Huh?"

"Stick them in the vault and lock it."

Police commissioner Ned Warren said the recordings disclosed "a startling link between" cops and race-horse gamblers, police ownership of slot machines, and a "tip off system on [gambling] raids." But Chief Culligan was described by the *St. Paul Dispatch* as "genial and unperturbed."

Ramsey County attorney Michael Kinkead proclaimed, "This thing must be sifted to the bottom no matter who it hits." Mayor Gehan said he had "every confidence in Kinkead."

The accused cops were entitled to a hearing before the St. Paul Civil Service Board. Raasch, whose street nickname was "Hitler," offered

Inspector James Crumley and detective Fred Raasch at their Civil Service
Appeals Board hearing, August 20, 1935.

improbable explanations having to do with bowling balls. A police
stenographer, called as a character witness, spun a tale of Raasch giving
his overcoat to a naked, drunken female prisoner. On the stand, Raasch
admitted he knew there was gambling at the Riverview but didn't know
it was against the law.

"I'm not on the morals squad," he said.

On the witness stand, Crumley insisted he was a dutiful cop. "If I
got orders to enforce gambling I would do so with an axe, even at the
Hollyhocks," he said.

When questioned about his conversations with gamblers, his standard replies were, "I don't remember" or "I was only kidding."

The Civil Service Board upheld the firings of Crumley, Raasch,
Michael McGinnis, and Ray Flanagan. Former chief Tom Dahill and
detective Charles Tierney were suspended thirty days for neglect of
duty and lowered in grade.

In addition to the gambling charges, Raasch and Crumley were found
to have taken a $300 bribe from Irwin and Helen Koop, proprietors

of the Empress Hotel. That case offers a detailed look at how Crumley ran his shakedown.

The Empress was a wonderland of "sporting women," out-of-season carnival workers, criminals, and fugitives. One of the sporting women was named Babe High, and her activities supplemented the income of her husband's downtown cigar store. Other long-term residents included Marion Daly, who accepted gentlemen callers and lived in a single room, bathroom down the hall. The proprietors were as hard up as their residents: The Koops were eighteen months behind in their rent.

Crumley, inspector of detectives, had command of twenty men, including Raasch, whom he used as a "clerk or office boy." Responding to supposed reports that prostitutes were picking the johns' pockets at the Empress, Crumley sent Raasch to arrest Irwin Koop and four of his sporting women.

Koop testified at Crumley's 1936 trial on bribery charges. He said he had been held in jail all night, protesting to the cops, "I cannot understand this. My wife and I got plenty of money invested here." He had been making regular payments to the downtown bookie who moonlighted as police department collector.

According to Koop's testimony, Raasch suggested that a $300 payment would set him free. Some of the money would be used to repay the men whose pockets had been picked, Raasch told Koop. "Why don't you pay it off and straighten up those fellows?"

Koop said he then appealed to Crumley, who only "told me what a serious case I had." Crumley advised Koop that all of his prostitutes had "squawked."

As if there weren't enough forces arrayed against Koop, the cops set him up with criminal attorney Tom Newman, who was to get $100 of the $300 bribe.

"A hundred dollars for five minutes work?" Koop said he asked Newman.

"You know we attorneys have to get our fees," Koop recalled as Newman's answer.

Koop was a fly struggling in a web, all the greedy spiders surrounding him.

He called his wife and begged her to borrow $300 from friends.

"Where did you pay Mr. Raasch that money?" Koop was asked in court.

"Over in the police station."

Bribe paid, Irwin Koop and his sporting women walked out of the police station and back into the nightlife.

Like Crumley, detective Fred Raasch faced bribery charges in Ramsey County District Court following his dismissal. He was charged with tipping off gamblers at the Riverview Commercial Club and at the Royal Cigar Store. Before Raasch's fate was handed over to the jury, his attorney, Jerome Hoffman, made an eloquent plea for his client that summed up how St. Paul's rackets worked.

Hoffman said Raasch became "a secretary or handyman to the Inspector of Detectives [Crumley]. Naturally, he is going to preserve that position for himself. He has been around long enough to know that certain forms of gambling existed in the city of St. Paul. Every person who frequents the downtown area knew that such violations occur every day, and further that they were in accordance with policy of the [police] department. The defendant was put in a difficult position. He was between two fires."

"We know," Hoffman told the jury, "that the Commissioner of Public Safety [Ned Warren] is dependent on votes for his position. We know that he is not antagonizing a private club with several hundred members to take a simple gambling device [slot machines] away from them." Commissioner Warren "permits and authorizes such a device within limitations . . . and expects the men of his department . . . to do as they are told." With Warren and the police chief "getting away . . . Raasch becomes the goat."

During deliberations the foreman asked the judge whether the jury could consider that Raasch was "acting under orders." The judge said no. The jury convicted Raasch but "strenuously recommended clemency."

At Raasch's trial, the shiniest brass of the police establishment showed up to say he was fundamentally a good cop. Police commissioner Ned Warren said so on the stand, and so did former chiefs Edward Murnane and Thomas Dahill. Detective Charles Tierney chimed in, as did Ramsey County sheriff George Moeller. Even Gus Barfuss, the current police chief and the face of reform, swore that Raasch was a square guy.

But one name was missing from the roster of top cops: Tom Brown. He wasn't going anywhere near a witness stand. Wallace Jamie and his band of wiretappers didn't get a thing on Tom Brown, and Brown avoided all involvement in the resulting bribery hearings and trials.

"It was known at the time . . . that Tom Brown was running things in St. Paul," J. Edgar Hoover was informed by one of his agents, "and it was hoped ultimately that . . . evidence enough would be secured on him to at least get him out of the Police Department. However, about that time Brown was transferred to some outside detail and had no occasion to make telephone contacts from the police station." One informant whose name has never been revealed "claimed it was not that Brown was tipped off but it was merely that things broke in his favor just at the time this investigation started."

But many did not believe it. The Jamie wiretaps had gone on for months. Tom Brown was, by reputation, the most corrupt and feared cop on the force. Jamie, Warren, and Kahn could not have been ignorant of the rumors about Brown swirling around St. Paul. Could it really have been a coincidence that Brown, month after month, stayed off the target list?

"It was noted during the recent police investigation at St Paul," said one FBI memo, "that Brown's name was conspicuously absent and agent was confidentially advised by [name redacted] that Brown was associated with commissioner Warren and Mr. Kahn of the *Daily News* and knew that the investigation was in progress."

It was well within Warren's power to transfer Brown to a post where the wiretaps didn't reach.

Months after the wiretap stories broke in public, FBI agent John Brennan and St. Paul detective Charles Tierney squared off. Tierney "stated that it was quite noticeable that Brown's name was never mentioned in the police [wiretap] investigation." Tierney said "the reason for this was that Brown was in on it."

Noted the *Union Advocate,* "People wonder where Tom Brown, Howard Kahn's buddy, comes into the picture. Could it be that [Police Commissioner] Warren did not suspect him . . . ? Is Brown's police reputation of such a high order that Warren, Kahn and Jamie did not think it necessary to work their mechanical stool pigeons on the former chief?"

Brown was a valuable source of police information for Kahn's paper, the *St. Paul Daily News,* which had set up the investigation. Brown had repeatedly used the *Daily News* to send messages to kidnappers, to embarrass Chief Dahill and his enemies, and to polish his own image.

The *Daily News,* a tabloid-style paper that emphasized coverage of crime, obtained "exclusives" from Brown. It also, over the years, ran stories that portrayed Brown as a hero.

A *Union Advocate* columnist wrote that a nice addition to the Jamie wiretaps would have been a "traveloge of Tom Brown following the beaten trail between Harry Sawyer's joint and Kahn's office" during the Hamm kidnapping.

In public perception, Police Commissioner Warren and editor Kahn may have been reformer-heroes. But in a system so deeply corrupt, perhaps no one was unstained.

Although Warren and Kahn were the public face of police reform, they drew their ultimate power from the businessmen who bankrolled it. Kahn had ties to banker Richard Lilly and through him to many other wealthy men. Lilly was the true power behind the move for police reform. Ned Warren's run for office had been bankrolled by Charles Ward, an ex-con who had risen to become president of Brown & Bigelow publishing company. There were many other wealthy and influential St. Paul men who, looking to protect their interests or to keep a secret, could have put out the word that Brown was untouchable.

However it worked, Brown's miraculous escapes from justice were just beginning.

36

HARRY TAKES THE STAND

On January 5, 1936, three outsized mug shots were splashed across page one of the *St. Paul Daily News.* Harry Sawyer was photographed in squat, grim profile. Lapland Willie Weaver looked like a dead-eyed punk with chipmunk cheeks and short hair. Cassius (Cash) McDonald, with silver hair and dark eyebrows, could have passed as the suave president of an insurance company. McDonald looked sorry, as if he were about to deliver disastrous news to his stockholders.

The occasion was the second trial of Bremer kidnappers. Ultimately, more than twenty people would be implicated in this abduction. Only three remained on the Most Wanted list: Harry Campbell, Alvin Karpis, and Doc Moran.

Moran, the self-taught plastic surgeon, would never turn up alive or dead, but the FBI had not yet given up on finding him. Karpis and Campbell had split up, with Harry going to ground in Toledo and Alvin celebrating New Year's Day with a 90 mph car chase and gun battle with Kansas City police.

Harry Sawyer arrived smiling for his date with justice. Dressed in an overcoat and a white fedora and surrounded by deputies, Harry entered the courtroom like the genial host of a party. He hailed his friends. Gladys rushed over and kissed him.

For the first days of the trial, Harry maintained a front of cheery denial. When he took the stand, it was like a homecoming. The courtroom was packed with reporters who had hung out at his Green Lantern. Harry could hardly deny he'd been a bootlegger. He described his clientele as coming from "all walks of life, from senators to attorneys to bootleggers to businessmen" to "newspapermen and printers." With that, he smiled at press row. Reporters giggled.

Harry said he'd known Edward Bremer since the early 1920s: "I had done business with the bank that Edward George Bremer was in since I was in town. Edward Bremer knew me pretty well. He and his father used to come down [to the Green Lantern] occasionally and drink. I handled their beer exclusively."

Gladys, a squarely built woman with deep sad eyes, sat in the front row watching intently as Harry admitted his acquaintance with the underworld. He said he'd known shoplifter extraordinaire Myrtle Eaton for twelve years. He admitted knowing Bolton, Ziegler, Curly Davis, the Barker brothers, and "Ray Hunter." He claimed he did not know that "Ray Hunter" was actually Public Enemy Number One, Alvin Karpis.

"I had nothing to do with [Bremer's kidnapping]," he testified, "either directly or indirectly. I first knew of it when I read it in the newspapers. I never met [with the kidnappers] in any apartment whatsoever." He and his lawyers crafted a story that portrayed him not as a fugitive from justice but as an entrepreneur scouting the nation for nightclub opportunities.

U.S. district attorney George Sullivan put Ed Bremer on the stand and slyly asked who had been with him just before his abduction. Bremer answered: his innocent daughter, Betty. Then he began sobbing.

Harry's lawyer leaped up to object to "the witness putting on that kind of demonstration." But the government had made its point: that the kidnapping had turned Ed Bremer from a confident young executive into an emotional wreck. It sharpened the point when his father Adolph, sick and weak, walked into the courtroom on crutches.

On the stand, Ed Bremer said his abductors had promised to reveal the finger man but never did. He testified that he barely knew Harry Sawyer, just enough to say hello. The government did not challenge that evasion in court, but the family had already admitted to the FBI that Ed Bremer "had considerable contact with underworld characters" and had been "perfectly willing to do business with them."

Bremer also testified that he was still haunted by the twenty-two-day ordeal. He said he was "nervous and could not sleep. I lost considerable weight. I couldn't be left alone."

One witness for the prosecution never made it to the stand. Father John Deere had been one of the intermediaries the gang had used to contact the Bremers. On the eve of his scheduled testimony, Father Deere was called to a higher court, dying of natural causes in his sleep.

On each day of the three-week trial, huge crowds gathered outside the federal building. The gawkers endured an arctic blast such as hadn't been seen in a generation. St. Paul temperatures plunged to 33 degrees below zero, and in the hinterlands it reached 55 below.

Just as this arctic weather moved in, fourteen Cubans arrived to testify against the ransom launderers. Huddled in overcoats the FBI bought them, many had never seen snow and likely returned to Havana with teeth-chattering cautionary tales of the northland. Room and board for the Cubans was expensive, so the government moved up their testimony. These bankers, money changers, and hotel clerks told how Cash McDonald had shown up in Havana with loads of cash. He approached gold dealer Rene Bolivar in a café, looking to exchange $10,000. That was a test for the next exchange, of $72,000. Having changed the $5 and $10 ransom bills into gold, McDonald exchanged that gold for $1,000 in U.S. Federal Reserve notes. That transaction occurred at the Chase National Bank, where McDonald told cashier Jose Zalacain he was in Havana to open a horse-race track.

Some of those $1,000 bills, FBI agents testified, were found at the house where Ma and Fred Barker had made their last stand.

With the Cuban portion of the testimony over, the government focused on the Ohio confab the Barker-Karpis gang had called for the purpose of splitting the ransom.

Cubans brought to testify in the Bremer trial endure some of the coldest weather in the state's history. The Department of Justice provided them with identical overcoats.

Mug shots of four "molls" appeared in the newspaper. Dolores Delaney flashed a defiant smile. Wynona Burdette looked defeated. The gawky Edna Murray was sick with cancer. Myrtle Eaton looked as she did in every one of her photos: creepy and hard.

When the "molls" arrived, so did Alvin Karpis's dad. He had been hoping to talk with Dolores Delaney, mother of the toddler he was raising. But Delaney was held in jail during the trial and never was called to testify.

John Karpowicz was used to disappointment. Alvin Karpis's hardworking immigrant parents could never figure out what they had done wrong, nor that the answer might be "nothing." Karpowicz was described by reporters as "a little old man with piercing eyes."

He pleaded with reporters: "Why do you fellows haunt me?"

He told them his grandson "will never be told about his father" and he intended to "raise him up to be a useful citizen." It was not to be. Raymond Karpis, son of Alvin Karpis and Dolores Delaney, embarked on a long criminal career while in high school.

When Edna Murray began to testify, Harry seemed to realize he was in serious trouble. She described a scene from a kidnap planning meeting at her apartment: "They were in the living room and I was in the kitchen. I served some beer to them. Harry Sawyer was standing up in the middle of the room and he was talking to Fred Barker, and he was talking about the heat being on over that radioman [Roy McCord] being shot. He said 'The town is hot. You'd better wait a while.'"

On the morning after the kidnapping, Murray testified: "Volney and I went to Sawyer's farm, arriving there about 10 o'clock, and I saw Sawyer in the back yard, standing against the back porch . . . I overheard Sawyer tell Volney that the town was full of G-men, that it was hot."

The Kissing Bandit said Harry had journeyed to Cleveland for the sole purpose of splitting the ransom. News reporters noted that the cancer-stricken Murray seemed "near collapse on the stand." The court recessed to give her time to recompose.

When she returned, she testified that the ransom money was hidden "in my bedroom, under my bed" in Cleveland. Fred Barker had brought it to her apartment. He entered carrying a Gladstone bag, in the company of Harry Sawyer, wife Gladys, and "adopted" daughter Francine. Murray told of the gang's tense arguments and said Ma Barker had

Elmer Farmer, left, the tavern owner who helped the Barker gang in Bensenville during both the Hamm and Bremer kidnappings, is handcuffed to Volney Davis as they leave the courthouse accompanied by G-men.

strong opinions on how the money should be divided. "I talked with Harry Sawyer in Weaver's back yard. He was talking about the boys all quarreling among themselves, he said he was going to check out and as soon as he got his dough he was leaving."

After Murray's four hours on the stand, the government had tied Harry Sawyer and Lapland Willie Weaver to the kidnapping by direct eyewitness testimony.

Then the government brought in its stalwart, Byron Bolton. A tall, pale, handsome man with jet-black hair combed straight back, Bolton testified that after week one of the kidnapping, Harry Sawyer and Shotgun George Ziegler met in Chicago to try to get the ransom plan back on the rails. It was devastating to Harry's prospects when Bolton said Ziegler had once suggested ditching the plan and robbing Bremer's bank instead, but Harry insisted on a kidnapping.

About four months after Bremer's release, in June 1934, Bolton testified that he met with Fred Barker and Harry Sawyer in a private room at

Elmer Farmer's tavern in Bensenville, Illinois. "I asked Sawyer if he had been, if he had just come from St. Paul and he said no, that he had left St. Paul in April because he had heard government agents wanted to question him about the Bremer kidnapping." Fred, Bolton said, complained about the difficulty of laundering the Bremer ransom and talked about a Cuban solution, and said this in the presence of Harry Sawyer.

In his defense, Harry said he barely knew this Murray woman. "Every time I saw her she was drunk" and spent whole days in bed, he testified.

So he did in fact see Edna Murray in Cleveland. Why was he there?

Harry said he'd journeyed to Cleveland to meet "Ray Hunter" and discuss going into the slot machine business with him. He admitted moving in with "Ray Hunter" and Dolores Delaney and later with Fred Barker and Paula Harmon. Then, he said, he left with Willie Harrison for Florida, looking for opportunities to start a nightclub.

He didn't mention Cash McDonald or Cuba.

"What did you do in Miami?"

"Drank beer and drove around a little."

Harry had to cover up that ransom-laundering trip to Cuba. So he copped to the Florida heat, claiming he'd stayed in his room, filling his bathtub with ice and beer and taking occasional trips to scout nightclub locales.

Then, Harry testified, he got quite the shock: "I read that my wife had been arrested in Cleveland."

His story was already falling apart. He moved in with the most wanted fugitives in America in order to close a slot machine deal? He was well acquainted with the underworld but did not know Alvin Karpis by sight? Karpis, whose second home had been the Green Lantern? Dozens of people could testify that they'd seen Harry in St. Paul with Karpis.

Did Harry expect a jury to believe he didn't know Fred Barker was wanted by the FBI? That Harry was ignorant of what everybody else in America knew: that the Barker gang was wanted for two kidnappings?

And when his wife was arrested in Cleveland, Harry didn't leave Florida to help her? He didn't immediately fly up to take care of Francine, the girl he hoped to adopt?

And the reason for this neglect, he expected the jury to believe, was not because he was running from an indictment, but because . . . because . . .

Harry was starting to sputter. He denied he knew he was a wanted man when he left his farm in spring of 1934. His former maid Betty Baerwold would later contradict that testimony. When asked why he stayed on the run, Harry said, "After I found out what they did to my wife in Cleveland, I didn't feel like giving myself up." He complained that the FBI "stripped people of their clothes and held them for hours."

Then he changed his story and said he'd driven to Ohio to borrow money from Fred Barker and that his ultimate purpose was to open a nightspot in Vegas "because it was booming."

Lapland Willie Weaver did not put up much of a defense. While Harry Sawyer had a thousand local connections and was a danger to many of them, Weaver was just an Ozarks thug who happened to be a boyhood pal of Fred Barker. He didn't know many secrets and so wasn't a threat to very many people. After the ransom split, he and his reluctant paramour Myrtle Eaton had fled to Florida, purchased a chicken ranch, and essentially bought a child from a desperate mother. Federal agents tracked Eaton and Weaver down through a Washington, DC, criminal and carefully prepared a raid that would have echoed the shootout with Ma and Fred Barker. But Hoover, always sensitive to publicity, was under pressure to avoid bloody episodes. Questions had been raised about whether the violence at Lake Weir had been necessary. FBI agents surprised Weaver while he was going out to buy a Sunday newspaper and took him peaceably.

Weaver on the stand was described as looking "more like a clerk than a gunman." While he testified, the 2-year-old child who had lived with him and Eaton frolicked in the courthouse in the care of government matrons.

There's never a good time to be on trial for kidnapping, but the winter of 1936 was inauspicious for all the defendants. The Lindbergh case had caused a national backlash against criminals. Screaming headlines called for the execution of the man accused of murdering the Lindbergh baby: BRUNO MUST DIE! The governor of California was calling for vigilante action against criminals. In Minnesota, the citizens of White Bear Lake declared that if the cops couldn't enforce the law, they would.

On January 24, 1936, Cash McDonald was found guilty and would be sentenced to fifteen years in prison. Lapland Willie Weaver and Harry Sawyer were saddled with life terms.

A sobbing Ed Bremer thanked the jury.

Reporters wrote that Weaver's face wore a "cynical leering smile" after the sentence. Tears flooded "the hard-bitten eyes" of Cash McDonald. Harry Sawyer and Gladys cried as they embraced for the last time, surrounded by the antiseptic white tile walls of the county jail.

"It's a bum rap," Harry muttered. Then he speculated about whether he'd be sent to Alcatraz: "I wonder if this means the Rock?"

A reporter for the *St. Paul Daily News* recorded Harry's "tearful embrace" of Gladys "as he looks over her shoulder out the window, his last glance at the city whose underground he ruled."

Weaver, Sawyer, and McDonald were escorted to the Union Depot for the long train ride to the penitentiary. St. Paul attorney John DeCourcy reported to investigators that Gladys "became intoxicated after her husband's conviction and said that if Harry has to go to the pen she was going to see Tom Brown go there also."

37

"DID YOU TELL THEM YOU KNOW ME, DAD?"

By 1936, when St. Paul's underworld was being exposed in the courts, the FBI suspected Tom Brown of kidnapping conspiracy. But Brown had been careful to deal indirectly with the Barker gang. His medium in the Bremer case was Harry Sawyer, and only if Harry cracked could Brown be convicted. But the greatest danger to Brown's freedom was the Hamm kidnapping, because he'd been a more active mole and gotten the largest share of the ransom. In the Hamm case, it was Jack Peifer whose testimony might send Brown to Alcatraz.

Brown's brother-in-law, George Rafferty, fueled the FBI's suspicions. Rafferty, a St. Paul cab driver, was judged to be "very bitter against Tom Brown" by FBI agents.

During the Bremer kidnapping, Rafferty dropped in to FBI headquarters to suggest that Brown's Crane Lake property was the most likely place for the victim to be held. The FBI noted that Brown had "given money to Rafferty's wife and children, has five or six boats at his lake, tried to get Rafferty on the police force and said he would get him a downtown beat and show him how [the bribery system] works."

Although he had never witnessed Brown accepting a bribe, Rafferty said, "he must be on the take to have all the money he has."

The FBI also reported that, "During the trial of [detective James] Crumley, Rafferty carried a woman passenger who said she hoped Crumley was acquitted, since Brown was much worse and nothing was ever done to him. She said Brown was a murderer in addition to being a crook, that he had killed five or six men and that her husband had told her stories about Brown that would make a person's blood run cold."

A hearsay conversation that took place in a taxi is worthless as evidence, but it does tell of the rumors swirling around St. Paul. According to Crumley, even St. Paul cops were afraid they would be killed if they crossed Brown.

Hearsay evidence, FBI agents noted, could under some circumstances be allowed in a conspiracy trial, and there was a chance that Byron Bolton's testimony could be used to convict Brown. But agents wanted to find direct evidence or an eyewitness to Brown's crimes. Brown had been cagey enough to limit his exposure to the underworld and, therefore, his risk of prosecution. In the fall of 1935, J. Edgar Hoover wrote the agent in charge at St. Paul: "I have a very personal interest in developing all the information which is available with regard to the participation of Tom Brown" in the Barker gang's crimes. The FBI's best hope of prosecuting Brown was to crack Jack Peifer's connection to the Hamm kidnapping.

Bill Hamm couldn't escape, no matter how much distance he put between himself and the judicial circus in St. Paul. In late winter of 1936, he, his wife, his child, and a nurse encamped at the Halekulani Hotel on Waikiki Beach. St. Paul FBI agent C. W. Stein, welcome or not, flew in to visit their palmy refuge.

For years, the Hamm case hung over the FBI, unsolved. Now agents were interested in learning what Hamm had heard when he'd visited Byron Bolton in jail. Hamm's motive for that visit had been to explore rumors that Jack Peifer, a man he considered a friend, was the author of his kidnapping.

During that jailhouse talk, Hamm told FBI agent Stein, Bolton had identified Peifer and Brown as setup men. Hamm said he had relayed this to detective Charles Tierney and chief Tom Dahill. "Hamm stated that Tierney and Dahill are bitter enemies of Tom Brown and in his opinion would do anything to help convict Brown in this case," Stein reported.

But Hamm, mortally afraid of the underworld, insisted he could not identify Doc Barker as his kidnapper. When Stein showed him pictures of Doc, Hamm said sure, he recognized him, but only because he'd seen his picture in the newspapers. When Stein's report confirming that Peifer was a suspect reached the mainland, agents embarked on an arresting comedy.

When Jack Peifer had been subpoenaed to testify at the Bremer kidnapping trial, he'd disappeared. An informant told the FBI that Peifer had been raging against the Barker gang. It seemed to Peifer that he had gotten away with the Hamm kidnapping, and now, this heat over the Bremer case was causing the cops to focus on him. Alvin Karpis's ascent to Public Enemy Number One added to the pressure. Peifer began threatening to have Karpis "bumped off."

A few weeks later, Peifer, having calmed down, resurfaced in the Twin Cities. He explained his absence by saying he'd been fishing up north and then, what the heck, he'd decided to marry his longtime girlfriend Violet Nordquist and make her a Peifer.

The couple had driven to romantic Pierre, South Dakota, and gotten hitched. Once they had been gambling's godfather and his beauty queen. Now they were husband and a wife who could not be compelled to testify against him.

FBI agents, itching to get Master Jack into an interrogation room, gathered around the Hollyhocks. Peifer, chauffeur-driven, roared down his driveway and blasted past them. The agents followed the car, driven by Sam Tanaka. In downtown Minneapolis, Tanaka veered into a parking garage. Its electric door closed out the agents.

After a while, Peifer's lawyer, Archie Cary, appeared and brought the feds up to his office. There they found Peifer "semi-intoxicated" and arrested him.

Now FBI agents raided the Hollyhocks, looking for the new bride, Violet Peifer. She was no shrinking violet, but a tall, tough athletic beauty with striking blue eyes. As her husband fell into the FBI's trap, Violet wriggled out.

Agents raided the Hollyhocks but were road-blocked by a "distinctly uncooperative" Sam Tanaka. During the search of the nightclub and Peifer's quarters, the FBI found a list of people serving on the current grand jury. That information was supposed to be secret. How had it come into Peifer's possession?

Sam Tanaka said he didn't know. When agents left the Hollyhocks at 2:00 AM, they took a handcuffed Tanaka with them.

Violet Peifer holed up with relatives in St. Paul, and the FBI could not figure out exactly where. A drunken lawyer named A. R. English called the FBI, claiming he could lead them to Violet. Agents followed him to the Hotel St. Paul and waited to arrest her, but she didn't show up.

Jack Peifer, hung over and facing the hot lights of the FBI interrogation room, proclaimed his innocence in the Hamm kidnapping. He must have been mighty sobered by the news that Charles Fitzgerald, the gang's "greeter," and Edward Barthelmy, the Bensenville postmaster, were both in custody. Testimony from either man, but especially Fitzgerald, might sink him.

Peifer insisted he had never paid protection money to either the Minneapolis or the St. Paul police. He admitted that many cops frequented the Hollyhocks. He knew Brown and Crumley well, but they were "just coppers." Peifer claimed his dealings with Shotgun George Ziegler were limited to a discussion on how to turn Ziegler's Cranberry Lake property into a resort.

When the questions turned to his rental of the Idlewild cottage at Bald Eagle Lake, Peifer's glib façade broke. He realized the FBI had tangible evidence linking him to the Barker gang's hideout. He lawyered up.

Agent Earl Connelley, the public-enemies hunter who'd led the raid on Ma and Fred Barker, saw a chance of getting Peifer to talk about Tom Brown. Peifer "did not indicate hostility to the suggestion that possibly he should tell us the full details of any and all persons involved in this case, particularly the activities of the police officer who was alleged to be furnishing the tip-off to the gang through him."

Meanwhile, the feds were pressuring Charles Fitzgerald, whom they'd arrested in Los Angeles. At first he was defiant: "I'll never go to jail for this you can depend on that," he told the FBI. He joined the chorus of crooks who denied knowing Alvin Karpis. He denied, but with a wink, knowing Tom Brown and Jack Peifer. But when he realized the evidence was stacked against him, he begged the cops to spare his girlfriend, Belle Born, from hearing the truth. He wanted Belle to be told that he'd merely been a ransom launderer and otherwise uninvolved in kidnapping.

The FBI, hoping for an incriminating conversation, left Peifer and Charles Fitzgerald alone in a room, monitored by Dictaphone.

Peifer asked Fitz: "Did you tell them you know me, Dad?"

The reply wasn't audible. Fitzgerald, who'd been wounded during the Swift payroll robbery, needed a cane to gimp around. He thumped that cane on the table.

Peifer encouraged him: "Make a noise with it."

They finished in whispered conversation, Fitzgerald thumping the table.

Before they led him back to a cell, Peifer told agents that he had never committed a serious crime and could take whatever was coming to him. The events of the next few months were to prove him wrong.

Spectacularly wrong.

On the last day of April 1936, William Hamm was visited at the brewery by Peifer's one-eyed bouncer, Saph McKenna. McKenna tried to convince Hamm that Peifer was not the mastermind of his kidnapping. Then they talked about W. W. Dunn, the lifelong "friend" of the Hamm family. McKenna told Hamm that the Hollyhocks had long used Dunn as a bagman to shuttle bribes to St. Paul cops and politicians. Hamm then joined those who suspected that Dunn played a hidden role in his kidnapping. He told McKenna that he felt Dunn had "sold him out" and felt betrayed because "they had been intimate in the past."

The fact that the underworld solicited Peifer's victim for help showed their desperation. Peifer's defense, led by Archie Cary and backed by powerful friends, would "move heaven and earth" to defend him, a St. Paul cop told the FBI. Peifer had the potential to expose a great swath of the Twin Cities' seamy side. The underworld even sent an emissary to Edward Bremer, asking if he could bail Peifer out. Bremer demurred, but the Free Jack fund finally topped $100,000 on May 1, and Peifer was let out of jail.

38

"AT PEACE WITH THE WORLD"

As Peifer was sweating out bail, James Crumley's corruption trial was held in a stuffy St. Paul courtroom. Crumley—a shambling, massive, mess of a man in a rumpled suit—mopped his brow frequently during his testimony. The jurors wore headsets, listening to recordings of police issuing tip-offs to gamblers. They heard how Crumley had taken a bribe to protect a shoplifting gang run by one Pearl Miller.

Crumley had been asked by Wisconsin police to arrest Miller. She was also wanted by police in Detroit, Philadelphia, Omaha, and Kansas City. Instead of arresting Miller, Crumley invited her to "see me at the house tonight" and eventually sent detective Fred Raasch to collect a bribe from her.

As his wife, son, and daughter watched from the gallery, Crumley tried to shift blame for the lax enforcement of gambling laws to Ned Warren, the elected police commissioner. Warren "called me in and said I'm a craps shooter myself, go easy on the gambling," Crumley said.

According to Crumley, Warren said: "Now there is a guy in town I want to run. He spent a lot of money in my campaign and two weeks before the election I got him to switch over [to support Warren's side]. He has a policy game and I want him to run."

The policy game was a numbers lottery in which people tried to divine the last three figures of the daily "bank clearings" that appeared in the newspaper. This racket was boosted by shills, who loudly claimed to have won and spread chump change around the bars and cafés to further that impression.

According to Crumley, Commissioner Warren wanted him to strictly enforce the law against those who wouldn't pay bribes. Warren supposedly said, "Now there's a Negro coming over from Minneapolis to Rondo Street, and I want you to give it your personal attention."

"I said, 'All right,'" Crumley testified. "'I'll see he doesn't start.'"

Crumley also said Warren told him which horse-racing parlors could "go" and which should be shut down. Under the circumstances, Crumley said, "I held down as much as I could on crime." He said he mediated gamblers' conflicts "because I was afraid somebody would get hurt."

When Warren took the stand, he declared Crumley's testimony "too ridiculous for comment."

Crumley also told the jury that his chief, Michael Culligan, approved of his every corrupt action. Then came a parade of seven character witnesses and testimony by Mary Crumley, his wife of forty-two years. Crumley's lawyer, William Green, told jurors Crumley had served St. Paul "twenty-one years without a black mark, keeping the town free of murderers, kidnappers and thieves."

No, he had done just the opposite. He and his cronies had run a shakedown and criminal protection racket that had encouraged those very crimes. Because of Brown, Crumley, Sawyer, Peifer, Gleckman, Kinkead, et al., the city was overrun with criminals. Had Crumley and Brown simply done their jobs in 1932, Fred Barker and Alvin Karpis would have been captured in the house on Robert Street, sent to prison, and possibly executed in Missouri. Since their escape from Robert Street, at least four cops and three civilians had been killed by the Barker gang.

But Crumley resented being prosecuted while Tom Brown, the big fish, swam through the net. At one point during Crumley's trial, his attorney asked wiretapper Wallace Jamie, "You at no time tapped the phone of Detective Brown?"

"Objection!" roared the prosecution.

Sustained.

The prosecutor who objected happened to be Michael Kinkead.

On April 23, Crumley was acquitted of all criminal charges. It took the jury forty-five hours to reach that verdict. Outside the courtroom, Crumley, surrounded by newsmen, "sighed and lighted a large black cigar."

Blowing cigar smoke, he said: "I'm at peace with the world. See my attorney."

But he was not at peace with the world. He was a disgraced 65-year-old cop on a $75-a-month pension, with gambling and drinking habits to support. As a cop, whenever he needed cash, he'd arrest people and release them in return for a fee. One of his acquaintances remembered a Crumley arrest, where he'd put "a bum" behind bars and released him when the man agreed to buy a ton of coal for the Crumley home furnace.

That wasn't going to work now that he had no badge.

A few months after his acquittal, Crumley got involved with a drug dealer, gambler, and thief named Stuttering Bill Hildebrandt. Born in Brooklyn, New York, Hildebrandt was 45 and had an erratic criminal career that included going broke while operating a bookie joint in the St. Francis Hotel. Hildebrandt and Crumley approached federal narcotics agent John Wall with an offer of $400 to win leniency for a woman who'd been arrested for dealing "opium and yen shee."

Crumley added that a piece of that $400 would have to be rebated to him. After all, he was the fixer. But he was walking straight into another electronic trap.

Federal agent Wall recorded long conversations with Stuttering Bill and with Crumley. As Wall laid his trap, he and Stuttering Bill talked about Crumley. Stuttering Bill complained that Crumley was "getting a little simple, childish."

"Well," Wall said, "he's close to 70 [years old]. He's undergone a change lately. I don't think I've ever come in contact with a fellow in my life that only thinks in terms of dollar and cents."

"He's always been that way," said Stuttering Bill. "Every time I see the man he wants me to get him a new suit of clothes. 'Get me an overcoat.' I can't see the man without him asking me to give him some money."

"Yes," Wall agreed, "there is something phony about him."

"He does so much talking," complained Stuttering Bill.

Wall noted that whenever he'd gone to Crumley's house, the disgraced detective was "sitting around playing solitaire," so bored he'd beg Wall to take him for a ride, anywhere, just to get out of the house.

Eventually, both Stuttering Bill and Crumley were too talkative for their own good. Crumley was charged with bribery and conspiracy. He wanted to be his own attorney, he told reporters, "so convinced is he of his innocence."

Reason, or perhaps fear, prevailed, and he hired a lawyer. On the way to the courthouse, Crumley complained to his attorney, "I don't feel so good." So his lawyer bought him a pint of whiskey. They stopped at a tailor shop to pick up a suit for the court appearance, and Crumley drained the whiskey. He sat down and removed his shoes and socks. "I'm going to end it all," he said, and took out a .38 pistol. The lawyer wrestled it away from him. Crumley drew a straight razor from his pocket, but the tailor snatched that away.

On the witness stand, Crumley leaked tears when his lawyer prodded him to tell about the death of his son fourteen years before. He cried again when answering questions about his scant education. The jury may have been moved, but they found him guilty of bribery.

On June 15, 1938, Crumley appeared for sentencing. He told the judge, "My greatest regret is that they said I was a stool pigeon." This referred to his testimony against others involved in the case. "I don't care about myself or my pension," he said, "but I have grandchildren growing up and I don't want that hanging over me."

"You're not charged with being a stool pigeon," the judge reminded him, "but with a serious offense."

"It is evident," his attorney said, "the defendant believes he has lost all his friends." Crumley, "trembling and depressed," was sentenced to serve seven months in jail. His daughter, in the gallery, wept.

39

"SIT HERE, ALVIN"

Since abandoning his wounded and pregnant wife in Atlantic City, Alvin Karpis had been on the run for eighteen thieving months. His most spectacular act was to hold up an Ohio mail train. But he was so desperate for partners that he recruited, among others, a local heroin addict. For a while, Karpis sightings were a form of American amusement. The FBI was deluged with bad tips. In Chicago, his mom issued a plea through the press: "Give up son, don't let them shoot you down."

In 1936, he slinked into Hot Springs, Arkansas, a resort town renowned for gambling, prostitutes, and public baths. He rented here, boarded there, always on the move—and, by the way, seeking treatment for gonorrhea. For a while he came under the protection of a prostitute who was a bed buddy with the chief of police. He fished by day and nightclubbed in the evening, but it must have been a dispiriting time. All his reliable partners were dead or in prison, as was Dolores. His baby son was being raised by his parents, whom he dared not visit. Every word spoken in his parents' home was heard by the FBI and translated from their native Lithuanian.

In Hot Springs, one woman claimed she married him on short notice. If so, the marriage did not outlast the honeymoon. Karpis kept moving south, eventually renting an apartment off Canal Street in New Orleans. Neighbors knew him as a mild-mannered fellow with a slight speech impediment who loved to go fishing. He impressed his landlady as a "nice, quiet little man. He is just a boy. I can't imagine such a slim fellow being as bad as they say he is."

J. Edgar Hoover was still under pressure from members of Congress who abhorred the idea of a federal police force. In an effort to humiliate Hoover, one senator asked if he'd ever personally made an arrest. Hoover admitted he hadn't.

When agents discovered that Karpis was in New Orleans, Hoover flew down to take credit for his first arrest. Karpis and Hoover tell different stories about this arrest, and each man is naturally the hero of his own story. Each accused the other of being a coward. Karpis said Hoover only moved in when the other agents had him tied up. Hoover said that Karpis turned into a quivering "yellow rat." However it actually went down, the result is indisputable: with Karpis in chains, Hoover and a well-armed crew of FBI agents took him on an airplane ride to St. Paul.

A Northwest Airlines flight attendant said that on the plane, Karpis was trembling and Hoover talked to him as if he were a child. "Now come in here, Alvin," Hoover cooed to Public Enemy Number One. "Sit here, Alvin."

In St. Paul, reporters were delirious, spreading hysterical rumors, racing across the Mississippi River to the airport.

G-MEN CAPTURE KARPIS
WITHOUT FIRING A SHOT
IN RAID LED BY HOOVER
PLANE THOUGHT TO BE ENROUTE HERE
FROM NEW ORLEANS

Hoover and his agents, toting machine guns, hustled a shackled Karpis through a mob of reporters, photographers, and newsreel men and into a dark car that sped toward the federal courthouse, a building that resembles a castle out of a German fairy tale. Karpis was shackled to a radiator in FBI quarters. Hoover told his men, "If he starts to lie, kick his teeth in for him."

Number one on the FBI's agenda was to persuade Karpis to turn on Jack Peifer.

Karpis admitted he'd chosen to operate from St. Paul because police were crime friendly. "I'd be a sucker if I didn't take advantage of that," he said. "Particularly if the thieving copper is the head of the kidnap squad."

After a few days in custody, Karpis began whining about his civil rights. He was being held like . . . like . . . a hostage. FBI agents, he complained, were no better than kidnappers. The irony of his complaints seemed lost on him.

Out the window he could see the corrupt city where he once roamed a free criminal, a legend. He could see the cigar-store horse-racing parlors, the taverns now operating openly, the cafés, the pool halls. Across Rice Park stood the stylish hotels, the Lowry and the St. Paul, where he and his gang lived the high life of glamorous, free-spending rogues.

Karpis on the run had worried himself ever skinnier, down to a waist size of twenty-six. Leading his parade of nightmares was the gallows in Missouri. Just behind that was Jack Peifer and what might escape from his lips. Now Harry Campbell had been snared by the FBI, so the feds had another potential stool pigeon. Bail for Karpis was set at $400,000, or as much as $8 million in today's money. News reporters exclaimed that this was the highest bail in American history.

40

HEAT WAVE

The heat wave of 1936 provided a sweaty background for the legal dramatics in downtown St. Paul. It brought a heat so intense that newspapers reported the daily death toll along with the temperatures. Highs hit 104 and 107 degrees. People, unable to sleep in their apartments, camped out at city parks. In the Twin Cities alone, forty or fifty people died of the heat every day. On the worst day, more than a hundred souls perished. Before the heat wave passed, it took more lives in the city than the Spanish flu epidemic of 1918.

The legal heat was intense too. Having been publicly chastised and demoted, former chief Tom Dahill turned in his badge. It would be six years until he could collect a pension, so he opened a café in downtown St. Paul and took over the contract to feed the prisoners at the Ramsey County Jail. There were plenty of them, and during the kidnapping trials, Dahill's kitchen would feed the most infamous survivors of the public enemies era.

Whoever could get out of town during that torrid summer did, and one of the vacationers was Dr. Nippert, the Bremer family physician who came crashing into the story when a bottle was thrown through his glass door. The doctor, swimming alone within sight of his vacation cabin, drowned.

Larry DeVol met his end as well. DeVol, the most dangerous man the warden at Stillwater Prison had ever known, had been transferred to the prison for the criminally insane in St. Peter, Minnesota. There he led a breakout of fifteen inmates. Weeks later, police in Enid, Oklahoma, cornered him in a tavern. DeVol, drinking with a woman he'd just met, chugged the last beer of his life, whipped out a pistol, and shot patrolman Cal Palmer dead and wounded his partner. Five cops chased, cornered, and killed him as he crawled underneath a car.

On July 14, Alvin Karpis was escorted into federal court. His jailers observed that he'd been nervous, pacing his cell, babbling about hunting in the South and how he loved to drive fast cars at night. Reporters were unimpressed by Public Enemy Number One. One described him as a "timid, dapper little man."

Asked for a plea in the Hamm kidnapping, Karpis mumbled. When the judge asked if that mumbling constituted a guilty plea, Karpis said, "I guess so. I plead guilty." Later Karpis joked with reporters, saying that he only pleaded guilty because he didn't want to sit in a hot courtroom during a long trial. But Karpis's joke covered his real fear. By placing himself in the custody of the federal government, he hoped to avoid the hangman in Missouri.

The day after Karpis's plea, Edward Barthelmy, postmaster of Bensenville, Illinois, admitted he had allowed kidnappers to sequester Hamm in his home. Then U.S. district attorney George Sullivan revealed that the government was certain Jack Peifer had brought $40,000 of the

G-men hustle Alvin Karpis from car to courthouse in St. Paul, 1936. Photo retouched by the *Pioneer Press*.

Hamm ransom back to St. Paul from Chicago. That money was for himself and "others unspecified."

That phrase must have sent a chill through Tom Brown. Even in corrupt St. Paul, it was becoming harder to pretend that the former chief wasn't in on the kidnapping.

On July 16, with the heat wave cranking as big ceiling fans turned to no effect, as cops guarded the courtroom with shotguns, and as huge crowds gathered outside waiting for news, Gladys Sawyer took the stand. She testified that Jack Peifer and certain members of the St. Paul police split the Hamm ransom.

The courtroom erupted. Spectators gasped and murmured. Lawyers leaped to their feet.

When things quieted down, Gladys was re-examined. She seemed frightened by the vehemence of the reaction. She changed her mind. Why no, actually, she hadn't heard that at all, about Peifer and the cops splitting the ransom. It was stricken from the record.

Ed Barthelmy was called to testify, and he minimized his involvement. He knew Shotgun George Ziegler only as a cultured friend, he said. They often attended lectures and concerts together. One day Ziegler offered him $20 so that he could use Barthelmy's house for a vacation spot. Why anyone would vacation in a suburban Chicago railroad town was never explained.

Next thing he knew, by golly, Barthelmy said, Ziegler and his buddies were leading a blindfolded man into his house.

Barthelmy was anything but a career criminal. His wife was the president of the PTA. His son had starred that spring in the high school play. Up until the day he hosted the kidnappers, he'd lived as a "respected citizen" in the suburbs. "His only fault is that he likes to talk a little too much," one Bensenville citizen told a reporter. Now he was doomed to a long prison sentence unless he could portray himself as an accidental kidnapper.

"Looking back on it," he testified, "I suppose I was just dumb but I was very friendly with [Ziegler]. It didn't strike me as unusual that he would want to come out here." He claimed he was threatened by Bolton and Ziegler and forced to cooperate once it was evident they'd engineered a kidnapping. The judge, inundated with pleas for clemency from Barthelmy's family, neighbors, and friends, sentenced him to six years in federal prison.

On July 17, Byron Bolton told the court of a crucial conversation between Jack Peifer and Shotgun George Ziegler. Peifer told Ziegler, "I want you to meet a man at the police department who can give us some dope" during the kidnapping. He meant dope in the 1930s sense: information. After that meeting, Ziegler told Bolton, "I just met a hell of a good copper on the kidnap squad. He will tip us off on any police activities."

Bolton testified that when Charles Fitzgerald heard about this arrangement, he groused that "twenty-five thousand is too much for a cop."

"Not if he does what he says he can do," Ziegler replied.

That afternoon, the new police commissioner, Gus Barfuss, announced the suspension of Tom Brown. Barfuss noted that the kidnap squad consisted of only Charles Tierney and Tom Brown. No evidence suggested that Tierney had conspired with the kidnappers, but there was a growing accumulation of pointers to Brown.

The kidnapping and conspiracy laws at the time were weak, and in the Hamm case, the statute of limitations was about to kick in. Prosecutors scrambled to prepare six John Doe indictments, planning to fill one out in the name of Tom Brown.

One reporter noted that "the most unperturbed character in the Twin Cities, apparently, is Tom Brown." The day after his suspension, Brown was stopped by the reporter on a downtown street.

"I have nothing to say either in confidence or for publication," Brown said.

"Are you going to fight the suspension?"

"I love everybody," Brown said.

"Who is your lawyer?"

"Why do I need a lawyer?" Brown said. "I told you everybody is my friend. I love them all. See you some other time."

It was beginning to look as though Tom Brown's many escapes from justice were more than luck. The message, sent through this news reporter, might be interpreted as Brown's intention to protect his influential friends. He didn't need a lawyer because he expected that his friends, frightened by how much he knew, would make the charges go away.

Mayor Gehan appealed to the FBI. He wanted a conference with J. Edgar Hoover on the subject of Tom Brown. Hoover, who felt that every official in St. Paul was corrupt, brushed the mayor off.

Back in the courtroom, William Hamm appeared, sick and trembling with the chills in that monstrously hot courtroom. It had been three years since the kidnapping, but Hamm couldn't seem to escape it. Doc Barker, although locked up in Alcatraz, had contacts with thugs everywhere. The underworld was still shaking Hamm down years after the kidnapping. Hamm now realized that it was the seemingly affable Jack Peifer who had threatened him via cousin Benz. There was good reason for William Hamm to feel afraid, on and off the witness stand.

When Byron Bolton was put back on the stand, he recounted the day when Peifer arrived in Chicago for the Hamm ransom split. Shotgun George Ziegler asked Peifer to stay a few days and pal around. Peifer replied that he was carrying $40,000 "and a lot of it doesn't belong to me. I want to get back to St. Paul with it."

Ziegler, Bolton testified, chastised Peifer for going to 204 Vernon and cleaning up after the Barkers. Peifer shrugged that off, saying that Tom Brown had given him plenty of time to clean up. Former chief Tom Dahill took the stand and related the story of how Tom Brown had failed to investigate at 204 Vernon and had lied about it afterward.

On the same kind of evidence, the gangsters' girlfriends were being sentenced to prison terms for harboring and enabling. Prosecuting these "molls" was an obsession of J. Edgar Hoover's. Brown's behavior in twice enabling the Barker gang's escape was provable beyond doubt. Yet harboring and enabling charges were never lodged against him.

Now that Bolton's testimony had provided legal foundation, Gladys Sawyer was called back to the stand and testified that yes, she had heard that Brown had gotten a piece of the ransom. Prosecutors began writing indictments naming Brown in the Hamm and Bremer kidnappings.

41

"OH! I WANTED TO SEE HIM"

Jack Peifer had influential friends. When his bail was pegged at $100,000, it set off a citywide scramble to raise money from sources legitimate and otherwise. Many people feared Peifer would crack in jail.

Alvin Karpis called Peifer "yellow" and predicted "he would talk if held long enough."

A retired Minnesota Supreme Court chief justice, Samuel Wilson, joined Peifer's defense team. Wilson had enormous prestige, but not even Oliver Wendell Holmes could have saved Peifer. Bolton's testimony against him was direct evidence, not just hearsay. Bolton testified that before that fateful flight to Chicago, he and Peifer's man Saph McKenna wrapped up $75,000 in stolen Liberty bonds to be laundered down there. Those bonds had nothing to do with the kidnapping, but laid groundwork, since they were evidence that Peifer was in the money-laundering business.

Then Bolton testified about Peifer grabbing the ransom money in Chicago. The FBI corroborated Bolton's accounts at key points. His story of the flight to Chicago, for instance, was backed by the flight manifest. Peifer would later delude himself that, had he never taken that flight, the feds could not have convicted him.

Jack Peifer with his team of attorneys. Left to right: Mortimer Boutell, Adrian David, Peifer, former state supreme court chief justice Samuel B. Wilson, and Archie Cary. The photo was published in the *Pioneer Press* on July 22, 1936.

Peifer's respectable family sat through much of the trial. His brother Richard, a turkey farmer and the mayor of a small Minnesota town, was president of the state's Egg, Butter, and Poultry Association. Another brother was a St. Paul dentist. They sat on either side of their elderly mother, who was dressed entirely in black. Also in the front row sat his wife Violet, described in newspapers as a "beauty contest winner" a "fashion model" and a "striking blonde."

Peifer's attorneys planted favorable stories in the press. One columnist lobbed in a softball: "Peifer's chief means of livelihood is a chicken and turkey ranch he owns with his brother." Peifer's attorney and partner in nightclub businesses, Archie Cary, told the jury Jack was "an ordinary citizen of a good Minnesota family. In no way shape or form" did he help the kidnappers. One newspaper photo showed Violet sitting on Jack's lap and supplied a pseudo quote: "There's nothing to worry about, honey, it's just a Byron Bolton frameup."

Throughout the ten-day trial, Peifer seemed at ease, often joking with friends or attorneys. Reporters described him as "dapper" in court, "good natured," and "scoffing."

Once Peifer said to a friend in the gallery: "What's the odds?"

"It's a toss up," the friend said.

"What!" Peifer said. "They haven't got a thing on me."

Oh yes, they did. The jury retired and at 8:20 the next evening, a Saturday, found Jack Peifer guilty of kidnapping William Hamm. Violet Peifer, exquisitely dressed, sobbed on her husband's shoulder, then fainted.

On the following Monday, Alvin Karpis and Charles Fitzgerald were sentenced to life in prison. Both made a great drama of declaring that Jack Peifer had been wrongly convicted. "Jack Peifer had nothing to do with the Hamm kidnapping," Fitzgerald barked in court. But time would reveal that the purpose of this sideshow was to entice Peifer to repay money he'd owed Karpis.

According to the FBI, Karpis once considered kidnapping Peifer's wife until the debt was paid. Soon after he was brought in handcuffs to St. Paul, Karpis asked FBI agents if he could talk to Peifer's lawyer. The message was: If Jack coughed up the money, Karpis would declare him innocent. If not, Karpis would testify to his guilt. Karpis's father attended the trial and went home with a package of cash from Peifer.

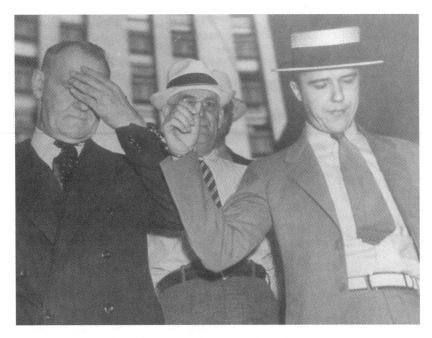

Karpis and Fitzgerald (covering his face) brought in for sentencing in 1936 after their guilty plea in the Hamm kidnapping.

Alvin Karpis intended that money for Dolores Delaney when she got out of prison. A portion was to be saved for the college education he hoped his son would attain.

After Karpis and Fitzgerald declared him innocent, Peifer asked his lawyers to seek affidavits from them but was told such documents would be worthless.

Before Peifer's jury had retired, former justice Samuel Wilson treated them to a rant against the prosecution. Perhaps his anger got the best of him because the justice, seemingly out of nowhere, added, "Tom Brown is a big shot in this case and he is just as guilty as Peifer, if Peifer is guilty."

Police commissioner Gus Barfuss publicly promised that Tom Brown would be fired. Well, absolutely maybe. City attorney John J. Connolly hedged. Conveniently enough, Mayor Gehan had left town. Connolly said he was "studying" charges against Brown and would decide whether to proceed when the mayor returned.

On July 30, Tom Brown, who'd asked a reporter why he would need a lawyer, hired one. He announced he would fight his dismissal.

On the next day Jack Peifer went to court for his sentencing. He'd been free on bond, and obviously he'd spent the night drinking. His eyes were bloodshot, he looked pale, and he was chewing gum. He greeted reporters and friends as if he were popping in for a chat with the judge. He'd instructed his wife Violet to stay home and assured her that whatever the sentence, he would be free on appeal.

But he had secretly prepared for the worst.

The judge gave him thirty years, canceled his bond, and ordered him to prison immediately. Peifer's sangfroid disappeared. In a daze, he turned to his lawyer, Archie Cary. "We will fight this as long as we can," Peifer declared. Ever the showman, Peifer summoned up one more burst of denial, wishing the press and courtroom spectators a cheerful good-bye.

"Peifer was seen to reach into his rear trouser pocket, pull out a handkerchief and pass it quickly over his mouth," a news reporter wrote. "He appeared shaken, but talked to his attorneys and was able to walk out of the courtroom when taken to his cell. He refused his lunch. He brought down one of the bunks and lay down."

In that handkerchief had been a stick of cyanide-laced gum. Peifer lay in his cell, sick and sweating, at first sobbing and moaning, and then quiet. His cellmates figured he was having a normal reaction to the shock of being sentenced.

He was dead within two hours.

Reporters told Violet Peifer the news. "Oh! I wanted to see him," she cried. She rushed by taxi to the county morgue, and there burst out weeping. She stroked her dead husband's hair and cried, "Jack, this is what you get for being good to people."

Back at the Hollyhocks, following instructions Jack had given her, she ripped up a floorboard to find $25,000 in cash.

That evening, C. W. Stein of the St. Paul FBI was getting a call "every five minutes" from the judge in the Peifer case. Judge Matthew Joyce was "considerably upset by Peifer's suicide, and is fearful lest he be attacked by some of Peifer's friends when he goes home tonight."

"The Judge is getting the jitters and wants to go home but is afraid to," an agent cabled to Washington. J. Edgar Hoover okayed an FBI bodyguard for Judge Joyce.

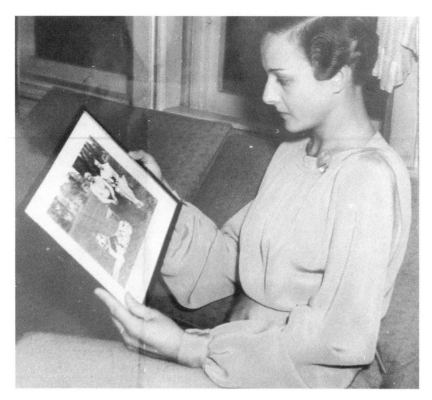

After her husband's suicide in jail, Violet Peifer looks back at happier times during an interview that was published in the *St. Paul Dispatch* on August 5, 1936.

Jack Peifer was 43 when he killed himself. He was buried with military honors, marking his Great War service. More than a thousand people showed up for his funeral.

With the death of Jack Peifer, Tom Brown's lucky streak grew longer. The only survivors of the gang who could have spoken against him, Doc and Karpis, weren't talking, and there was no way the government would bargain down their prison terms. Jack Peifer was as silent as the grave. And Harry Sawyer, the man most likely to put Tom Brown in Alcatraz, was already locked up there.

But somebody was working on Harry, urging him to talk about Tom Brown.

42

"WILL YOU PLEASE TALK TO MR. McKEE?"

As April turns to May, the most anticipated event in Minnesota is the Governor's Fishing Opener. Minnesota actually has far more than its advertised 10,000 lakes, and the most boats per capita of any state. At the fishing opener, the governor motors out in a boat, catches a walleye or pretends to, and summer fun officially begins.

But in the spring of 1936, a more grim and determined fishing expedition was undertaken in the capital city. It was becoming obvious to the FBI and St. Paul reformers that one big fish had escaped them: Tom Brown.

They put the squeeze on Tom Filben, who gave glib answers on a variety of subjects. Filben said he was a "very old friend" of Tom Brown's. Filben told agents he "did not think Brown got any more [payoffs] than any others at the PD, that for the last few years there was little money to be had, and that there are three or four cliques at SPPD fighting for their cut."

When W. W. "Billy" Dunn returned from the 1936 Kentucky Derby, agents put him under the hot lights. Dunn told the FBI he "considered the Hamms to be the best friends he had in the whole world."

Agents noted that Dunn "vehemently denies he was a collector for Tom Brown." Good-time Billy admitted he knew "all the underworld characters," but only because they hung out at his billiards parlor. He acknowledged flitting in and out of Leon Gleckman's bribery headquarters at the St. Paul Hotel but said it was purely social. Tom Brown? Why Billy hardly knew the man. But he did allow that after the kidnapping, Brown borrowed $500 from the Hamm brewery on "three separate occasions." Billy said he handled the cash for William Hamm, who approved the loans. These were his only transactions with Brown, he claimed.

Why Hamm would loan money to the man who'd helped engineer his kidnapping was never explained.

Meanwhile, the enemies Brown had made on the St. Paul police force were urging the FBI to target Brown. Former chief Tom Dahill and Brown's erstwhile partner Charles Tierney said gambling payoffs were split among Tom Brown, James Crumley, and others. Tierney told federal agents that Brown was the only cop in St. Paul whose fingerprints were not on file and that when the whole department was fingerprinted during the Hamm kidnapping, Brown refused. He also refused when fingerprints were taken during the Bremer kidnapping. Agents, prodded by J. Edgar Hoover, began to intensify the pressure on their sources for information about Brown.

St. Paul's city hall is housed in a gorgeous art-deco tower. It overlooks the Mississippi docks and is graced with artwork and gleaming marble floors. On the last day of April 1936, the FBI's C. W. Stein was escorted up the elevator and into the mayor's office. There Stein met with mayor Mark Gehan, police commissioner Ned Warren, and John J. Connolly, the city's attorney.

Stories about Brown were surfacing in public. The mayor said a newspaper reporter had told him "there was quite a rumor to the effect that Tom Brown of the St. Paul Police Department got $25,000 of the Hamm ransom money." The mayor also told Stein that "at the time Homer Van Meter was killed (Tom Brown being one of the men who killed him) he had $8,000 on his person"; that "after he was taken to the morgue they found only $1400."

Commissioner Warren said that his term was expiring and that he would like to suspend Brown because "he had always prided himself on a clean police force," Stein reported. No commissioner could have run a clean police force in St. Paul in the early 1930s, and Warren was not above suspicion. He was accused by some of taking payoffs from gamblers. Given St. Paul's shadowy politics, it's not easy to tell which men were true reformers and which were merely fighting on behalf of their own factions.

The mayor and police commissioner told Stein that two unnamed St. Paul cops "would probably be inclined to talk if Brown was not on the force, but as long as he is on the force they are afraid of being killed if they talk."

City attorney John J. Connolly said that only by filing charges with the civil service commission could Brown be removed from the force. He also warned that the statute of limitations made it imperative to indict Brown by June 19, which would mark three years since the end of the Hamm kidnapping.

After the meeting, Stein wrote to FBI headquarters: "It was quite likely that our agents will pick [Brown] up within the next week or ten days."

FBI supervisor K. R. McIntire wrote J. Edgar Hoover: "Investigation is now going forward to develop further information implicating Tom Brown and [W. W.] Dunn. It is interesting to note that during the spring of 1934 Bessie Green . . . advised agents at St. Paul that Dunn was in fact an underground intermediary between the [Barker gang] and Hamm's family . . . Dunn is reported to have received a portion of the ransom money."

The FBI turned up the heat on James Crumley, who by now had been bounced off the police force. Could Crumley help them snare Brown? Crumley confirmed that Dunn had been a bagman for years and asserted that he "no doubt shared in a ransom split with Brown," according to a Stein memo sent by FBI Teletype.

Crumley may have been among those St. Paul cops who feared being killed if they talked about Brown. He played a cagey game with the FBI. He suggested that Pat Reilly, the former Green Lantern bartender, could bring down Big Tom.

FBI inspector Hugh Clegg thought so too. He was quoted in an FBI memo as saying, "Pat Reilly is the man to get." Informers had told Clegg that if agents would "drug him or hit him in the head with something . . . that he would give them more information than anyone else possesses in the Twin Cities."

Reilly had been arrested under the new federal harboring laws. The feds had determined that Reilly had connected the wounded John Dillinger with local doctors. Sentenced to twenty-one months, Reilly protested that he was only a "chump" who found it difficult to say no when asked for favors. He claimed he had never met this guy, what's his name, Dillinger. He publicly apologized for "disgracing his family."

Reilly was locked up in Leavenworth. Crumley begged the FBI to take him to see Reilly. He promised he could persuade Reilly to talk, especially if Reilly "could do so without harming Harry Sawyer."

"Crumley appears bitter against Brown," an FBI Teletype said, "holding him responsible for his expulsion from St. Paul Police Department and states [he] will cooperate but probably will furnish only hearsay in fear or involving self in unlawful practices." Crumley, said the FBI, "expressed considerable contempt for Tom Brown, calling him a murderer and a double crosser." Crumley volunteered to "do anything in his power" to snare Brown.

Actually, Crumley wanted somebody else to do the dangerous work of ratting out Brown. He suggested that former chief Frank Cullen was closest to Brown during the Hamm kidnapping and "would know the whole setup." Crumley said officer Jeff Dettrick was also close to Brown but was not "considered smart enough to be let in on any of the inside information."

Crumley told the FBI that W. W. Dunn had been "collecting for gamblers for 10 years and had been getting his cut with those fellows" and certainly would not be left out of his share of the ransom. Crumley said he always thought Dunn had some connection with the Hamm kidnapping, "particularly as the delivery of the ransom was made so safe."

"Crumley emphatically stated numerous times during the interview that he was no angel himself but that he was not a murderer and that he had never received any money from any kidnapping case," according to the FBI. He admitted, though, that he had "helped (criminals) out when they might have been prosecuted."

Crumley said Brown was still a power to be feared. Indeed, after Dunn had been questioned by the FBI, Brown visited his office at Hamm's brewery "to see what information he had given."

In Chicago, FBI agents were questioning an informant whose identity they've kept confidential to this day. Earl Connelley, Melvin Purvis's successor in Chicago, telegraphed Hoover that the Chicago underworld had told him that "W. W. Dunn during period Tom Brown was police chief was payoff man between Brown and gamblers. That Saph McKenna delivered payments weekly to Dunn for Hollyhocks gambling. Dunn [is] financially interested in nightclub in Minneapolis with Peifer."

Further, underworld rumors said that "Dunn made payoff to police in this [Hamm] case and [there is a] possibility he received share of ransom." The FBI informant also said that McKenna had been ordered to tell William Hamm that "the 'boys' wanted him to lay off making any identification and the message was delivered."

With Dunn denying all, the FBI went to work on Harry Sawyer's wife, Gladys. An agent in Omaha found her "slightly under the influence" and "very garrulous."

Gladys had fallen a long way since the Sawyers scrambled to leave their Minnesota farm, one jump ahead of the FBI. Only two years back she'd had two homes, a powerful husband, and a precocious almost-adopted daughter. Her life was all luxury autos, diamonds, furs, and servants, set against the background of a glamorous nightlife.

After Harry's conviction, she lived for a while with his relatives in Lincoln, Nebraska. But the Sandloviches had a "deep family pride and Harry's behavior has wounded them greatly," reported a local social services agency. When Gladys began "gossiping around Lincoln" about her gangster days, the family paid her $1,000 to leave town.

Apparently she used this money to buy a small grocery/deli/confectionary in Omaha and lived alone in the back room. She was bitter. She was drinking. She wanted revenge.

She especially wanted revenge on Tom Brown, an informant told the FBI. According to Gladys, the most corrupt of the St. Paul cops were Brown, Crumley, and William McMullen. She said they worked their scams by phoning either Harry Sawyer or Jack Peifer with tips for the underworld. She said she believed the FBI could get Harry to implicate Brown since her husband "was taking his imprisonment hard."

When she, Harry, and Francine were on the run in Cleveland, Gladys said, she overheard the Barker gang wondering why Brown had gotten "an awful lot of money" out of the Hamm kidnapping.

During the Bremer kidnapping, she said, Crumley came to see Harry on the farm, but she did not know what they discussed.

When Harry was arrested, she told FBI agents, his underworld friends assured her they would bail him out. Jack Peifer came up with $1,000, but the rest of Harry's pals told Gladys to "go to hell." She said Harry was "always too easy to get along with, that friends have taken advantage of his good nature and that as a result, he has nothing but a life sentence to serve." She did not ask Tom Brown for help after Harry's arrest because "she did not want to get him in trouble at that time."

But she did now, in May of 1936. She was seething with anger that the crooks with badges had not been prosecuted. She had a $250 loan out to Detective McMullen's wife and wrote to collect, threatening to tell all if she didn't get her money.

McMullen's wife wrote back: "Your threats create antagonism which, if carried out, benefits neither of us. Have patience. As soon as humanly possible."

The FBI reported: "Mrs. Sawyer said that the Bremer family are as rotten as any of the underworld in St. Paul and have worked hand in hand with the underworld for years. She said the [Bremers'] Commercial State Bank got its start with the proceeds of the Denver Mint Robbery. Her information was that Danny Hogan had made a deal with Adolph Bremer . . . money secured in the robbery was passed through this bank on a percentage basis." She told the FBI that the Hamm family "was not mixed up with the underworld like the Bremers were."

Gladys believed that Tom Brown "will talk if he is confronted with the definite information that the government knows his connection with the underworld and his participation in the kidnapping."

She urged Harry to talk freely to the FBI, even though she feared retribution. She gave FBI agent Sam McKee a letter to deliver to Harry in Alcatraz.

> Darling: Will you please talk to Mr. McKee?
>
> With the deal you got along with myself why should we try any longer to protect some people.
>
> He is bringing you a note that I received from Clara McMullen regarding the money they owe. Honey I have been trying every way possible to get money from people in St. Paul and this note is just a sample of the answers. The ones that Uncle Sam is mostly interested in now, I think, is Tom Brown and the Bremers.
>
> I am working 18 hours a day and not making ends meet.
>
> I have been talking to Mr. McKee just what little I know through hearsay conversations about some of the things in St. Paul. I am only doing this to try to help you.
>
> You know you shouldn't be there, so why stay if you can help yourself? I don't think it is going to get you out but it may mean you can come back to Leavenworth where I can see you.
>
> Life isn't worth living the way it is now.
>
> All my love
>
> GLADYS.

Tom Brown, avid hunter and fisherman, had enjoyed many a summer day on the lake near his Boundary Waters cabin. But it seemed Brown might soon join another avid fisherman, Alvin Karpis, staring down from that stony prison at the fishing boats on San Francisco Bay.

43

"She must be crazy"

At Alcatraz, doctors had categorized Harry Sawyer as a "considerably overweight" prisoner with a stubborn case of gonorrhea. He was judged "of average intelligence, alert, stable, cooperative and well-adjusted." He told doctors he'd had "severe alcoholism" for the past twenty-five years. He said he "attributes his current situation to the fact that he was intoxicated at the time of his involvement."

In prison, Harry tried to reconnect to the Sandlovich family in Nebraska. When their rabbi, Maurice Solomon, visited as family emissary, Harry sent him back with a pitiful request: Would his brothers and sister please answer his letters?

When FBI agent Sam McKee arrived at Alcatraz, the warden told him Harry was "maintaining an arrogant attitude and insisting he's unjustly imprisoned." Harry figured his only crime was letting the Barker gang hang out in his café.

Sam McKee was a "sawed-off little character with jug ears" who had a reputation as a tough interrogator. He spent three hours trying to pry information from Harry. But the prisoner was obsessed, endlessly replaying the trial in the theater of his mind. Harry, instigator of the Bremer kidnapping, could never put the blame on himself.

Byron Bolton had lied on the stand, Harry told McKee. So had Edna Murray. Because of their lies, he said, his sentence was far more severe than it should have been. McKee found Sawyer "bitter toward the FBI, double-crossed by his friends, in ill health and unlikely to live long."

Regardless, Sawyer insisted he "will do his time and never double-cross anybody." He said that if Tom Brown or Jack Peifer had anything to do with either kidnapping, he didn't know about it.

McKee showed Harry the letter Gladys had written. Harry read it and said, "She must be crazy." McKee reported that "when asked if he did not have any regard for his wife, he said that she was on the outside and had her store and if she couldn't get along she could 'jump in the lake.'"

Harry sent a message back to Gladys through McKee, asking her to quit urging FBI men to see him. Gladys should know that Harry "was carrying a pretty heavy load as it is, being sentenced to life on perjured testimony, and that [FBI] agents were well aware of this fact." If the FBI expected him "to tell a lot of lies, like Bolton did, they were badly mistaken." He advised Gladys to "take care of her business and stay sober."

Perhaps Harry was simply being true to the code of silence that had served him all his life. Being locked up with the most notorious criminals of his time, and knowing what happened to men who talked, he may have been simply looking after his own safety. Alcatraz was in turmoil. In the months before Harry's arrival, there'd been a prisoner revolt. Al Capone, Harvey Bailey, and Machine Gun Kelly refused to join the rioters. The prisoners who'd fomented the revolt called them "yellow rats." Capone, in fear of being stabbed, began wearing an inch-thick homemade canvas vest.

When the FBI told Gladys the results of their interview, they said "she gives up. Her husband does not know what's good for him. If he could he would probably give her a good punch in the nose."

McKee wrote: "Mrs. Sawyer stated that she did not care whether she ever heard from him again." Harry, she said, "is not as smart as he thinks he is." His mobster friends have "given him the run around," she said, "and when the crisis came, they left him penniless and without assistance."

Gladys was beginning to grasp that Harry was delusional. She recalled that when she had visited him in Leavenworth, he told her to go back to Omaha and start a beer joint. This new fantasy tavern would be a reincarnation of the Green Lantern, Harry hoped, "where his erstwhile friends could call on her."

On May 28, agent Sam McKee took the disgraced detective James Crumley to see Pat Reilly in Leavenworth. In a prison interview room "Crumley very frankly told Reilly that we wanted information" on Brown, "since he was the cause of Crumley's demise in St. Paul." Crumley made a "strong personal appeal" to Reilly based on their long friendship, McKee reported.

But Reilly would not talk "because it won't help him and all he wants to do is finish his time and return to St. Paul." Reilly was due for parole in eighteen months and didn't want to "rile the underworld." He claimed he planned to go straight and work for his mother's laundry as a truck driver.

While McKee was at Leavenworth, he also interviewed Leon Gleckman, Brown's former godfather. Gleckman told the FBI he quit bootlegging in 1928 with lots of cash and with the ambition of becoming mayor of St. Paul. He believed he could make more money by peddling political influence than from booze. He considered both Dunn and Brown personal friends. He told the FBI he was "responsible for Brown being appointed Chief in 1930, and said that Brown was his man." He said he had bought the allegiance of city councilmen Clyde May and Irving Pearce.

Until 1932, Gleckman was kingmaker and de facto mayor of St. Paul, and labor candidate William Mahoney was the first true opposition he'd faced. In 1934, Gleckman had been convicted of tax evasion, shadowed by the same agents who nailed Al Capone. Gleckman had tried to bribe a juror in his IRS case and was convicted of bribery as well as tax evasion.

Regarding his own kidnapping in 1931, Gleckman said friends had told him he'd be surprised to learn who was behind it. Gleckman was beginning to suspect what others had long assumed: that Peifer had engineered it. He told McKee he would "take care of it in his own way" if he confirmed his suspicions. Gleckman recalled bitterly the kidnapping of his daughter Florence in 1932, which had ended with her release when the plan went awry. Gleckman said he despised kidnappers. Even so, the FBI could not persuade him to help snare the kidnapper's friend, Tom Brown.

44

"I AIN'T BEEN SO FAR WRONG"

J. Edgar Hoover's men never arrested Tom Brown. The only legal proceeding he faced was one he could have avoided simply by accepting his dismissal from the St. Paul police. But he insisted on a hearing before the city's Civil Service Board. It began in August 1936, as the last kidnapping sentences were being handed down in federal court.

Brown's attorney, Lewis Anderson, launched a public relations campaign, denying his client's role in either kidnapping. Brown sought out

Described as the "most unperturbed person in St. Paul" during the time he stood accused of conspiring with criminals, Brown sits calmly at his hearing before the Civil Service Appeals Board in September 1936.

reporters and predicted that once the facts were known, "The public will be completely convinced of my innocence."

On August 21, the gangsters' nightmare, Byron Bolton, appeared before the appeals board to testify against Brown. Bolton repeated the testimony he'd given in federal court, saying that during the planning of the Hamm kidnapping, he kept hearing the other gangsters say they had help from a local cop and that Fred Barker reserved $25,000 for "Brown's share."

The Hamm money "was all in large piles and stamped with the various amounts on it just like it came from the bank. $500, $1000 etc. They got a pencil and figured the expenses and then Fred Barker counted it out. First they took out [the shares of] Tom Brown and then Peifer."

Splitting up the money, "there was no bones about it," Bolton said. "It was Tom Brown this and Tom Brown that."

As he had in the Karpis trial, Bolton testified that he heard Shotgun George Ziegler tell Peifer that he had "been a fool" to clean up 204 Vernon Street after the Barkers left. Peifer replied that Tom Brown would give him time to do it. Bolton said in the Bremer case, Brown's share was cut from $20,000 to $5,000 because he didn't provide much information once the FBI had figured out he was a mole. Then the gang cut Brown's share to zero "after he killed Homer Van Meter."

Brown's attorney sneaked in references to the St. Valentine's Day Massacre, hoping to smear Bolton.

Objection!

Sustained, but the point was made.

The Brown hearing was the last time Bolton would take the witness stand. He was shuttled back to federal court for sentencing. He had been calm throughout the trials but now broke out in tears. He never really had recovered from tuberculosis and had lost forty pounds since his arrest. He stood before the judge with head bowed, hands clasped. He was sentenced to three years in prison. On his way out of court, he muttered, "I am very glad it is over with."

Meanwhile, two days after Bolton identified him as a prime actor in the kidnappings, Tom Brown took the test to become, once again, police chief of St. Paul.

The gangster trials had concluded just in time for the State Fair. As Mardi Gras is to New Orleans, the State Fair is to Minnesota. The fair may be the closest thing Minnesotans have to a state religion. Agriculture is the very soul of the state, but the fair is more than a celebration of farm heritage. It's a place where Minnesotans go to enjoy the last days of summer, eating foolishly, drinking too much, dancing under the stars, riding on Ferris wheels, roaming the lit midway.

So the Brown hearing, like much else in Minnesota, was suspended for the fair and Labor Day weekend. There was just too much fun to be had. To add to the general excitement, the St. Paul Saints were taking on the Minneapolis Millers in the baseball finals. It was all enough to drown out the ominous headlines coming out of Germany:

HITLER SAYS REICH WANTS LOST LANDS

After the holiday, when the Brown hearing reconvened, James Crumley took the stand. Prodded for his opinion, Crumley said he didn't like Brown and at one point hadn't "spoken to him for 10 years."

While Bremer was a captive, Crumley said, he drove to the farm to see Harry Sawyer. Crumley was then an inspector, a higher rank than Detective Brown. But somehow Brown had made Crumley his errand boy, and Crumley resented his power.

At Sawyer's farm, Crumley told Harry, "They grabbed Eddie Bremer."

"To hell they did," said Harry.

"Walter Magee got a phone message to look under his steps and he did and found a note."

"That big so-and-so," said Sawyer. "The first thing he did was run to the police."

Crumley made a second visit to the Sawyer farm during the kidnapping. He was again carrying a message from Tom Brown: St. Paul cops and FBI agents were flying up to Detroit Lakes, Minnesota, following a tip that Bremer might be held there.

Brown did not know where Bremer had been sequestered and apparently worried that the hideout might actually be at Detroit Lakes. He wanted Harry to know what the cops were up to. He needn't have worried: "I don't care where they go," said Harry, who knew Bremer was in the Chicago suburbs.

During the Bremer kidnapping, Crumley was sent around St. Paul to interview the usual suspects. Among them was Jack Peifer, who had taken off for Florida.

"Did you go to Florida to find him?" the prosecution asked.

Crumley got in a shot at detractors who said he'd enriched himself with bribes.

"No, I didn't have no money, like I'm supposed to have now."

"Then what did you do?"

"I went to McCormack's Restaurant to find Harry Sawyer, and Pat Reilly said, 'Don't you know where he lives? He's across the street from Tom Brown's farm.'"

Crumley testified that during the Bremer kidnapping, "Brown asked me if . . . Myrtle Eaton knew anything about the kidnappers." Crumley said Eaton probably did. "I said they are pretty high class people and if they are tough she certainly is connected with it," he testified.

"You weren't so far wrong, were you?" asked the prosecutor.

"I ain't been so far wrong in a lot of things, and you know it."

Then Crumley added a note that demonstrated how casually he took the kidnapping of Ed Bremer: "I'd see Pat Reilly on Wabasha Street and I'd holler at him to bring Eddie Bremer back."

Crumley then launched a defense of himself, saying he wasn't as bad as Tom Brown: "I didn't know none of them murderers, only high class thieves. I ain't one of those guys who says I like a guy when I don't."

"How well do you like Tom Brown?"

"Huh?" Crumley, his mammoth form slumped in the witness chair, sat up straight. "No, I don't like him."

The hearings took another weeklong break. During this one, Tom Brown left St. Paul, destination undisclosed.

45

A Stranger Comes to Omaha

Among the most dangerous of potential witnesses against Tom Brown was a middle-aged woman running a store in Omaha. Gladys Sawyer had given up on Harry but retained enough bitterness against Brown that she agreed to give a deposition for his hearing.

On September 10, 1936, St. Paul detective Charles Tierney, accompanied by two city attorneys, journeyed to Omaha to take that deposition. One of those attorneys advised the FBI that "Tom Brown had arrived in Omaha about 24 hours" before the deposition team got there and "registered at the Paxton hotel."

The deposition team visited Gladys's store and made an appointment to take her statement. In the intervening hours, Gladys was visited by a friend who said he had been sent by a local police officer. "This friend of mine doesn't know Mr. Brown," Gladys said, "but it seemed the officer [who had arranged the meeting] was acquainted with him." Gladys pretended she wasn't interested in damaging Brown. She told this visitor, "I had had trouble enough and didn't want to be involved in anything at all."

When asked by this friend what she might reveal in the deposition, Gladys hedged: "I won't do him any good, and I'll try not to do him any harm." The friend then "suggested I leave town." Gladys said she wasn't going anywhere, especially at the urging of that "double crossing son of a bitch Tom Brown." She gave Charles Tierney and the lawyers the deposition they had come for.

On September 16, when the hearing reconvened, John. J. Connolly, attorney for the city of St. Paul, pointed a finger at Brown. He charged that Brown made a "deliberate attempt" in Omaha to "get Gladys Sawyer out of town so she could not give a deposition."

Brown attorney Lewis Anderson blustered that the prosecution's charge was "erroneous and malicious."

Anderson and Connolly began a shouting match.

"Keep quiet!" Anderson roared.

That echoed, no doubt, the feeling of some in the St. Paul establishment. Tom Brown knew many secrets. For an entire generation, St. Paul had thrived on the dark profits of bootlegging, gambling, and money laundering.

In her deposition, Gladys Sawyer said, "I think the first time I ever talked to Mr. Brown was the night Frank Ventress was killed."

Brown had helped deflect attention from Harry and the Green Lantern in the aftermath of that murder. After that, Harry Sawyer and Tom Brown seemed to grow closer. Brown phoned the Sawyer home often enough that Gladys began to recognize his voice. On the day in 1932 that the Barkers escaped from Robert Street, Gladys answered the phone. Harry took the call and left in a hurry. "I think when he came home for dinner that night, he said . . . he'd had to go up and get somebody out of a house. He said it was raided."

Gladys also recalled the time she drove to Grand Avenue, on orders from Harry, to warn the Barker gang of a raid. Her most damaging testimony centered on a conversation she'd had with Harry after the Bremer kidnapping. Harry had told her, "I have $36,000 to split with Tom Brown." "He did not say," Gladys added, "what money it was."

The hearing shifted focus to 204 Vernon and the Barker gang. Landlord James McLaren testified to an embarrassing tale of police cowardice and incompetence. When he discovered that his tenants were the Barkers, he rushed home to find his house surrounded by St. Paul cops. "The police told me to look out or I might get shot."

But McLaren insisted on going in. Cops boosted him in through the window.

The public enemies were gone. McLaren let the cops in. Did they dust for fingerprints? Collect evidence? No. McLaren said, "They helped themselves to beer and stuff in the ice box."

McLaren testified that Tom Brown, in charge of the investigation, never questioned him about the Barkers.

When former chief Tom Dahill took the stand, he described St. Paul's police department as a festering mess of jealousy, rivalry, greed, and ambition. Contributing to the chaos was a system of rotating police chiefs, which kept ambitious men scheming for the job.

Dahill gave examples of information he suspected Brown had passed on to kidnappers: W. W. Dunn's inability to drive a truck and Dahill's remarks about wanting to shoot the kidnappers. He also related the story of Dr. Nippert's broken window and how his milk bottle trick had proved that Brown was leaking information to the press.

Dahill denied personal animosity toward Brown. News reporters noted that, judging by the tone of his answers, Dahill had a lot more animosity toward Brown than he would admit.

After Dahill stepped down, witnesses against Brown delivered one hit after another. Miss Betty Baerwold, the Sawyers' maid, said she had seen him often at Harry's farm.

Edward Bremer said that shortly after the abduction of William Hamm, detectives Tom Brown and Charles Tierney warned him to look out for kidnappers and offered him protection. Only in retrospect did Bremer begin to wonder whether Brown had researched him in order to set him up. Two years after the kidnapping, detective James Crumley told the FBI that Bremer's guess was accurate: Tom Brown "secured knowledge of Bremer to be used in his kidnapping" while supposedly performing his duties on the kidnap prevention squad.

Walter Magee testified that the contents of the "proof of life" note he and Brown had drafted had somehow gotten to the kidnappers. Nick Hannegraf's mother showed up to tell of the failed raid at her property. Former detective Fred Raasch testified that Brown ordered him to stall that raid.

"The Kissing Bandit" made an appearance by deposition. Edna Murray, suffering with cancer and locked up for a long sentence, testified that during the time that the FBI was looking for Baby Face Nelson, she saw Tom Brown talking with him in a car parked behind the Green Lantern.

Murray's deposition said that three weeks before the Bremer kidnapping, "Fred Barker came over to my apartment in the evening and I was alone." He "said I should get out of the apartment for that night. [The cops] were coming out to raid somebody in the building. He said that Brown . . . asked Sawyer if any of the gang was living at the Edgcumbe and it would be better to get them out because [the cops] were going to investigate a man who lived in the building."

Murray also said that a day after the McCord shooting, Sawyer visited her in St. Paul. He warned her that Brown thought it was foolish that the gang intended to go through with the kidnapping so soon after the McCord shooting.

Murray's deposition was devastating. She said she had on various occasions seen Brown in the Green Lantern speaking with Harry Sawyer and members of the Barker gang. She said that during Bremer's captivity, her boyfriend Volney Davis said "Tom Brown was keeping the gang informed of the activities" of the FBI. She said Davis told her that in return, "Brown was to get a cut of the ransom money."

Murray also testified that when the federal government was considering using the imprisoned Larry DeVol as a trial witness, Brown leaked to Karpis the route that agents planned to use. The idea was that the gang would free DeVol or kill him trying, a scenario chillingly similar to the Kansas City Massacre.

If Murray's testimony was true, Brown's motive could be read as pure self-preservation. In prison, DeVol had been telling inmates and guards that he had paid $100 a week in protection money to Harry Sawyer, which ultimately went to Tom Brown and James Crumley. DeVol also said Brown and Crumley had gotten a 10 percent cut from the Barker gang's robberies. In the end, however, the government decided not to use DeVol as a witness.

Edna Murray's deposition was too much for Brown's attorney. He erupted, complaining about hearsay evidence and bellowing that the hearing had "degenerated into a witches' plot."

Shouting matches broke out.

"Go ahead and badger me," Dahill shouted at Brown's attorney. "It's time I lost my temper, some of the things that are going on around here."

Finally Brown took the stand and portrayed himself as a humble family man. He said that a few weeks before the Hamm kidnapping, he had taken his son and two other boys to his Crane Lake cabin to prepare it for summer. Returning to St. Paul, Brown said, he cleared his vacation time with Chief Dahill.

A huge load of groceries was delivered to the Brown house on the day before the Hamm kidnapping. Brown offered this as proof of his intent to go north to his lake cabin. But just then one daughter got a fever. His wife also contracted it, and then another daughter was quarantined with scarlet fever. Brown postponed his drive to the cabin.

Brown offered all this as proof that, had it not been for chance, he would have been out of town during the Hamm kidnapping.

He told his persecutors how often he had checked on his ailing loved ones during the Hamm kidnapping. When he wasn't nursing the sick, he was working around the clock to bring the kidnappers to justice, crashing exhausted on a cot in the police station. A photo of Brown appeared in the September 22 edition of the *St. Paul Dispatch,* during the time he was presenting his defense. It showed him calm, hands folded, alone at a table in a paneled hearing room.

He was asked about that crucial Monday, June 12, 1933, when he was suspected of meeting with Shotgun George and Jack Peifer while the Barker gang was planning the Hamm kidnapping at White Bear Lake.

Well, no, he was busy that day, taking his feverish daughter to the doctor after she was sent home by a school nurse. He had spent the evening at home, in the company of detective Tom McMahon, druggist Emil Benson, and a couple of farmer friends from outstate.

"Did Peifer come see you that night?"

"No sir."

"Did Goetz [Shotgun George] come see you that night?"

"No sir."

"Did they call you that evening?"

"No sir."

His alibi meant little, though, since a round-trip to White Bear Lake and a brief talk with someone there could have been accomplished in under an hour.

It was pointed out to Brown that in 1925 he had paid $6,475 in cash for his home on Maryland Street. By that time he had been on the force six years. That $6,475 represented nearly his entire salary over that time. How had he paid cash for that home, raised five children, bought cars, clothes, groceries, cigars? A lake resort? A farm? Boats?

Brown could not answer. He had an Al Capone problem. He had spent far more money than he could have legitimately made.

He was asked about bank "transactions changing $50 or $100 bills by you or your son?"

"To the best of my recollection, I did. I probably exchanged $20, $50 and $100 bills."

"Did you or your son?"

"I don't remember my son doing anything."

"In the past have you loaned any money on mortgages?"

"Yes."

"To whom?"

"Alex Walker [St. Paul police chauffer]."

"How much did you loan?"

"$3,300."

"What security did he give you?"

"His house."

Brown admitted he had loaned Chief Dahill $750 to buy a car. Also, he had invested in "stock market speculations" with James Filben, a venture that coincided with the payment of the Hamm ransom. He had three safety-deposit boxes. He'd hoarded $700 in gold. Sometime in 1933 or 1934, the kidnapping years, he had changed a $1,000 bill at the American National Bank. In today's money, that bill would be worth about $20,000.

That last admission led to screaming headlines in the city's three newspapers.

This testimony would soon cause the IRS to open an investigation of the Bank of Tom Brown. In the meantime, he was asked about his criminal connections. Did he know Harry Sawyer, Myrtle Eaton, and Jack Peifer?

Yes he did.

"Didn't you take Crumley to task for calling up Myrtle Eaton and asking about the kidnapping?"

"No!" Brown shouted.

Asked about Nick Hannegraf, Brown said, "I never saw him."

"Didn't he show you pictures [of the Barkers]?"

"I told you I never saw [Hannegraf]. Crumley was in charge [of the Robert Street investigation]. I don't know anything about it. It was already investigated when it came to me."

Asked whether he knew that Barker and Karpis were wanted for murder of a sheriff, he said, "I believe so."

He admitted trying to keep the FBI out of the Bremer and Hamm kidnapping probes. "When one works on a case he likes to get credit for it," he explained.

He denied knowing Harvey Bailey, bank robber extraordinaire and one of the nation's most wanted men. He denied FBI reports that he and Bailey had gone deer hunting at Crane Lake.

St. Paul Dispatch

68th YEAR—NO. 314.   24 PAGES   ST. PAUL, MINN., WEDNESDAY, SEPTEMBER 23, 1936.   THREE CENTS IN ST. PAUL

TOM BROWN ADMITS CHANGING $1,000 BILL; REVEALS $3,300 LOAN TO POLICE ASSISTANT

STATE LABOR RAPS GOVERNOR IN STRIKE CASE

Peterson, at Same Time, Withholds Proposal to Use Troops.

CONFERENCE DEFERRED UNTIL THIS AFTERNOON

Mercury Drops 50 Degrees in North Region

Light to Heavy Frost Predicted for Upper Part of Western Minnesota.

WEED POLLEN COUNT POSITION CHANGED

PROTEST SENT TO GOVERNOR

PRESIDENTIAL VOTE HERE MAY BE RECORD

FASCISTS ADVANCE RAPIDLY ON MADRID

Fall of Capital and Toledo Imminent, Rebel Leaders Assert.

THRONGS FLOCK TO GET SEATS AT COOK SCHOOL

Buffet Entertaining and Dishes Suitable for Occasion Featured on Program.

COMMUNITY SING GIVES ZEST TO DAY'S SESSIONS

YOUTH IDENTIFIED BY GIRL IN KNIFE ATTACK

TAXI DRIVER HELD UP AND ROBBED OF $8.70

14 KILLED 36 HURT AS FRENCH TRAINS COLLIDE

Minneapolis Drivers Use Safety Lane Here

OLSON MEMORIAL SERVICE DELAYED TO NOVEMBER 11

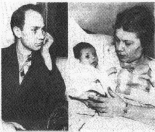

BABY GIVEN CHANCE TO LIVE

Fight With Death Bares Possible Hemophilia Cure

Chemical Compound Revives Boy Given Up for Dead After Lawyer Overhears Plaint of Jobless Parent and Orders Ambulance to Rush Lad to Last Chance.

CHRISTIANSON GIVES 6-POINT FARM PLAN

Outlines Republican Program in Address at Paper's Forum.

Father's Whip Cut Wounds in Back, Lad Says

Citizens' Views On Lights Asked

Deposit Box Also Rented In 3 Banks

Accused Detective Testifies Under Cross-Examination That He Lent Tom Dahill $750 and Other Department Men Smaller Sums; Corrects Testimony to Show That He Paid $6,475 Cash for House He Lives In.

EXCHANGED MORE THAN $700 IN GOLD COIN AT TIME PRESIDENT CALLED IN HOLDINGS

SHANGHAI AREA UNDER JAPS' MARTIAL LAW

International Police Ousted After 2 Marines Are Shot; Troops Landed.

NAVY MINISTER TAKES COMMAND OF FLEET

GERMAN PLANE REACHES AZORES ON HOP FROM N. Y.

The Big Fella makes big headlines at his hearing, September 23, 1936.

Brown's standard response to deniable inquiries was "I don't remember." He admitted being the guest of honor at a party at Harry Sawyer's, though. He'd been given a machine gun, it was rumored, a token of his secret membership in the underworld. However, Brown said, the machine gun was a gift from his hunting buddy and fellow ex–police chief, Truman Alcorn.

"Where were you on June 12, 1933?"

Driving with Jack Peifer and Shotgun George to see the Barker gang, perhaps?

"I don't remember."

Brown acknowledged that he'd known Shotgun George Ziegler since 1929. He said that back then, he'd received a tip from Ziegler that the Hamm family was a kidnap target. Brown relayed this information to William Hamm Sr., the patriarch, and the old man took this news gravely. He asked Brown to tell nobody else. Brown said that's why he never mentioned it to Edward Murnane, chief of police at the time.

Had he heard it was the Barker gang that had killed two Minneapolis cops during a bank robbery?

"That came out recently."

"But you hadn't heard it before?"

"I might have."

How well did Brown know bootlegger Leon Gleckman?

"All I knew was what I read in the papers."

But history leaves no doubt that Gleckman was a personal friend and Brown's criminal mentor. The FBI had already learned that Adolph Bremer and Gleckman were the hidden forces that powered Brown's rise through the police ranks.

Thomas O'Connell, former police commissioner, stood up in the hearing and barked that Brown was "dragging the whole city into this mess in a fight to prove his guilt or innocence." He and Brown nearly came to blows, reporters said, and O'Connell was dragged out of the room by detectives.

Big Tom had long used the press to his advantage, and now *Daily News* city editor Fred Strong, called to the witness stand, hinted at prosecutorial "intimidation."

Suddenly Brown bellowed, "If anybody wants a fight, we'll have a fight." He stood up. "I want it understood there's nobody going to push me around this courtroom," he shouted.

Prosecutor Connolly got in his face.

"You're not going to bluff me, Tom Brown."

When things calmed down, Strong testified that the *Daily News* had gotten the Dr. Nippert milk bottle story from Leon Gleckman. So if Strong's testimony was accurate, Brown had at least in this instance used Gleckman as his conduit to the *Daily News.*

46

THE DISAPPEARING ACT

On October 8, 1936, the Civil Service Board judged Tom Brown guilty of conspiracy in the Hamm and Bremer kidnappings. The board wrote Brown that witness "statements have been fully investigated and as a result of said investigation, you are hereby discharged for inefficiency, breach of duty, misfeasance and malfeasance."

Specifically, the commissioners found that Brown had

- conspired with the Barker gang and Harry Sawyer to kidnap Edward Bremer
- failed to properly investigate the Hamm kidnapping
- disclosed confidential police information to the kidnappers of William Hamm

Brown's firing from the St. Paul police department was upheld. He was 46 and would be eligible to collect the standard police pension of $75 a month at age 50.

Brown filed an appeal with the district court. Newsmen pestered officials about criminal charges. John Pearson, assistant county attorney, said "evidence is not sufficient to support a serious criminal charge." Pearson's boss was Michael Kinkead, who had every interest in keeping the pressure off Brown. Had Brown turned state's evidence, Kinkead was looking at disgrace and possibly prosecution.

Under Kinkead's direction, a Ramsey County grand jury took up the Brown charges but refused to indict. A few weeks after his firing, the Brown case, and the man himself, disappeared from public view. For a while, federal officials pursued a Brown investigation. Treasury men studied his earnings and spending. It seemed that the fate of Al Capone and Leon Gleckman might befall Tom Brown: both of them were serving long sentences for tax evasion. Ultimately, despite evidence that Brown spent far more than he officially earned, tax charges were never filed against him.

The most likely place for Brown to cool out after his dismissal was his cabin at Crane Lake. Deer season was only weeks away. The lake property Tom Brown shared with slots king Tom Filben was unusually isolated. The entire area is thinly populated and has since become national forest. There are no roads to Crane Lake, and in Brown's time the closest anyone could get by car was thirty miles. From the end of the road, it was at least a two-hour boat ride to a portage, a trek through the woods, and another boat trip to the cabin itself. Here was the perfect place for a wanted man to hide.

When the FBI began seriously investigating Brown, they dispatched agents to Crane Lake. Ross Daugherty, the local game warden, was the man who had told the feds that Brown and Filben owned adjoining properties on the Canadian border and had built a two-story lodge they shared. St. Paul detective William McMullen also owned a cabin on that lake.

Daugherty had told the FBI that the Brown-Filben property was known locally as a hideout for wanted men. He had said he was "certain he saw" Brown deer hunting with Harvey Bailey. Daugherty also said he saw Verne Miller, cop killer and bank robber, hiding at the Brown-Filben place. Other local people told similar tales. Agents had returned from Crane Lake wiser, perhaps, but with nothing they could take to court against Tom Brown.

By the time the Civil Service Board had passed judgment on Tom Brown, the FBI had vanquished the public enemies, earning a new respect in Washington and around the nation. Unlike Baby Face Nelson, Pretty Boy Floyd, John Dillinger, and Ma Barker, Tom Brown had attained no national reputation. It cost the FBI nothing, in terms of prestige, to let him go. Why the IRS let Tom Brown get away with tax evasion is a mystery. The agency had astonished the nation and set a precedent by bringing down Al Capone, and later Leon Gleckman and other bootleggers. Tax evasion in another form would someday bring

Brown to the brink of imprisonment. But the IRS probe of Brown's finances undertaken in 1936 fizzled out. Whether agents could not find enough evidence, or became distracted, or were pressured to drop the probe is unknown.

Michael Kinkead, an architect of St. Paul's protection rackets, was never charged with any crime, nor was his reputation publicly sullied. To readers of the local newspapers, he was portrayed as a thundering crime fighter. When rising reformer Harold Stassen took over the state government, Kinkead was moved aside to the politically harmless post of probate judge, which he kept until retirement.

For the St. Paul establishment, sending Tom Brown and his secrets out of town was a safe solution. The fact that Brown was repeatedly able to "borrow" money from William Hamm after the kidnapping indicates the level of fear and intimidation he inspired. In a city whose political economy had been built on systematic corruption, many in public life had something to hide, and Brown knew where it was hidden. On a police force where many suspected that Brown was a cold-blooded murderer, no cop was willing to risk talking. So Tom Brown left St. Paul, punctuating with a full stop the era of speakeasies, Tommy guns, and kidnappings.

A little more than a year after Brown left public life in St. Paul, he filed an application for a liquor license in Morris, Minnesota. Morris is a college town 170 miles northwest of the Twin Cities. The recipient of the application was William Mahoney, the man who as St. Paul's mayor had demoted Brown after the Barker gang's escape. Mahoney was now state liquor commissioner. He approved the license, transforming Big Tom from kidnapper to booze merchant.

The next public mention of Brown's name occurred on September 28, 1941. St. Paul newspapers briefly reported that Brown's boat had capsized while he'd been fishing with friends on a Minnesota lake. Brown struggled to shore, but a fishing buddy drowned.

In the meantime, St. Paul appointed police commissioner Gus Barfuss, who began rousting the remnants of Brown's clique.

With Jack Peifer dead and the Hollyhocks shuttered, Violet Peifer paid Tom Filben to drop his claim to the property and sold it in 1938. It is now a magnificent private home on the Mississippi. Violet married defense attorney Eugene Rerat and died in Florida in the 1980s.

Harry Sawyer, after a transfer to Leavenworth, was released in an ambulance on February 11, 1955. He was sick with cancer and cirrhosis. He was in a wheelchair, his pain dulled by narcotics, until he died in Chicago on June 23.

Alvin Karpis served the longest in Alcatraz of any man ever remanded there. He learned to play the guitar in Alcatraz and started a band that featured Al Capone on the accordion. Released in 1969, Karpis, who was born in Montreal, was deported to Canada. He hooked up with a Canadian crime writer and produced two autobiographies, charming audiences on the attendant book tours. His books were a mix of shrewd observations and glib self-deception. His writings kept in place a psychological mask that had served him all his life. He claimed to be an honorable professional thief. He blamed the bloodshed on somebody else. In 1979, he died in his sleep in a Spanish resort town. The cause was an overdose of sleeping pills and liquor.

Dolores Delaney ran out of sympathy for Karpis once he was locked up in Alcatraz. No longer able to deny he was a kidnapper and a killer, all she had to show for her years with Karpis was a bullet wound, a prison term, and a son she hardly knew. In her last public pronouncement, she told a reporter that Karpis had "made his bed and now he has to lie in it." She then disappeared into private life.

In Alcatraz, Doc Barker became "one of the worst troublemakers" ever locked up there. In 1939, he and four cohorts managed to tuck saw blades into harmonicas and slip them past prison guards. On a night so foggy that boats in San Francisco Bay were running aground, Doc and his buddies made a 3:00 AM break. They sawed through their window bars and ran to a raft they had assembled out of driftwood and strips of clothing. There on the rocky shore, Doc was shot to death by prison guards.

Ma Barker and each of her sons met a violent death. Ma was inflated into a caricature of a bloodthirsty gangster by the FBI, which needed to muffle the embarrassing fact that they had killed an old woman who had committed no crime. The myth of Ma Barker, spread by imaginative books, movies, and websites, proved far stronger than the truth of her life.

Fred's girl Paula Harmon, having suffered a nervous breakdown in the hands of the FBI, went home to her parents in Port Arthur, Texas, and in late 1934 attempted suicide several times. A few days after Fred and

Ma were gunned down by the FBI, Paula was locked up at the State Hospital for the Insane at Rusk, Texas. For the rest of her life, she was an emotional invalid, shuttling between her parents' home and a sanatorium.

Super-witness Byron Bolton served three years in prison and then went into hiding. Edward Bremer died in Florida in 1965. His family exited the brewing business but is still prominent in Minnesota banking. William Hamm Jr. became a gloomy and paranoid man who never fully recovered from the psychological effects of his kidnapping. He died in 1970 in Minneapolis. The family sold the Hamm's brand, which was subsequently produced by other breweries.

James Crumley died of heart failure in 1939. Failed reformer Tom Dahill ran a restaurant in downtown St. Paul until he was able to retire on a police pension. He died in 1960. W. W. "Billy" Dunn became general manager of the Hamm's brewery, despite William Hamm's suspicions of him. He died in a St. Paul nursing home at age 89.

In July of 1941, Leon Gleckman, facing another prison term on tax charges, got stinking drunk and rammed his car into a bridge abutment in downtown St. Paul. He did not survive. Gladys Sawyer divorced Harry, closed her Omaha grocery, and lived the rest of her life in Denver. Of all the underworld characters from the Tom Brown era, his pal Tom Filben enjoyed the most luxurious afterlife. Filben and his wife moved to a hilltop estate in Indian Wells, California. His wife dabbled in antiques, while Filben relaxed around the swimming pool. According to one report, Filben's fortune came from slot machines he'd placed in Cuba.

Although Tom Brown seemed to be living quietly in small-town Minnesota, trouble erupted in Morris just after the end of World War II. The town had five liquor stores, including Tom Brown's. In June of 1945, the citizens got up a petition drive that would cancel all liquor licenses and sell alcoholic beverages only from a municipally owned store. The weekly newspaper, the *Morris Sun,* only noted that it was an "intense campaign." Exactly what motivated the citizens of Morris to shut five liquor stores is unknown. News stories avoided mentioning the issues, motives, and personalities involved. In August, the petitioners won "by 180 votes out of 1430."

The case ended up in the state supreme court, but on New Year's Day, the five stores were forced to cease selling liquor. Brown soon left Morris for the North Woods resort town of Ely.

In January of 1947, a grand jury indicted Brown on nine counts of vio-
lating federal liquor laws. Upon learning this, Brown went into hiding
and was "subject to a statewide manhunt" for several days. Ultimately
he surrendered to Frank Sommer, the police chief who had taken over
the O'Connor System and passed it on to Brown. Sommer was now a
U.S. marshal.

Brown hired attorney Jerome Hoffman of St. Paul, who worked out a
deal with the federal courts. Brown pleaded guilty to avoiding the federal alcohol dealer's tax and failing to register as a liquor seller. In return,
the government dropped eight charges of failing to report liquor sales to
the IRS. For the entire time it had been open, Brown had operated his
liquor store in disregard of federal laws.

Brown paid a $3,500 fine on the one count and had a year in prison
and all probation suspended. Attorney Hoffman asked the court for
leniency because Brown was "a sick man" and was "out of the liquor
business and intended to stay out."

But not really. After that case was settled, Brown opened Tom Brown's
Bottle Shop in Ely.

Tom Brown's Bertillion card. Before fingerprinting became reliable, police
agencies used the "Bertillion system" to track and identify criminals.

Ely was a fitting town for an outdoorsman like Brown to retire in. The town served as outfitter for hunting, canoeing, and fishing expeditions into the Boundary Waters. Brown ran his liquor business until January of 1959, when he died, at age 69, of a sudden heart attack while walking along a street.

In St. Paul, Brown's successors in the police department cleaned up his mess. In the fall of 1936, under commissioner Gus Barfuss, police cracked down on dice, punchboards, and other forms of gambling. That crackdown caused a real estate crash downtown. Many saloons, pool halls, and cigar stores, deprived of illegal income, folded. By 1945, according to an FBI crime survey, St. Paul had become a low-crime city with an effective police department.

The Green Lantern, the portal for so many of the era's most notorious crimes, was razed in a spasm of urban renewal that removed the streetcar lines, and much of the life, from downtown St. Paul. No interior photograph of Harry Sawyer's legendary tavern is known to exist, and the building has been replaced by public housing apartments. A popular gangster-era tour of St. Paul visits many of the sites that do remain, including Jack Peifer's Mystic Caverns casino. The federal courthouse where the Bremer and Hamm kidnapping trials were held has become a National Historic Landmark, and its halls are lined with interpretive displays, including reminders of the gangster era and a mention of the role of Big Tom Brown.

47

ONE PATH THROUGH THE WOODS

Those who see the public enemies era solely as a time of gangsters, Tommy guns, and molls are missing a great deal. Underneath that flashy surface lay a tangle of greed, selfishness, and callous indifference on the part of public officials and a great many supposedly respectable citizens.

The gangsters were, like actors in a play, merely the most noticeable characters in a larger production. Unnoticed by the audience was a much bigger cast of writers, directors, producers, technicians, financiers, and so forth. Likewise with the public enemies. Their part was violent and sensational, yes, and acted with breathtaking audacity. But corrupt policemen and political fixers stood just behind the curtains. Backstage milled a shadowy group of prosecutors, sheriff's deputies, private detectives, defense attorneys, judges and jailers, politicians, merchants, money launderers, bankers, brewers, fences, and messenger boys.

In the gangster era, the true power was held by men in business, law enforcement, and politics who, to the casual observer, might seem wholly legitimate. The gangsters only *seemed* to be shooting their way to wealth and freedom with a Tommy gun. In truth, many purchased a "license" to commit their crimes.

It is often said that in this broke and broken-hearted era, the public admired and even rooted for the gangsters. But that is only a slice of truth, and not the whole pie. It had to be discouraging when citizens learned they could not trust the police. The honest cops on the force must have been demoralized, knowing that their authority could be undercut by a cash payment to a superior. The police were to be feared: Corrupt cops would sometimes arrest suspects not for the purpose of solving crimes but to extort money from them. Innocent and marginally guilty people were roughed up. Murders and other serious crimes were answered with little or no investigation. People were railroaded to prison, confessions extracted under torture or coercive detention.

Many citizens and some dissident politicians complained that children were becoming addicted to slot machines, that speakeasies and bordellos were opening in genteel neighborhoods, that gun battles were erupting in the night. Ordinary families feared random street violence; wealthy ones hired bodyguards to protect against kidnapping. Rumors spread that the police were not just greedy but murderous. The atmosphere became so threatening that judges sent their families out of town during high-stakes trials, and others begged for FBI protection. Even FBI agents feared attack by the underworld.

In St. Paul, the behavior of inspector James Crumley was frightening in its implications. Crumley spent much of his energy seeking shakedown victims, arresting them, and then extracting favors: *Buy me a ton of coal. Buy me an overcoat.* What citizen could feel safe from such a predator? Who knew, once in his clutches, when you might escape and at what cost? It's known for certain that Crumley pressured at least one man to perjure himself for the purpose of sending another fellow to prison—for a life term.

So much for the glamour of the gangster era.

Many other cities had police officials who were also criminals: Chicago's Tubbo Gilbert; chief Dutch Akers of Hot Springs, Arkansas; and captain George Timiney of Toledo are just a few who became legends of corruption. As far as is known, however, Tom Brown is the only police executive of the era to have conspired in kidnapping. Brown not only violated the public trust with these crimes but betrayed two wealthy families who relied on him for advice on keeping themselves safe from kidnappers.

Brown had much in common with the men of the Barker-Karpis gang. His origins were in the poor, somewhat backward countryside, among farmers and miners. Like the Barkers and Karpis, he had little schooling. He and his secret partners greatly enjoyed outdoor sports, and perhaps Brown did go duck hunting with the Barker brothers, as was reported to the FBI. But the most striking affinity between the police chief and the gangsters was a compulsive greed coupled with an utter lack of conscience.

Consider the words of Alvin Karpis, the only one of this bunch who wrote a memoir. In it, Karpis gloated about the $33,000 the gang stole in their 1933 payroll holdup in South St. Paul. Their wild gunfire killed policeman Leo Pavlak and wounded John Yeaman so seriously he never fully recovered. Gangster Charles Fitzgerald took a bullet in the hip, which caused him to stump around with a cane for the rest of his life. But by Karpis's assessment, the robbery amounted to "a good day's work even if it did cost one wounded crook . . . and one wounded and one dead cop."

That evaluation is astounding in its coldness, its lack of empathy, the utter soullessness of its calculation. But this was the Barker-Karpis ethos. Money, and the freedom to spend it wildly, was their motivation. The death, destruction, fear, and pain they caused troubled them not at all.

And so, Tom Brown. Apparently, the ghosts of Frank LaPre and Homer Van Meter did not spook him. The flaming corpses of Sadie Carmacher and Rose Perry evoked only an evasive shrug. The deaths of his fellow officers in Minneapolis gave him no pause: he continued his partnership with the murderous Barker gang, which soon killed patrolman Pavlak. Neither the panic shooting of the hapless Oscar Erickson nor the cold execution of Arthur Dunlop penetrated the well-armored psyche of Tom Brown. The lifelong sufferings of patrolman John Yeaman and airline dispatcher Roy McCord, if they registered with Brown at all, were excused by the profits obtained. Johnny Quinn languished for years in Stillwater Prison on dubious charges because Brown needed to protect the Green Lantern. Four hapless Italian immigrants were incarcerated at that same prison while Brown's benefactor Jack Peifer reaped the rewards of their crime.

And so Tom Brown had this in common with his secret partners: human pain, grief, and suffering were meaningless if they resulted in a cash payoff.

Criminal history is limited in scope because it only encompasses those who were caught. The smartest criminals go into the books as successful, perhaps even admired, members of society. Of all the figures considered in this narrative, the shrewdest criminal may have been county attorney Michael Kinkead. Whatever his contemporaries said about him in living rooms, cafés, and taverns, his public reputation was spotless. Yet there is no doubt he played a significant role in St. Paul's corruption. Given the opportunity to prosecute Tom Brown for kidnapping conspiracy, Kinkead passed. It would have been an interesting trial, since prosecutor and accused would have had full knowledge of the other's crimes. Many supposedly respectable men would have sweated that one out. But the moment passed, Brown left town, and Kinkead eventually retired, untroubled by public controversy, on a state pension.

Another clever escapee was Tom Filben, king of the slot machine and renowned practical joker, whose crimes were largely financial. He was, however, at least an auxiliary in the gruesome murder of Sadie Carmacher and Rose Perry and a silent witness to many other crimes. Filben never spent any serious time incarcerated and enjoyed a long, sunny retirement in the desert of Southern California.

But the most spectacular Houdini acts were pulled off by Tom Brown. His shrewdest habit was to insulate himself by creating the fewest possible witnesses to his crimes. When Jack Peifer came to trial there were, by his defense attorney's count, forty witnesses against him, including six who presented direct evidence. Had Tom Brown come to trial in that summer of 1936, only one man, Harry Sawyer, might have provided direct testimony against him. Two potentially strong witnesses, Jack Peifer and Shotgun George Ziegler, were dead by the time the FBI got wise to Brown.

Brown realized early on that simply refusing to cooperate with the justice system was the surest way to avoid punishment. He alone of St. Paul cops refused to be fingerprinted. During the mid-1920s, when indicted for aiding bootleggers, he would not be dragged into court. Grand juries were no danger to him, since Michael Kinkead was in charge of the jurors. For all his contact with the justice system, Brown was rarely on the witness stand, as if he realized the dangers presented by the rules of cross-examination. He continued in this spirit of noncooperation even after his public disgrace, when he'd been reduced to mere liquor merchant. He'd refused to pay federal taxes on his booze for the whole time he'd been in business. In this case he relied on friends from his old network to make a deal for a fine and suspended sentence, minimizing for one final time his contact with justice and the risks therein.

Tom Brown was also one of the luckiest criminals of the gangster era. His bagman, Billy Dunn, given the chance to sandbag Brown, told the FBI one glib lie after another. The messenger boy Pat Reilly, a repository of gangster knowledge, kept it all to himself even though ratting on Brown might have sprung him from Leavenworth. Leon Gleckman, imprisoned there too, wouldn't give the FBI a thing on Brown. Harry Sawyer, rotting with cirrhosis and cancer, sat silent in Alcatraz. Disgraced cop James Crumley suggested the names of others who might talk but declined to provide direct evidence. There was certainly an element of luck in all these outcomes. But fear may have played a role too, since Brown's reputation for ruthlessness intimidated even fellow cops.

Brown got lucky too, with the FBI. Just when the case against him was coalescing, the agency began to focus on snaring every person who had harbored the fugitive Barker-Karpis gang. Hoover seemed determined to turn the Bremer case into a series of show trials, a warning not just to kidnappers but to all who would aid the wanted man. Pat Reilly was locked up for aiding Dillinger. Doctors and nurses were prosecuted. Wives and girlfriends were imprisoned for the crime of not betraying their men. While his agency was expending its energy on those investigations, Hoover famously let the Chicago mob get away with murder. Tom Brown, too, benefited from Hoover's selective enforcement.

It's possible, though far from proven, that Brown's escapes from justice were aided by political connections. His cryptic remarks to a reporter that "everybody is my friend" hint of a connection to power. Why did Mayor Nelson, in 1923, rescind his promise to fire Brown? Why did the federal government not pursue bootlegging charges against him a few years later? Why did the IRS drop its 1936 investigation against him? Were those all mere coincidence?

Brown certainly was practiced in witness intimidation, as evidenced by the threats he had delivered to Gladys Sawyer, so that may account for some of his escapes.

But it's interesting to note FBI document number 12176 in the Bremer investigation. Page nine discusses Brown, the 1935 wiretap investigation of the St. Paul police, and crusading editor Howard Kahn. It begins a discussion of Brown's role and then . . . page ten is missing. It's possible that this omission is the result of a clerical error. But the FBI's Bremer kidnapping files amount to well over 500,000 pages, and missing pages are extremely rare. The odds against a clerical error seem high. Also, that 1936 IRS investigation into Brown's finances could not be found in a preliminary search of the National Archives. Whether these are mere coincidences, or the result of political skullduggery, cannot now be known.

But it's possible to trace, without descending into speculation, how Brown escaped J. Edgar Hoover, who was once so determined to indict him. After the last kidnapping trial, and the suicide of Jack Peifer, Hoover's focus shifted from St. Paul to Toledo and Hot Springs. He became obsessed with using his new legal cudgel, the harboring law. "In regard to my plan to investigate crime conditions in several of the cities in which bad conditions exist, such as St. Paul, Toledo and Hot Springs," Hoover wrote, " . . . Toledo would be the best place to start because of the fact that so much information would be obtained while investigating harboring charges." His agency squandered energy on fruitless investigations of prostitutes, bartenders, drug addicts, cab drivers, gamblers, housewives, bystanders . . . Hundreds of reports came in from exhausted agents in Ohio and Arkansas, and little was accomplished.

Meanwhile in St. Paul, FBI men concluded that "the most damaging testimony [against Brown] no doubt would be excluded in federal court as hearsay." The conversations Bolton reported having with Ziegler were a possible exception because hearsay evidence may be allowed if a conversation took place "in furtherance of a conspiracy." But the FBI was satisfied when Brown was fired from the police force. After three spectacular kidnapping trials, each a marvelous success from the federal point of view, they shifted their focus away from St. Paul.

In the court of reason, however, the case against Brown might well stand. The witnesses would range from the raving madman Larry DeVol to the former state supreme court justice Samuel Wilson. The well-connected gang women Bess Green, Edna Murray, and Gladys Sawyer told similar accounts of Brown's involvement in crime. His former partner detective Charles Tierney and his supervisor/rival Tom Dahill both said Brown was deeply involved in the kidnappings. St. Paul's mayor and city attorneys visited J. Edgar Hoover to further the case against Brown. George Rafferty, Brown's brother-in-law, and James Crumley, his one-time friend, recounted their suspicions of Brown to the FBI. Brown certainly used delaying tactics at least twice to give the Barker gang time to skip town. He admitted cashing a $1,000 bill but could not explain where he got that, or his surplus of money and property. In the most dramatic and controversial cases of his career, the Gleckman kidnapping and the Van Meter shooting, his contradictory stories created doubts about his actions and motives. And finally there was Byron Bolton, who said his friend Ziegler had delivered $25,000 to Brown for his role in the Hamm kidnapping. Hearsay, yes. But time has proven that the information Green, Bolton, Dahill, and Tierney gave the FBI was highly accurate. All that corroborating testimony cannot be simply dismissed.

Big Tom's mysterious connections remain intriguing. Why was Brown not among those stung in the Jamie probe? The answer provided by Charles Tierney, soon to become chief of St. Paul police, was that Brown was let in on the secret by the investigation's designers, Ned Warren and Howard Kahn. Saloonkeeper Frank Reilly told the FBI that Warren and Kahn had gambling interests with Brown. Whatever the truth of that, Warren, who posed as a reformer, enjoyed Brown's political support. Editor Kahn and his *Daily News* used Brown and Gleckman as a source of inside information.

So when we sum up a clever and lucky criminal-cop, a distracted federal government, and a corrupt police and court system, it all amounts to Tom Brown's escape. With Jack Peifer dead by his own hand, with Harry Sawyer and Alvin Karpis locked up in Alcatraz, with Doc Barker shot down on that island's stony shores, and with the bodies of Fred and Ma Barker shipped back to the Ozarks, their secret partner Tom Brown retired to his sportsman's paradise, drinking, hunting, and fishing up north, where the woods are dark and quiet and deep.

ACKNOWLEDGMENTS

This book and its author were helped along the way by many people, including Elizabeth Burnes, archvist at the National Archives in Kansas City. She located, among other things, a long-buried transcript of the Bremer kidnapping trial. It's tempting to mention several librarians at the Minnesota Historical Society Library by name, but the entire staff has proven so helpful and knowledgeable that only a collective thank-you will do. Staffers at the St. Paul Public Library, Ramsey County Historical Society, and Dakota County Historical Society also propelled this book in the right direction.

This book had four editors. The first draft was rewritten using feedback from *Pioneer Press* reporter Doug Belden. The resulting manuscript was worked into final form by Ann Regan, editor in chief, and Shannon Pennefeather, managing editor, at the Minnesota Historical Society Press. In between, freelance copy editor Sally Heuer raised many good questions. The help of all on matters large and small is appreciated.

Pat Thraen, *Pioneer Press* newsroom researcher, proved a cheerful guide to that newspaper's wonderful photo archive. Thanks also to the *Pioneer Press* and its editor Mike Burbach and publisher Guy Gilmore for permission to use the photos.

NOTE ON SOURCES

All matter within quotes is taken from written sources. Except where noted, all newspaper stories referenced in this work were printed on page one. A phrase with capitalized words indicates that a headline is being quoted.

The journalists who were the first recorders of this history are not credited by name because news articles of the 1930s generally appeared without bylines. Only columnists were regularly identified.

Everyone who researches or writes about this era, especially its midwestern phase, owes a debt of gratitude to St. Paul writer and researcher Paul Maccabee. His decade-long struggle to pry information out of the FBI led the bureau to eventually release thousands of documents about the public enemies era. His book *John Dillinger Slept Here* manages the neat trick of being both a careful history and an entertaining read. It is indispensable to an understanding of the era. Maccabee's voluminous research is now preserved as the St. Paul Gangster History Research Collection (GHRC) at the Minnesota Historical Society.

The era covered in this book saw an identity change for the nation's top police agency. In the early 1930s it was called the Division of Investigation, Department of Justice. In 1935, its name was changed to the Federal Bureau of Investigation. Because many of the investigations cited here straddle that name change, and because it is the identity familiar to most readers, the agency is called the FBI throughout.

Where FBI sources are listed below, they refer to three primary file groups: the Dillinger File (DF), the Hamm Kidnapping File (HKF), and the Bremer Kidnapping File (BKF). These massive files are broken into sections, and each document is meant to have a serial number, although it is missing on a few documents. In some cases, particularly in the Bremer Kidnapping File, when the serial number is missing it is possible to identify the documents via their digital versions, available at the FBI Freedom of Information Act website. Those online documents are identified (in parentheses) by part number and document number. Researchers will note, however, that the FBI's online documents about the

Bremer kidnapping have entire sections missing and that the numbering system can be confusing.

Preserved court transcripts from the 1930s are rare, usually found only with cases that have been appealed. One such document provided a significant foundation for this book: it recounts the January 1936 trial of Harry Sawyer, Cassius McDonald, and William Weaver. McDonald's guilty verdict was appealed to the 8th Circuit Court of Appeals in St. Louis and is preserved by the National Archives in Kansas City as case #10587.

Daily newspaper sources were primarily the *St. Paul Pioneer Press* (PP), its sister publication the *St. Paul Dispatch* (DISP), and the *St. Paul Daily News* (SPDN). At the dawn of the 1930s, the *Pioneer Press* and the *Dispatch* were owned by the Ridder family. In 1933, that family bought the *Daily News,* and so all three of the city's dailies were under the same ownership. In 1938, the *Daily News* was folded into the other two papers. The *Daily News* is the most cited newspaper in this work because it was a tabloid in spirit, if not in format, with a special interest in covering crime.

The weekly newspaper with the most impact on politics was the *Union Advocate,* edited by labor leader William Mahoney until his 1932 election as mayor of St. Paul. After he lost his bid for re-election, Mahoney returned to the *Advocate* as a flame-throwing writer behind the column "Lifting the Lid on City Hall." Many of the *Advocate* references cited in this work were taken from that column.

Readers will note that, by coincidence, there were two men named Farmer involved with the Barker gang. The Missouri fixer Herb "Deafy" Farmer hid them after they shot the sheriff of West Plains. The Illinois tavern owner Elmer Farmer was their contact man when choosing hideouts in Bensenville.

Readers will also note that St. Paul had a bewildering succession of police chiefs in this turbulent era. From the beginning of 1930 to the end of 1936, eight men served as chief, some of them serving twice. They are, in order of their first appointment: Edward Murnane, Tom Dahill, Tom Brown, Frank Cullen, Michael Culligan, Gus Barfuss, Charles Coulter, and Clinton Hackert. The source of this information is the St. Paul Police Historical Society.

A selected list of interesting and helpful books on the era follows.

BOOKS AND ARTICLES

Burrough, Bryan. *Public Enemies: America's Greatest Crime Wave and the Birth of the FBI.* New York: Penguin, 2004.

Cooper, Courtney Ryley. *Ten Thousand Public Enemies.* Boston: Little, Brown and Co., 1935.

Ernst, Robert R. *Robbin' Banks and Killin' Cops: The Life and Crimes of Lawrence DeVol and His Association with Alvin Karpis and the Barker-Karpis Gang.* Baltimore: Publish America, 2009.

Gentry, Curt. *J. Edgar Hoover: A Man and His Secrets.* New York: W. W. Norton, 1991.

Hoffman, Dennis. *Scarface Al and the Crime Crusaders: Chicago's Private War Against Capone.* Carbondale: Southern Illinois University Press, 2010.

Hoover, J. Edgar. *Persons in Hiding.* Boston: Little, Brown and Co., 1938.

Karpis, Alvin, with Bill Trent. *Public Enemy Number One: The Alvin Karpis Story.* New York: Coward-McCann and Geoghegan, 1971.

Kessler, Ronald. *Bureau: The Secret History of the FBI.* New York: St. Martin's Press, 2002.

Kobler, John. *Capone: The Life and World of Al Capone.* Boston: Da Capo Press, 1992.

Maccabee, Paul. *John Dillinger Slept Here: A Crooks' Tour of Crime and Corruption in St. Paul, 1920–1936.* St. Paul: Minnesota Historical Society Press, 1995.

Okrent, Daniel. *Last Call: The Rise and Fall of Prohibition.* New York: Scribner, 2010.

Poulsen, Ellen. *Don't Call Us Molls: Women of the John Dillinger Gang.* Oakland Gardens, NY: Clinton Cook Publishing, 2002.

Purvis, Alston. *The Vendetta: Special Agent Melvin Purvis, John Dillinger, and Hoover's FBI in the Age of Gangsters.* New York: PublicAffairs, 2009.

Purvis, Melvin. *American Agent.* New York: Doubleday, Doran and Co., 1936.

Severeid, Paul. *The People's Lawyer: The Life of Eugene Rerat.* Minneapolis, MN: Ross and Haines, 1963.

Summers, Anthony. *Official and Confidential: The Secret Life of J. Edgar Hoover.* New York: G. P. Putnam Sons, 1993.

Touhy, Roger, with Ray Brennan. *The Stolen Years.* Cleveland, OH: Pennington, 1959.

Wingerd, Mary Lethert. *Claiming the City: Politics, Faith, and the Power of Place in St. Paul.* Ithaca, NY: Cornell University Press, 2003.

ARTICLES

Federal Bureau of Investigation. Barker-Karpis Gang Summary File #7-576, November 19, 1936.

High, Stanley. "St. Paul Wins a War." *Current History* (September 1938).

Karpis, Alvin. "Karpis Recalls St. Paul." *Capital Magazine, St. Paul Pioneer Press* and *St. Paul Dispatch,* March 7, 1971, 4–6, 9.

NOTES

1. HISTORY'S SHADOWS

Basic background on the Barker gang: FBI, Barker-Karpis Summary. Available at the FBI's Freedom of Information Act website.

"My life in crime was minor league stuff": Karpis and Trent, *Public Enemy Number One,* 42.

"First genuine major league stickup": Karpis and Trent, *Public Enemy Number One,* 45.

"Would have all been caught in St. Paul": Volney Davis confession, August 9, 1935, BKF Sec. 134 #7453, supplement, 1–2.

"In jail a long time ago": Edna Murray on Tom Brown, October 17, 1935, BKF Sec. 138 #7744, 33.

The FBI summarizes its case against Brown in an unsigned memo dated November 10, 1936, HKF Sec. 11 #1082.

Brown's criminal influence: C. W. Stein to Hoover, June 12, 1936, HKF Sec. 10 #824x.

2. "EVERYTHING COULD BE FIXED"

O'Connor System: Max Burger, 6211743, June 25, 1926, File 48-39-10, RG 60, National Archives, Kansas City, MO.

Richard O'Connor quotes: George C. Rogers, "Richard (Dick) Thomas O'Connor: manuscript biography," C-1-5, Minnesota Historical Society, St. Paul.

Chief O'Connor quotes: SPDN, July 24, 1924.

Not one bank robbery in St. Paul; bootleggers' income; home deliveries of liquor: Wingerd, *Claiming the City,* 254–55.

"Forty percent of our people on welfare.": recalled by Mayor Mark Gehan, DISP, December 21, 1959.

Wisconsin, in 1932, became the first state to make payments to the unemployed. Through the Social Security Act of 1935, the federal government essentially coerced the states into adopting unemployment insurance. See Social Security Board, *Unemployment Compensation, How and Why,* Publication No. 14, U.S. Government Printing Office, March 1937.

St. Paul payoff system described: T. G. Melvin, June 16, 1936, HKF Sec. 10 #86; also R. T. Noonan, May 14, 1936, HKF Sec. 9 #761, 9–10.

"Everything could be fixed": Volney Davis quoting Doc Barker, Newman, November 15, 1935, BKF Sec. 144 #8116.

3. THE RISE OF BIG TOM

"He must be on the take": FBI report on Rafferty's visit, R. T. Noonan, June 18, 1936, HKF Sec. 10 #880, 46, 47.

Mayor Nelson reports that he had hired Chicago operatives to probe St. Paul vice: PP, December 18, 1923.

Rust shooting and Larson's quotes: SPDN, August 17, 1923.

Mayor's operatives describe bordellos, speakeasies, gambling dens, and Leon Gleckman's speakeasy-casino: PP, December 18, 1923.

Chief Sommer reports his detectives unable to detect much vice in the city: SPDN, PP, December 18, 1923.

Grand jury recommends establishment of state police force: PP, December 15, 1923.

Mayor tells Sommer to resign or be fired, calls Brown, et al., in for interrogation: PP, December 14, 1923.

Sommer resigns: PP, December 17, 1923.

Sommer to return to job with Secret Service: PP, December 16, 1923.

"Brown, it's a remarkable thing": PP, December 15, 1923, 5.

Mayor changes his mind on Brown's dismissal: PP, December 18, 1923.

Summary of shooting cases involving Brown: SPDN, August 24, 1934.

Brown's Cleveland indictment and arrest on theft charges: C.W. Stein, March 18, 1936, HKF Sec. 6 #444.

Raasch asked to provide false alibi: SPDN, September 17, 1936, 2.

"Not worthy of belief:" Judge John B. Sanborn district court ruling, July 23, 1926, included in FBI report, HKF Sec. 6 #444.

Sudheimer quote: PP, November 11, 1930.

Murnane quote: DISP, November 22, 1927. On the same day, the newspaper carried the story that liquor conspiracy charges had been dismissed against Brown.

For details on Brown's connection to Gleckman and the Bremers, see chapter 24. For Brown's connection to Peifer and the Hamm kidnapping, see chapter 16. For testimony on his connection to Sawyer and the Bremer kidnapping, see chapter 44.

Talbot and Dahill's withdrawal: SPDN, January 22, 1932.

Brown and bribery: S. K. McKee, June 3, 1936, HKF Sec. 9 #800.

Brown's focus on traffic enforcement: SPDN, January 31, 1932, 2.1.

Minnesota Crime Commission reported: DISP, July 13, 1927.

Bremers as Gleckman bankers: SPDN, March 1, 1932.

Bremer business ties to the Green Lantern: Harry Sawyer testimony, *Cassius McDonald vs. United States,* 8th Circuit Court of Appeals, case #10587, p336, RG 276, National Archives, Kansas City, MO.

Adolph Bremer's political support for Brown: Nathan memo to Hanni, date and serial number obscure (PDF Part 13, doc. #23–25).

FBI learns of Bremer connection to underworld: FBI summary, February 23, 1934, BKF Sec. 8 #711; also FBI memo, S. L. Fortenbury, February 8, 1934, BKF Sec. 4 serial number obscure (PDF Part 6, doc #78–80).

4. ROARING THROUGH THE OZARKS

The account of Thomas Sherrill's murder, including "it would ruin": Michael Koch, *A Murder in Tulsa. The Sherrill Murder Case and the Rise of the Barker-Karpis Gang* (Baltimore: Publish America, 2009), 24–47.

Lloyd Barker's imprisonment and its effect on the Barker family; also "loose morals": FBI, date obscure, BKF Sec. 184 #8823, indexed January 6, 1936. This document also includes interviews with George Barker and others close to the family.

Reunion of Fred and Herman at Ma's Tulsa home: Robert Winter, *Mean Men: The Sons of Ma Barker* (Danbury, CT: Rutledge Books, 2000), 50–58.

Herman Barker's last crime and suicide: FBI, date obscure, BKF Sec. 184 #8823, indexed January 6, 1936, 10.

Volney Davis on Ma Barker's jailhouse visit: BKF Sec. 134 #7453, 4–5.

Description of Ma Barker's home in Tulsa: Karpis and Trent, *Public Enemy Number One,* 82–84.

5. MURDER AT THE GREEN LANTERN

Dan Hogan: a profile of "Dapper Dan" appears in the SPDN Sunday magazine, February 4, 1934, 6.

Harry Sawyer background: FBI, July 10, 1935, BKF Sec. 118 #6666x.

"After Hogan's death": Harry Sawyer testimony, *Cassius McDonald vs. United States,* 335.

Green Lantern's gambling Blue Room: PP, May 30, 1931.

Green Lantern's deal with the Schmidt's brewery: *Cassius McDonald vs. United States,* 335.

Sawyer characterizes the Green Lantern as a journalist's hangout: *Cassius McDonald vs. United States,* 335.

Schmidt's Brewery underground pipeline: Maccabee, *John Dillinger Slept Here,* 188.

Dorothy Ventress, "a striking brunette": PP, June 3, 1931.

Dorothy Ventress testimony: trial transcript, Ramsey County District Court case #13602, 300–305, Minnesota Historical Society, St. Paul.

Witness Lund's quotes: PP, March 22, 1931.

"I lifted his head, and he just coughed" and other Ventress shooting details, St. Paul police department, March 20 and 23, 1931, and Frank Ventress file, GHRC.

St. Paul police interview with Dorothy Ventress, March 21, 1931, Frank Ventress file, GHRC.

Brown closes the Green Lantern: DISP, March 29, 1931.

Kremer tells of his background: Ramsey County District Court case #13602, trial transcript, 19–21, 48.

Detective Crumley barges into Kremer's soft drink parlor: Ramsey County District Court case #13602, trial transcript, 39.

Kremer's time in jail: Ramsey County District Court case #13602, trial transcript, 45.

An affidavit casting doubts on the strength of the case and the credibility of the witnesses, including White and Kremer, was filed by county attorney Michael Kinkead on May 15, 1939. It is included in Ramsey County District Court case #13602.

Brown admits he "held the witnesses" too long in Ventress murder trial: PP, May 31, 1931.

White's testimony: Ramsey County District Court case #13602, trial transcript, 260–89.

Quinn's testimony: Ramsey County District Court case #13602, trial transcript, 304–66.

McKenna backs up Quinn on alibi: Ramsey County District Court case #13602, trial transcript, 391–92.

Testimony of ballistics expert Colonel Calvin Goodard: Ramsey County District Court case #13602, trial transcript, 176–79.

"I would poke you in the nose": Ramsey County District Court case #13602, trial transcript, 275.

"I saw a gun in his hand": Ramsey County District Court case #13602, trial transcript, 365.

Character witnesses describe Ventress as foul tempered and Quinn as easygoing: Ramsey County District Court case #13602, trial transcript, 376–90.

Kremer tells of Ventress murder: SPDN, March 30, 1931.

Brown closes the Green Lantern: DISP, March 29, 1931.

Green Lantern "owner" George Hurley arrested in downtown St. Paul murder: SPDN, February 5, 1930.

Pat Reilly background: E. A. Tamm, March 28, 1935, BKN Sec. 91 #5389.

6. Summer in the Ozarks

"Never hesitated to shoot his way out of trouble": Karpis and Trent, *Public Enemy Number One*, 17.

Fred's marijuana stash: Karpis and Trent, *Public Enemy Number One*, 41.

Note on Karpis's first wife, Dorothy Slayman: W. E. Miller, June 8, 1934, BKF Sec. 26 #2146 (PDF 21 Part 49, doc#10).

Karpis-Barker jewelry robbery and its consequences: W. E. Miller, June 8, 1934, BKF Sec. 26 #2146 (PDF 21 Part 49, doc#11).

Fred and Karpis join forces, the resulting jewelry store burglary, imprisonment of Karpis and Barker, and Dorothy Slayman's return of the jewels: Winter, *Mean Men*, 106–11.

"Dorothy enjoyed the quiet life in Chicago": Karpis and Trent, *Public Enemy Number One*, 108.

7. Where's Leon?

Gleckman and partner Morris Roisner owned an interest in the Mill Creek Distillery in Havana: James N. Sullivan, Internal Revenue investigation report, December 3, 1936.

"Tribute on legitimate businesses": William Mahoney, unsigned column, "Lifting the Lid on City Hall," *Union Advocate*, February 4, 1932, 2.

Gleckman's legal troubles: SPDN, March 1, 1932.

Frank Reilly's account of how the Gleckman scheme worked and assertion that even candy companies had to pay bribes: R. T. Noonan, June 18, 1936, HKF Sec. 10 #880, 47–48.

Gleckman's men on the city council traded favors in return for power to name the police chief: William Mahoney, unsigned column, "Lifting the Lid on City Hall," *Union Advocate*, March 24, 1932, 2.

Gleckman responsible for Brown's promotion to chief; Gleckman speaks of "intimate friendship" with St. Paul councilmen May, Pearce: K. R. McIntire, HKF Sec. 10 #834, June 15, 1936; also S. K. McKee, June 5, 1936, HKF Sec. 9 #776, 2–4.

Cimin, Tallerico abduct Gleckman: Joe Jurley testimony in Ramsey County Circuit Court, case #13788, October 20, 1931, SAM 47, Minnesota Historical Society, St. Paul.

Cimin takes $1,400 from Gleckman, has him write letters; Cimin and Tallerico return to St. Paul; Cimin offered "$7000 or $8000" as ransom: Albert Tallerico testimony in Ramsey County Circuit Court, case #13788, October 20, 1931.

Gleckman fishing and other details of his captivity: Tony Scandale testimony in Ramsey County Circuit Court, case #13788, October 20, 1931.

The appearance of a mystery "big man" and Gleckman's release: Joe Jurley testimony in Ramsey County Circuit Court, case #13788, October 20, 1931.

Tallerico drops Cimin at train station, meets him the following Tuesday, takes him back to kidnap hideout, and then drives to St. Paul: Albert Tallerico testimony in Ramsey County Circuit Court, case #13788, October 20, 1931.

Gleckman's kidnapping revealed in the press: SPDN, September 29, 1931.

Chicago cops know nothing of Gleckman's disappearance; Brown blames Chicago gangs: SPDN, September 30, 1931.

Crumley's arrest of "Minneapolis negress": SPDN, September 30, 1931.

Report of caddies, Keller Golf Course, Gleckman at barber shop: SPDN, October 1, 1931.

Gleckman escorted home by Brown, Peifer and gives "I was fishing" explanation; Brown says he can do no more: SPDN, October 2, 1931.

Gleckman keeps his golf date: SPDN, October 3, 1931.

Discovery of Frank LaPre corpse: SPDN, October 4, 1931.

Scandale beaten by St. Paul police: Tony Scandale testimony in Ramsey County Circuit Court, case #13788, October 20, 1931, 46.

Jurley beaten by St. Paul police: Joe Jurley testimony in Ramsey County Circuit Court, case #13788, October 20, 1931.

Tallerico says St. Paul cops never struck or threatened him: Albert Tallerico testimony in Ramsey County Circuit Court, case #13788, October 20, 1931, 16.

Robbins and the Ten Thousand Lakes Fur Farm; investigator for state securities commission fired, SPDN, February 10, 1930.

Robbins claims shakedown by state officials, SPDN, February 14, 1930.

Robbins's role in Gleckman kidnapping: Albert Robbins testimony in Ramsey County Circuit Court, case #13788, October 20, 1931.

Press wrap-up of the kidnapping and praise for Brown's work: SPDN, October 5, 1931.

8. THE SHOW

"Reenactment" of Gleckman kidnapping: SPDN, October 6, 1931.

The kidnappers said Gleckman was blindfolded until he reached Rest Lake. None of them wore masks: Albert Tallerico, Joe Jurley, and Tony Scandale testimony in Ramsey County Circuit Court, case #13788, October 20, 1931.

LaPre's funeral: SPDN, October 7, 1931.

Newspapers praise Peifer's "errand of mercy": PP, October 3, 1931.

Interview with Tallerico, including "mortal terror" quote and his attorney's quotes: R. T. Noonan, June 18, 1936, HKF Sec. 10 #880, 43.

"You will have to pay"; Saph McKenna reveals details of County Attorney Kinkead's shakedown of Jack Peifer's Hollyhocks casino: R. T. Noonan, May 14, 1936, HKF Sec. 9 #761, 10.

Kinkead, Brown accuse Robbins: SPDN, October 5 and 7, 1931.

Crumley finds guns, says one belongs to Cimin: SPDN, October 7, 1931.

"Not one year but 40 years" and other details from interview with Tallerico: R. T. Noonan, June 18, 1936, HKF Sec. 10 #880, 44.

Brown, LaPre's widow, and Gleckman in lawsuit over money taken from LaPre's safe: SPDN, November 6, 1931.

Brown admits taking money from LaPre's safe: Thomas Brown testimony in Ramsey County Circuit Court, case #13788, October 20, 1931, 62.

Frank Reilly says Brown, et al., killed LaPre: R. T. Noonan, June 18, 1936, HKF Sec. 10 #880, 48–52.

Brown describes process of identifying kidnappers: PP, SPDN, October 5 and 6, 1931.

Robbins's twenty-five-year sentence: SPDN, October 7, 1931.

Robbins, Jurley, Scandale sentenced: Ramsey County Circuit Court, case #13788, October 20, 1931, 18–21.

Tallerico says cops never struck or threatened him; also Kinkead's plea for leniency: Albert Tallerico testimony in Ramsey County Circuit Court, case #13788, October 20, 1931, 16.

Tallerico sentenced: SPDN, October 27, 1931.

DeCourcy's indiscretions: FBI, BKF Sec. 167 serial number obscure, appears to be #9538 or #9539, 5 (PDF Part 197, doc. #121).

9. THEY SHOT THE SHERIFF

Murder of Sheriff Kelly described by a West Plains official: BKF Sec. 26 #2146 (PDF Part 49, doc. #8–10). This memo includes notes on Arthur Dunlop and his rental of a farmhouse in Thayer, MO, and the gang taking refuge with Deafy Farmer.

Background on West Plains sheriff shooting: FBI memo, February 21, 1934, BKF Sec. 8 #706.

An account of Sheriff Kelly's murder and the gang hiding out with Deafy Farmer and fleeing to St. Paul: Koch, *A Murder in Tulsa*, 109–11.

Dorothy Slayman's journey to West Plains and her arrest: Karpis and Trent, *Public Enemy Number One*, 110.

10. CAMBRIDGE, SADIE, AND ROSE

Inmate Newbern describes St. Paul's protection racket: T. G. Melvin, June 16, 1936, HKF Sec. 10 #864.

Ma a "nearly foolproof cover": Karpis and Trent, *Public Enemy Number One*, 91.

Cambridge robbery: DISP, SPDN, January 5, 1932. The St. Paul newspapers reported that well-dressed bandits stole $300 cash and $400 in merchandise.

Details of the robbery, including quotes: *Cambridge North Star,* January 7, 1932.

"A long string of small deals": Karpis and Trent, *Public Enemy Number One*, 34.

Detailed description of the Hannegraf episode, including interviews with family members: Maccabee, *John Dillinger Slept Here*, 104–9.

Fred Barker "always cheerful and friendly": Karpis and Trent, *Public Enemy Number One*, 41.

Karpis describes Dunlop as a drunk and an ingrate; Fred calls him "the old bastard": Karpis and Trent, *Public Enemy Number One*, 87.

Purvis quotes on Ma Barker: Purvis, *American Agent*, 152.

Hoover quotes on Ma Barker: Hoover, *Persons in Hiding*, 22.

"Evidently goes around" as their mother: This implies that, nine months before her death, the FBI was just realizing that Kate Barker was traveling with the gang: E. G. Peterson memo, April 7, 1934, HKF Sec. 4 #313.

Karpis description of Ma Barker: Karpis and Trent, *Public Enemy Number One*, 90.

Hannegraf background: S. K. McKee, May 20, 1936, HKF Sec. 8 #732.

The case of Rose Perry, including its connections to the Filbens, the Cambridge robbery, and the Denver Mint robbery: S. W. Hardy, January 17, 1940, BKF Sec. 270 #15142 (PDF Part 306, doc. #32–38).

Link with Denver Mint robbery: SPDN, March 10, 1932.

Peifer seen driving the two women away: R. T. Noonan, May 27, 1936, HKF Sec. 9 #759, 6.

Discovery of bodies and police theory: SPDN, March 7, 1932.

Brown's reaction to deaths of Perry, Carmacher: SPDN, March 8, 1932.

"No one from St. Paul": SPDN, March 9, 1932.

Filben, Brown connection: R. T. Noonan, May 27, 1936, HKF Sec. 9 #759, 9–11.

Melvin Passolt, chief of the Minnesota Bureau of Criminal Apprehension, theorized that Perry and Carmacher were murdered because of the Filben-Peifer-Brown connection: R. T. Noonan, May 27, 1936, HKF Sec. 9 #759, 6.

11. "MA, PUT YOUR GLASSES ON"

"Ma, put your glasses on": Helen Hannegraf testimony at Brown hearing, PP, September 17, 1936, and SPDN, September 17, 1936, 2.

Detective Fred Raasch's version of the morning Nick Hannegraf appeared at the police station: Raasch's statement made to Hilary J. Flynn, St. Paul assistant corporation counsel in April 1932, reported by FBI, August 18, 1936, HKF Sec. 11 #1037.

Barkers escape: R. T. Noonan report, May 27, 1936, HKF Sec. 9 #759, 18.

Barker gang's tip-off by Sawyer and escape from West St. Paul: Karpis and Trent, *Public Enemy Number One*, 89.

Crumley "crooked and had evil connections:" St. Paul Mayor Mark Gehan, SPDN, April 14, 1936.

Raasch version of Barker escape, as told at Brown hearing: SPDN, September 14, 1936.

Nick Hannegraf's visit to West St. Paul police: C. W. Stein, May 27, 1936, HKF
Sec. 9 #759, 20.

For Gladys Sawyer's testimony about the warning to the Barker gang, see chapter 45.

Sawyer's request for the Barkers' shotgun shells: Raasch's statement made to
Hilary J. Flynn, St. Paul assistant corporation counsel in April 1932, reported
by FBI August 18, 1936, HKF Sec. 11 #1037.

Nick Hannegraf had been drinking: Officer Roy Coffee testimony, PP, September 17, 1936.

12. DUNLOP'S LAST RIDE

Details of Dunlop murder: state police report to Passolt, BCA file 43030, Minnesota Historical Society, St. Paul.

State police seek "Andersons": SPDN, April 29, 1932.

State police give up on "Anderson" murder: SPDN, May 2, 1932.

Karpis on Dunlop murder. Karpis and Trent, *Public Enemy Number One*, 89.

Mahoney's "racketeer king" allegations: FBI, May 27, 1936, HKF Sec. 9 #759;
also SPDN, January 26, 1932.

Mahoney vs. Bundlie: SPDN, March 11, 1932.

Mrs. Clayton's accusations: SPDN, February 5, 1932.

Feud between the Reverend Eidson and Brown: SPDN, October 27, 1931.

Karpis on the political fallout of the Dunlop murder: Karpis and Trent, *Public
Enemy Number One*, 104.

Years after Dunlop's murder, FBI public-enemies hunter Earl Connelley concluded that Karpis had killed the old man. Fred Barker was out of town that
week, as Karpis had previously acknowledged: FBI, June 5, 1936, BKF Sec.
209 #1203.

Brown's "no jurisdiction" and "so-called killers": DISP, April 28, 1932.

13. WHITE BEAR LAKE

"Afraid of his own soul": Clegg to Hoover, February 12, 1934, BKF Sec. 5
#419.

Dunn the bagman: E. J. Connelley telegram to Hoover, May 1, 1936, HKF Sec. 8
#629; also Dunn a "collector for the police department": C.W. Stein to
Hoover, June 13, 1936, HKF Sec. 4 #292.

Roosevelt, Bremer friendship: J. Edgar Hoover memo, January 20, 1934, BKF
Sec. 1 #13.

Karpis: "I didn't ever deal": Karpis and Trent, *Public Enemy Number One*, 100.

"Rumor Makes Dahill Chief": SPDN, May 8, 1932. The paper also said Crumley
was in official disfavor because of his friendship with Brown.

McMullen promoted: SPDN, May 8, 1932.

McMullen's underworld connections: H. H. Clegg, June 22, 1934, HKF Sec. 4 #3.

Gladys Sawyer identifies Brown, Crumley, McMullen as St. Paul's most corrupt cops: Teletype from St. Paul to Hoover, May 15, 1936, HKF Sec. 4 #726.

A photo and story depicting the Bremer brothers greeting Franklin Roosevelt appeared April 18, 1932, in the SPDN.

Schmidt's ownership of Green Lantern: FBI interview with Gladys Sawyer, BKF Sec. 83 #5078.

Bremer ties to Sawyer, Green Lantern: *Cassius McDonald vs. United States,* 335–38.

Walter Magee testifies about arrest, release of Green Lantern criminals: SPDN, September 21, 1936.

Sawyer-Raasch conversation: Raasch testimony at Brown hearing, DISP, September 14, 1936.

DeVol a "great teacher": Karpis and Trent, *Public Enemy Number One,* 18. Over the years, DeVol has picked up the nickname "the chopper" for his propensity to chop people up with a Tommy gun. However, author Robert Ernst's biography of DeVol (*Robbin' Banks and Killin' Cops*) found that the nickname was bestowed on him by an imaginative magazine writer and that his fellow gangsters simply called him Larry.

The Barker gang's move to Kansas City; their robbery of the banks at Fort Scott and Concordia, KS: Koch, *A Murder in Tulsa,* 114–15.

Barker gang's Concordia and Fort Scott robberies: William J. Helmer and Rick Mattix, *The Complete Public Enemy Almanac* (Nashville, TN: Cumberland House Publishing, 2007), 464–65. A summary of the career of the Barker-Karpis gang and their methods is told on 449–74. Many of the gang's methods were used in the South St. Paul payroll robbery, described in chapter 20.

Paula Harmon background: FBI, February 3, 1934, BKF Sec. 2 #144; also H. T. Arterberry, February 17, 1934, BKF Sec. 6 #538.

Paula Harmon's disfiguring car crash: McCormack, January 27, 1934, BKF Sec. 2, serial number obscure (PDF Part 3, doc. #78).

Paula Harmon wildly spending insurance settlements: February 27, 1934, BKF Sec. 6 #548.

Paula Harmon's early life, marriages, and associations with the underworld: Winstead, February 27, 1934, BKF Sec. 10 #891.

Karpis evaluation of Paula Harmon: Karpis and Trent, *Public Enemy Number One,* 59.

White Bear revealed as gang hideout: DISP, April 22, 1936. As its source, the paper cited federal authorities.

"Expensively dressed": Maccabee, *John Dillinger Slept Here,* 113.

Nick had been drinking": state police report to Passolt, BCA file 43030, Minnesota Historical Society, St. Paul.

14. A ROBBERY AND THREE MURDERS

"Greenhouse"; Karpis describes the December 16 Minneapolis bank robbery: Karpis and Trent, *Public Enemy Number One*, 63–66.

Bank robbery description and shooting of Evans and Gorski: *Minneapolis Tribune*, December 17, 1932; PP, December 17, 1932; extended coverage in *Minneapolis Journal*, with many photos, December 19–21, 1932.

"Doc has been in the pen so much": Gladys Sawyer statement to FBI, September 15, 1934, BKF Sec. 35 #2869.

DeVol description and history: Minnesota BCA criminal file 29279, including records from St. Peter Hospital, Minnesota Historical Society, St. Paul.

"You son of a bitch" and other details of the robbery: Severeid, *The People's Lawyer*, 37–38. Rerat defended Leonard Hankins, who was unjustly convicted and imprisoned for this robbery. He also married Jack Peifer's widow, Violet.

Oscar Erickson details: St. Paul police homicide file, December 16, 1932, Oscar Erickson file, GHRC; also *Minneapolis Tribune*, December 17, 1931.

"All doped up": Mrs. James Bibeau, bridge player at Burton's apartment, quoted in the *Minneapolis Tribune*, December 19, 1932.

De Vol interrogation by Detective Tierney, Zachman testimony, doctor's report on Erickson injuries: Oscar Erickson file, GHRC.

DeVol arrested: *Minneapolis Tribune*, December 19, 1932.

Burton describes DeVol's behavior post robbery: *Minneapolis Tribune*, December 19, 1932.

Brown's association with criminals Harvey Bailey, Verne Miller: O. G. Hall, July 27, 1933, FBI Kansas City Massacre File Sec. 13 #401, 28.

15. THE LAST NEW YEAR'S EVE

Pig's Eye and history of St. Paul: John Fletcher Williams, *A History of the City of St. Paul, and of the County of Ramsey, Minnesota* (St. Paul: Minnesota Historical Society Press, 1983), 64–66.

Harry Sawyer takes over the Green Lantern: Clegg to Hoover, May 8, 1934, DF #7310.

Harry Sawyer background: FBI, July 10, 1935, BKF Sec. 118 #6666x.

Green Lantern's gambling Blue Room: PP, May 30, 1931.

Green Lantern New Year's: Karpis and Trent, *Public Enemy Number One*, 101–3.

Doc Barker, Volney Davis bribed out of prison: interview with former Barker gangster Harry Hull, J. V. Murphy, March 23, 1934, BKF Sec. 16 #1402.

Barker gang in Reno: Vetterli, April 11, 1934, BKF Sec. 20 #1679.

Ma Barker's panic attacks and heart palpitations: Karpis and Trent, *Public Enemy Number One*, 64.

Sawyers buy forty-acre farm: Dewey, March 15, 1935, BKF Sec. 83 #5078.

Gladys and Harry Sawyer took in Francine on January 21, 1933: Gladys Sawyer statement to FBI, September 19, 1934, BKN Sec. 36 #2919.

16. TARGET: WILLIAM HAMM

Peifer background: McKee, July 30, 1936, HKF #1002.

Peifer's preference for Japanese employees: McKee, June 9, 1936, HKF Sec. 9. #810, 90.

Hollyhocks phone line tapped: Hanni memo to Hoover, February 21, 1934, HKF Sec. 4 #292.

Interview with Mrs. Ogilvie: D. P. Sullivan, May 19, 1936, HKF Sec. 8 #723, 4–6.

Gleckman's fear of kidnapping: SPDN, October 22, 1931.

Peifer's recruitment of Karpis for the Hamm kidnapping: Karpis and Trent, *Public Enemy Number One*, 130.

Karpis can't understand why less money demanded in Hamm kidnapping: HKF Sec. 11 #1050.

Karpis's first job for Peifer: Karpis and Trent, *Public Enemy Number One*, 44.

Karpis puzzled over motive for Hamm kidnapping: S. K. McKee, July 1, 1936, HKF Sec. 10 #891, 8.

Hamm estate: SPDN, April 26, 1932.

Kidnap planning involved Brown, Ziegler, Peifer: Bolton statement to FBI, January 27, 1936, HKF Sec. 4 #365x. On page 4 Bolton says, "Goetz then told me that Peifer had introduced him to a police officer of the St. Paul police department, who was on the kidnap detail; that he and Peifer had talked with this officer, and it was the plan to pay him $25,000 of the ransom money." The St. Paul police kidnap squad consisted of two men: Charles Tierney and Tom Brown. See also FBI summary of Bolton's testimony at the Civil Service Board hearings, November 10, 1936, HKF #1082.

Ziegler sent to New York to murder for Capone: Brennan, July 24, 1935, BKF Sec. 121 #6793. This memo also includes details of how Ziegler planned the St. Valentine's Day Massacre.

Ziegler couldn't explain his rape of a young girl: Jack Peifer to Alvin Karpis, Karpis and Trent, *Public Enemy Number One*, 129.

Irene Dorsey, Ziegler's wife, tells the FBI her husband was involved in the St. Paul kidnappings: R. D. Brown, October 17, 1934, BKF Sec. 40 #3190.

Irene Dorsey interview: FBI memo, June 8, 1934, HKF Sec. 10 #823, 8.

Wide-ranging report on Hamm kidnapping, with details on Zieglers: S. K. McKee, HKF Sec. 5 #401. Includes neighbors' good opinion of the Zieglers (19); how the Zieglers "adopted" Bobby Perry and sent him to Catholic school (20); and Bolton seen by neighbors as a constant companion and maybe brother, Bobby living with the Zieglers until late November 1935, when he was taken back to St. Paul by Tom Filben (22). Also describes Bolton as "very sickly and delicate."

Bolton background: John V. Anderson, August 31, 1936, HKF Sec. 11 #1053.

Bolton's role at St. Valentine's Day Massacre: John Madala, May 19, 1936, HKF Sec. 9 #1738, 10–12.

Idlewild cottage revealed as Hamm kidnap planning site: PP, April 24, 1936.

Identification of Barker gangsters at Idlewild cottage: Henry Maihori testimony, S. K. McKee, April 27, 1934, HKF Sec. 8 #647.

Ma Barker, Helen Ferguson at Commodore: D. C. Suran, March 3, 1936, HKF Sec. 5 #401, 11.

"She wanted to be the only woman": Karpis and Trent, Public Enemy Number One, 84.

"Like getting money from home" and other testimony regarding Brown's involvement in planning the Hamm kidnapping: Bolton statement to FBI, January 27, 1936, HKF Sec. 4 #365x; also PP, July 17, 1936.

Filben-Ziegler connection: R. T. Noonan, May 27, 1936, HKF Sec. 9 #759.

Filben brings Bobby Perry to Hollyhocks, sends him away with Zieglers: D. L. Nicholson, October 16, 1934, BKF Sec. 40 #3176.

Bobby Perry living with the Zieglers: R. D. Brown, October 17, 1934, BKF Sec. 40 #3190.

Fitzgerald description and background: D. P. Sullivan, January 30, 1936, HKF Sec. 4 #371, 7.

Fitzgerald's confession: McKee, July 8, 1936, HKF Sec. 10 #913.

Karpis "sick of him": Karpis and Trent, Public Enemy Number One, 134.

17. "YOU ARE MR. HAMM, AREN'T YOU?"

William Hamm and Marie Hersey Carroll wedding: PP, January 2, 1934.

Letter from F. Scott Fitzgerald to Marie Carroll, quoted in John T. Flannagan, *Theodore Hamm in Minnesota: His Family and Brewery* (St. Paul, MN: Pogo Press, 1989), 84.

State of U.S. breweries: Okrent, *Last Call,* 29–33.

Hamm protection payments to gangsters: R. T. Noonan, October 26, 1934, HKF Sec. 4 #281.

Brown's office at Hotel St. Paul: E. J. Connelley telegram to Hoover, May 1, 1936, HKF Sec. 8 #629.

Hamm's account of kidnapping: interview, June 19, 1933, St. Paul police, included in Hanni FBI memo, HKF Sec. 1 #20, 20.

Karpis says Hamm named payoff men, but they were rejected, since the gang had Dunn in mind, given that he was a collector for the police department: Stein interview with Karpis, HKF Sec. 10 #853.

Summary and details of the Hamm kidnapping: R. C. Coulter, July 5, 1933, HKF Sec. 1 #30. In the conclusion, Coulter identifies Roger Touhy as the prime suspect.

Dunn, Brown connection: R. T. Noonan, May 27, 1936, HKF Sec. 9 #759.

Karpis narrates his version of the Hamm kidnapping: Karpis and Trent, *Public Enemy Number One,* 137–44. Note that Karpis's description is considerably more gentle—and perhaps less believable.

Bolton describes Hamm's captivity: Bolton statement to FBI, January 27, 1936, HKF Sec. 4 #365x.

Charles Fitzgerald's confession of his role in the Hamm kidnapping: S. K. McKee, July 8, 1936, HKF Sec. 10 #913.

A concise overview of the Hamm kidnapping: DISP, July 15, 1934.

18. "Too bad for Hamm and you"

Dunn's telephone conversations with kidnappers: interview, St. Paul police, June 20, 1933, included in Hanni FBI memo, HKF Sec. 1 #20, 3.

FBI's suspicion that Dunn received some of the ransom money: Clegg to Hoover, May 8, 1934, source: Bess Green, DF #7310.

Details of Hamm kidnapping and its mistaken links to the Touhy gang: V. W. Hughes, August 10, 1933, HKF Sec. 2 #127.

FBI's conclusion that Dahill was an honest cop who "did not have a free hand" in running the department: W. A. Rorer, February 20, 1934, BKF Sec. 7 #667.

Cab driver Allison's accounts: PP coverage of Touhy trial, November 1933; also, R. L. Nalls, June 29, 1933, HKF Sec. 1 #30, 3.

Fitzgerald tells of encounter with cabbie: McKee, July 8, 1936, HKF Sec. 10 #913.

Identification of Fitzgerald as kidnapper: Bolton statement to FBI, January 27, 1936, HKF Sec. 4 #365x.

Details of the ransom notes: St. Paul police files, June 16, 1933, included in Hanni FBI memo, HKF Sec. 1 #20, 6; also, R. L. Nalls, June 29, 1933, HKF Sec. 1 #30, 5.

Ziegler's visit to Rosedale Pharmacy: R. L. Nalls, June 29, 1933, HKF Sec. 1 #30, 5, 6.

Drugstores dispensing liquor: Okrent, *Last Call,* 45.

Brown's account of attending to his ill family: November 10, 1936, HKF #1082, 13.

Dunn's account of his drive with the ransom: SPDN, April 22, 1936.

19. Hidden in Plain Sight

Bess Green on Eaton: H. H. Clegg to Hoover, April 15, 1934, DF Sec. 12 #565, 12.

Myrtle Eaton background: PP, September 3, 1935.

Myrtle Eaton history and arrests: March 15, 1935, BKF Sec. 93 #5467.

Myrtle Eaton's circumstances: C. C. Dewey, April 16, 1934, BKF Sec. 20, serial number obscure (PDF Part 38, 40).

Myrtle Eaton's arrest for shoplifting on December 9, 1930, charges dismissed by county attorney: Ladd, November 10, 1934, BKF Sec. 42 #3339.

Bess Green talks with FBI about Weaver, Myrtle Eaton: E. G. Peterson, April 7, 1934, HKF Sec. 4 #313.

Crumley-Myrtle Eaton episode: HKF Sec. 9 #759.

The news account of Brown's Minnetonka raid was written before the raid took place, which suggests someone planted it in the press. It was printed in the PP and DISP on the day of the raid, June 21, 1933.

Barker gang at Vernon Street: E. E. Conroy to Hoover, March 19, 1934, HKF Sec. 4 #302.; also Bolton statement to FBI, January 27, 1936, HKF Sec. 4 #365x.

Karpis at 204 Vernon: Edna Murray statement to FBI, January 17, 1936, HKF Sec. 4 #365x.

Visit to try to convince the St. Paul police and other accounts of Charles Bradley and Mrs. Quick: R. T. Noonan, May 14, 1936, HKF Sec. 9 #761, 21–23.

Brown suspected of tip-off: O. G. Hall to W. A. Rorer, March 7, 1934, HKF Sec. 4 #312.

Gladys Sawyer tells of Vernon Street hideout: statement to FBI, September 15, 1934, BKF Sec. 35 #2869.

Brown's tip-off to Peifer: Bolton statement to FBI, January 27, 1936, HKF Sec. 4 #365x.

How reporter Glenn Harrison tried to alert police about 204 Vernon: O. G. Hall, March 7, 1934, BKF Sec. 15 #1376.

The McLarens return to Vernon Street: S. K. McKee, March 5, 1936, HKF Sec. 5 #400.

McLaren describes his return to his home, casual attitude of St. Paul cops: coverage of the Brown Civil Service hearings, PP, August 28, 1936.

204 Vernon dusted for fingerprints, eight-month delay: Noonan, May 27, 1936, HKF #759.

Dahill testifies regarding Brown, 204 Vernon: SPDN, July 2, 1936.

Brown, Barkers, Karpis go duck hunting: O. G. Hall memo for Hanni, February 6, 1934, BKF Sec. 3 #264.

20. THE FBI'S WRONG TURN

The notion that the modern FBI was formed in reaction to the Kansas City Massacre is the thesis of Bryan Burrough's *Public Enemies.* The summary of that shootout is taken from pages 48–50.

Resistance to a national police agency: Kessler, *Bureau,* 43–44.

Hoover's relationship with Purvis: Purvis, *The Vendetta*, 48–51.

Touhy identified as suspect: FBI memo, D. O. Smith, July 29, 1933, HKF Sec. 1 #27, 1–27.

"America's richest cop": Thomas A. Repetto, *American Police: A History, 1845–1945* (New York: Enigma Books, 2010), 22.

Brown's trip to Chicago; Hamm's uncertain identifications; Dahill's prediction: PP, July 25, 1933.

Karpis, Fred wary of return to St. Paul: S. K. McKee, July 30, 1936, HKF Sec. 11 #1002.

Touhy's release from prison and Judge John Barnes's conclusion he had been framed: United Press wire story, August 9, 1954.

Touhy describes his arrest in Wisconsin on suspicion of abducting Hamm, his meetings with Purvis, and beatings administered by shadowy police officers: Touhy and Brennan, *The Stolen Years,* 117–22.

Money laundering attempts and flight to Chicago details: Bolton statement to FBI, January 27, 1936, HKF Sec. 4 #365x.

Paula Harmon "downcast and drinking": Edna Murray statement to FBI, January 17, 1936, HKF Sec. 4 #365x.

Flight to Chicago details: S. K. McKee, March 5, 1936, HKF Sec. 5 #400.

Jack Peifer's testimony about the flight and the day that preceded it: PP, July 23, 1936, 4. Included is his story about Mrs. Harry Heide, who left the plane in Milwaukee, one stop after Bolton's exit.

The flight of Mrs. Heide: E. J. Connelley, April 24, 1936, HKF Sec. 8 #608.

Walker incident: *Wisconsin State Journal,* July 26 and 27, 1933.

"Brown's share": Bolton's statements to St. Paul Corporation counsel John Connolly, et al., August 4, 1936, HKF Sec. 11 #1037; also FBI memo, A. Rosen, April 5, 1936, HKF Sec. 6 #469x.

$36,000 to be split with Brown: Gladys Sawyer testimony, DISP, September 16, 1936.

Background on Delaney family: Dolores Delaney statement from Ramsey County Jail, Stein, January 28, 1936, BKF Sec. 163 #9282x.

"Nobody gets into her pants": Karpis and Trent, *Public Enemy Number One,* 111.

Delaney's abortion: Karpis and Trent, *Public Enemy Number One,* 114.

Description of Doc Barker, Byron Bolton, and the first moments of the payroll robbery: *South St. Paul Reporter,* August 30, 1933.

Pavlak, Yeaman hired by new chief: *South St. Paul Reporter,* August 30, 1933.

Yeaman dragged out of his car, shot a second time: *South St. Paul Reporter,* August 31, 1933.

Stassen suspected Crumley of confusing witnesses: Brennan, March 3, 1936, BKF Sec. 171 #9785.

Fitzgerald on his role in the Swift robbery: E. A. Tamm to Hoover, June 27, 1936, HKF Sec. 9 #752; also McKee, July 8, 1936, HKF Sec. 10 #913.

Doc Barker's shooting of Leo Pavlak: Minnesota BCA report, August 30, 1933, GHRC.

"No question," Crumley's quote on Brown's involvement in planning the payroll robbery: C. W. Stein, May 27, 1936, HKF Sec. 9 #759, 18.

Stassen said Alcorn was among the planners of the payroll robbery: O. G. Hall, February 20, 1934, no serial number apparent (PDF Part 16, doc. #77).

Alcorn and Brown connection: C. W. Stein, May 27, 1936, HKF Sec. 9 #759.

South St. Paul police chief Edgar McAlpine told the FBI Alcorn was in the liquor store: C. W. Stein, May 27, 1936, HKF Sec. 9 #759, 24.

Fitzgerald, et al., named in South St. Paul holdup: PP, April 22, 1936.

For interviews with the family of the South St. Paul policemen shot in the attack, see Maccabee, *John Dillinger Slept Here*, 166–69.

21. HARRY'S HARVEST

Summary of Sawyer's attempt to adopt Francine: United Charities of St. Paul Family Services report, February 28, 1936, GHRC.

Sawyers, Goetzs at Thanksgiving: Gladys Sawyer statement to FBI, September 15, 1934, BKF Sec. 35 #2869.

Edna Murray describes the Barker gang's return to St. Paul from Reno as Harry Sawyer lays the groundwork for the Bremer kidnapping: BKF Sec. 69 #4556, 4.

Plans rushed for opening of Touhy trial, heavy guard for trial: PP, November 5, 1933.

Touhy quotes, "Let's pretend we're all nuts," "Manacled and chained": Touhy and Brennan, *The Stolen Years*, 126–27.

Neckties sent to Touhy: DISP, December 4, 1933.

Benz delivers warning to Hamm on golf course: April 30, 1934, BKF Sec. 201 #11564.

"The long white finger" and other Touhy trial details and quotes: DISP, PP, November 11 and 12, 1933.

Hamm testifies at Touhy trial: PP, November 14, 1933.

Caretaker testifies regarding Touhy's car and threat from police: PP, November 23, 1933.

California alibi of "Gloomy Gus" Shaefer: PP, November 13, 1933.

Touhy verdict and Chief Dahill quotes: PP, November 29, 1933.

Dahill on lynching: PP, November 30, 1933.

San Jose lynchings: Clyde Arbuckle, *History of San Jose* (San Jose, CA: Memorabilia, 1986), 343.

Threats to the jury foreman: PP, November 23, 1933.

"Heat but none of the cash"; Gladys Sawyer's version of Hamm kidnapping and aftermath: FBI memo, J. Edgar Hoover, May 16, 1936, HKF Sec. 8 #715x.

Brown runs for sheriff: SPDN, January 1, 1934.

Retrospective on Touhy trial: PP, February 7, 1934.

Gangsters contribute to Brown's political campaign: Clegg telegram to Purvis and Hoover, May 6, 1934, HKF Sec. 4 #318.

Karpis's fantasy of Australia escape: Karpis and Trent, *Public Enemy Number One,* 159.

The account of Sawyer, Fred Barker, and Karpis meeting in Sawyer's kitchen: Burrough, *Public Enemies,* 173.

Details of Hollyhocks ownership: C. W. Stein, April 27, 1936, HKF Sec. 8 #613, 3.

22. "WITH OPEN ARMS"

Delaney quotes and account of journey to Nevada and California: Delaney statement from Ramsey County Jail, Stein, January 28, 1936, BKF Sec. 163 #9282x.

Chicago mail robbery and killing of Miles Cunningham: June 22, 1935, BKF Sec. 115 #6479.

"A pretentious gambling establishment"; Edna Murray describes the gang's fall 1933 jaunt to Reno: FBI, February 12, 1935, BKF Sec. 69 #4546, 34.

Bess Green on Dolores Delaney: H. H. Clegg, April 15, 1934, DF Sec. 12 #560.

A typical letter written by Delaney while incarcerated: September 1935, BKF Sec. 133 #7404.

Dolores Delaney's court testimony for Clarence DeVol: Karpis and Trent, *Public Enemy Number One,* 112.

Gangster Christmas at the Hollyhocks: Wynona Burdette statement to FBI, September 1, 1934, BKF Sec. 36 #2919.

Davis, Weaver in debt: Clegg telegram to Purvis, Hoover, HKF Sec. 4 #318.

Davis in debt to gangsters: Edna Murray statement from Wyandotte County Jail, February 12, 1935, BKF Sec. 69 #4546, 38.

Sawyer rejects suggestion that the gang rob Bremer's bank instead of kidnapping him: FBI interview with Edna Murray, October 17, 1935, BKF Sec. 138 #7744.

"Brewers have been forced": Nathan, February 17, 1934, BKF Sec. 6 #524.

Ed Bremer's Commercial State Bank was a "racketeer bank" according to an FBI report: H. H. Clegg, January 27, 1934, BKF Sec. 2 #99. It was "common knowledge" that Commercial State was a gangster bank: Clegg, January 29, 1934, BKF Sec. 2 #109. FBI public-enemies specialist Sam Cowley also concluded that Commercial State was a racketeer bank that kept accounts under false names. Ed Bremer was distinctly unhelpful when the government was looking into the finances of bootlegger Leon Gleckman, Cowley noted. February 16, 1934, BKF Sec. 10 #101.

"I don't know what Harry's beef was": Karpis and Trent, *Public Enemy Number One,* 163.

Brown, Tierney to trap kidnappers: SPDN, January 10, 1934.

"Brown has apparently been smart enough": John Brennan, February 15, 1936, HKF Sec. 5 #425.

Karpis's account of McCord shooting: Karpis and Trent, *Public Enemy Number One,* 165–66.

McCord shot, drugstore bandit sought: SPDN, January 13, 1934.

McCord shooters hunted: SPDN, January 14, 1936. The front page includes pictures of McCord's wife and children.

McCord victim stories, photos, and plea for donations: SPDN, February 19, 1934.

Shooters' car license number traced to Barker gang: O. G. Hall, March 7, 1934, HKF Sec. 4 #312.

Cops lack clues in McCord shooting: SPDN, January 15, 1934.

"Dumb yokel": Edna Murray testimony at Brown hearing, SPDN, September 15, 1936.

FBI solves McCord shooting: SPDN, April 2, 1935.

Brown promises a "clean, efficient and courteous" administration: DISP, January 3, 1934.

"The shooting of that radio man" and other details of the kidnap preparations: Edna Murray testimony, *Cassius McDonald vs. United States,* 120–22.

23. "WELL, I GOT EXCITED"

Edward Bremer's relationship with friends and family: E. N. Notesteen, January 25, 1934, BKF Sec. 1 #74 (PDF Part 1, doc. #165–69). This document describes the family's internal tensions and Ed Bremer's inability to get along with his father, sister, or brewery employees.

Ed Bremer "very apprehensive": Werner Hanni, January 19, 1934, BKF Sec. 1 #70.

Bremer's pre-kidnapping police escorts: Werner Hanni, January 19, 1934, BKF Sec. 1 #60.

Karpis wrote that the kidnap planning included tailing Bremer downtown, where he met his bodyguard daily at a garage near the bank. Just before the kidnapping, however, the gang was advised by Harry Sawyer that Bremer had fired his bodyguard. Karpis and Trent, *Public Enemy Number One,* 164–66.

Witnesses to abduction: *New York Times,* January 19, 1934.

FBI interview with abduction witnesses: R. C. Coulter, January 30, 1934, BKF Sec.1 #50.

"I got excited" and Karpis account of the Bremer kidnapping: Karpis and Trent, *Public Enemy Number One,* 167–71.

Bremer kidnapped: SPDN, January 18, 1934. Stories on page two note that the Gleckman kidnapping started a series of six high-profile abductions in St.

Paul. Also on the page, pictures of Tierney and Brown and a note about their anti-kidnapping squad.

Bremer's recollection of the abduction: *Cassius McDonald vs. United States,* 66–73.

Ziegler author of ransom notes: Bolton statement to FBI, January 27, 1936, HKF Sec. 4. #365x.

Bremer car found after phone tip: memo for Hanni, January 19, 1934, BKF Sec. 1 #60.

"Fear for Ed Bremer's Safety": SPDN headline, January 28, 1934.

Bremer describes his meals, other details of captivity: Clegg, February 10, 1934, BKF Sec. 4 #374; also *Cassius McDonald vs. United States,* 74–75.

Bolton account of kidnapping: DISP, January 17, 1936.

Bolton's testimony about his trip to the Bensenville hideout: *Cassius McDonald vs. United States,* 277–79.

Ziegler disposes of ransom typewriter: D. M. Ladd to Hoover, April 27, 1935, HKF Sec. 4 #346.

24. "ONE MORE CHANCE"

Walter Magee background: FBI summary, February 21, 1934, BKF Sec. 9 #711; also John E. Brennan, February 17, 1934, BKF Sec. 57 #524.

Magee a "rather shady character": E. N. Notesteen, January 31, 1934, BKF Sec. 1 #74.

Magee's road contracts: SPDN, October 23, 1931.

Bremer kidnapping details, Magee's testimony: *Cassius McDonald vs. United States,* 94–97.

Blood in Bremer's car: SPDN, January 19, 1934.

Karpis aware of Bremer political connections: Karpis and Trent, *Public Enemy Number One,* 163.

Tierney's assertion that Brown tried to keep the FBI out of the Bremer kidnap investigation: Stein, March 14, 1936, BKF Sec. 205 #9941x, 2.

"One of the most perfect things": H. H. Clegg, January 23, 1934, BKF Sec. 1 #61 (PDF Part 1, doc. #115).

Hoover "entirely dissatisfied" with Bremer investigation: letter to Hanni, January 19, 1934, BKF Sec. 1 #10.

Lumber camp and other bad tips: February 10, 1934, BKF #217; also January 27, 1934, BKF Sec. 2 #124.

Keenan's complaint about the press: FBI memo, January 22, 1934, BKF Sec. 2 #100.

Brown's leak of "proof of life" message: S. K. McKee, April 27, 1936, HKF Sec. 8, 29–31.

Dahill's testimony at Brown hearing: SPDN, September 2, 1936.

Brown, Crumley visit Sawyer during kidnapping: A. Rosen memo to Hoover, April 3, 1936, BKF Sec. 179 #10371x.

Dr. Nippert's story: FBI memo, February 9, 1934, BKF Sec. 3 #235; also PP, January 23, 1934.

Dr. Nippert testifies at Bremer trial: *Cassius McDonald vs. United States*, 86.

Ed Bremer's letters to wife, daughter: FBI summary, February 21, 1934, BKF Sec. 8 #711.

Photostats of the ransom notes and Bremer's letters: BKF Sec. 4, no serial numbers (PDF Part 6, doc. #185–224).

"If Dahill is so hot to meet us": BKF Sec. 4, kidnappers note, serial number obscure (PDF Part 6, doc. #204).

"In this instance": Edna Murray, October 17, 1935, BKF Sec. 138 #7744, 35.

Floyd Olson's platform: PP, April 18, 1934.

Ransom prepared: Phillip Smith testimony, *Cassius McDonald vs. United States*, 102.

Magee account of the bus station instructions and the time lock problem: *Cassius McDonald vs. United States*, 100.

Adolph Bremer in dire straits, worries about rival and that he might lose the brewery: E. N. Notesteen, January 31, 1934, BKF Sec. 1 #74.

"An embarrassed financial position": W. A. Rorer, February 2, 1934, BKF Sec. 7 #667, 3.

Details of the Bremers' financial dilemma: Fortenberry, February 21, 1934, BKF Sec. 8 #698.

Bremer's "You're crazy" quote: Karpis and Trent, *Public Enemy Number One*, 167.

"You can go fuck yourself now": FBI, Barker-Karpis Summary, November 19, 1936.

Leak of Dahill-rifle story, Dahill's milk bottle trap: S. K. McKee, April 27, 1936, HKF Sec. #647, 29–31.

"Blackmail," and the press and rumors: W. A. Rorer, February 2, 1934, BKF Sec. 7 #667, 3.

Magee on the Bremers' support for Brown; also Adolph Bremer's "considerable surprise" at Brown's involvement: Nathan memo to Hanni, date and serial number obscure (PDF Part 13, doc. #23–25).

Mulheran letter to Cummings: FBI copy received February 28, 1934, BKF Sec. 11 #1006.

Letter "Regarding the Hamm and Bremer": FBI copy received March 9, 1934, BKF Sec. 12 #1030.

Adolph Bremer's general distrust of St. Paul police department: H. H. Clegg memo to Hoover, January 23, 1934, BKF Sec. 1 #59.

Adolph Bremer suspects St. Paul police department of press leaks: W. A. Rorer, February 2, 1934, BKF Sec. 7 #667.

"Living hell": Fortenberry, February 19, 1934, BKF Sec. 7 #622.

Karpis's account of Bremer conversations: Karpis and Trent, *Public Enemy Number One,* 167–68.

25. "MOST UNBEARABLE"

Brown under suspicion, shut out of strategy meetings: H. Nathan, "Police Conditions in St. Paul," date and serial number obscure (PDF Part 13, doc. #23–25).

John Miller testifies about how he received a ransom note: *Cassius McDonald vs. United States,* 91.

Testimony on sale of flashlights: PP, January 21, 1935. Although clerk Florence Humphrey identified the flashlight buyer as Alvin Karpis, Volney Davis later told the FBI that he bought them. See Davis statement of October 1, 1935, BKF Sec. 76 #7606.

Florence Humphrey testimony: *Cassius McDonald vs. United States,* 92.

"Blackmail" by the press and rumors swirling in St. Paul: Rorer, February 20, 1934, BKF Sec. 7 #667.

"You don't have to say anything, Mr. Bremer" and other details of the press conference: SPDN, February 4, 1934.

Lillian Dickman's encounter with Volney Davis: *Cassius McDonald vs. United States,* 92.

Father Deere: H. Nathan, February 8, 1934, BKF; also FBI, Barker-Karpis Summary, November 19, 1936.

Father Deere interviewed, February 8, 1934, BKF Sec. 3 #238.

Volney Davis admits handing Father Deere a note: October 1, 1935, BKF Sec. 76 #7606.

Magee's actions as intermediary: FBI, February 9, 1934, BKF Sec. 3 #235.

Magee makes the ransom drop: *Cassius McDonald vs. United States,* 114.

"I know it is getting tough, Ed": *Cassius McDonald vs. United States,* 76.

Bremer freed: SPDN, February 8, 1934. In this issue, the newspaper printed on page one the mug shots of Fred Barker and Alvin Karpis. It took six more weeks (SPDN, March 23, 1934) for the FBI to publicly name Barker and Karpis as prime suspects in the Bremer kidnapping.

"All right, Bremer, beat it": Karpis and Trent, *Public Enemy Number One,* 170.

Bremer arrives home, other details of the kidnapping: FBI narration signed by Hoover, February 8, 1934, BKF Sec. 3 #212.

Bremer's testimony concerning his release and journey home: *Cassius McDonald vs. United States,* 78.

Adolph Bremer describes son's homecoming at trial: SPDN, April 18, 1935.

Bremer tells story to press: SPDN, February 9, 1934.

26. "TO HELL WITH DUTY"

County attorney Michael Kinkead and police chief Dahill were on opposite sides in the political fight for control of the police department. When Kinkead tried to insert himself into the Bremer kidnapping, a "battle royal" ensued, according to the FBI: February 8, 1934, BKF Sec. 3 #207. The FBI managed to keep Kinkead out of the process: February 8, 1934, BKF Sec. 3 #238.

"The attitude of Kinkead and the Bremer family": Clegg, February 9, 1934, BKF Sec. 5 #382.

Bremer arrives home, other details of the kidnapping: Hoover, February 8, 1934, BKF Sec. 3 #212.

Bremer tells story to press: SPDN, February 9, 1934.

"Never got a look" at captors; verbatim statement of Edward Bremer to the FBI: Nathan, February 8, 1934, BKF Sec. 4, serial number missing (PDF Part 7, doc. #162–67).

Dillinger blamed in Bremer case: *New York Times,* April 29, 1934.

"bunk": Clegg, February 9, 1934, BKF Sec. 5 #402.

"To hell with duty": Clegg, February 13, 1934, BKF Sec. 5 #491.

Discarded gas cans discovered in Wisconsin: memo to Hoover, February 23, 1934, BKF Sec. 8 #711.

Gas can discovery vaults Barker gang to top of suspect list: J. Edgar Hoover telegram to Hanni, February 17, 1934, BKF Sec. 6 #525.

Farmer's gas can discovery told at trial: SPDN, April 22, 1935.

Bremer brothers "personal friends of the President": Clegg, January 23, 1934, BKF Sec. 1 #61.

"Filled with fear" and "antagonistic to all who sought to solve the case": H. H. Clegg, February 12, 1934, BKF Sec. 4 #275.

Rorer interviews with Ed Bremer: FBI memo, February 13, 1934, BKF Sec. 4 #343.

Cops shut Green Lantern: DISP, March 20, 1934.

Ed Bremer on family, underworld: FBI summary, February 21, 1934, BKF Sec. 8 #711; also FBI memo, S. L. Fortenbury, February 8, 1934, BKF Sec. 4 serial number obscure (PDF Part 6, doc. #78–80).

"Knock the roof off": SPDN, July 9, 1934.

27. THE HEAT

Ransom brought to Ziegler's apartment: *Cassius McDonald vs. United States,* 280.

FBI's use of nascent computer technology: letter to banks from Hoover, February 18, 1934, BKF Sec. 3 #193; also memo for Tolson, January 31, 1934, BKF Sec. 2 #112.

The gang knew the bill numbers had been recorded: Karpis and Trent, *Public Enemy Number One,* 169.

Ziegler spends $5,000 of ransom in Chicago; Doc Barker exchanges only $10,000 on trip to Reno; Toledo casinos refuse to launder the ransom money: October 17, 1935, BKF Sec. 138 #7744.

Berg's story of Fred Barker in pain: SPDN, April 30, 1935.

Karpis on Doc Moran, surgeries: Karpis and Trent, *Public Enemy Number One,* 52.

FBI summary of case against Berg: undated, BKF Sec. 96 #5525, 66.

Berg in court testimony admits his role: FBI, May 6, 1935, BKF 104 #5692.

A comprehensive view of the connections among Doc Moran, the Barkers, and money launderers was supplied by Moran's assistant Jimmy Wilson: FBI, September 19, 1934, BKF Sec. 36 #2919 (PDF Part 41, doc. #4).

Joseph Moran and surgeries: FBI, Barker-Karpis Summary, November 19, 1936, 75–76.

Delaney quotes: statement from Ramsey County Jail, Stein, January 28, 1936, BKF Sec. 163 #9282x.

Unnamed gangsters say Goetz killed because he talked too much about the Bremer kidnapping: PP, January 25, 1935.

Murder of Shotgun George: Mars Eghigian, *After Capone: The Life and World of Mob Boss Frank "the Enforcer" Nitti* (Nashville, TN: Cumberland House Publishing, 2006), 258.

28. "NO CRIMINALS HERE"

SPDN campaign of front-page editorials begins January 19, 1934.

O'Farrell quoted: SPDN, February 2, 1934.

McMullen's underworld connections: H. H. Clegg, June 22, 1934, HKF Sec. 4 #3.

Cops watch for bandits from café: SPDN, March 15, 1934.

Kahn's "open friendship" with Gleckman: "Lifting the Lid on City Hall," *Union Advocate,* October 24, 1935, 2.

"Conversation between Kahn and Leon Gleckman": "Lifting the Lid on City Hall," *Union Advocate,* July 18, 1935, 2.

Mayor Mahoney's denials; McDonald's claim that gangsters had "killed each other off": SPDN, February 7, 1934.

"Poison spot": Stanley High, "St. Paul Wins a War," *Current History* (September 1938).

"No criminals here": SPDN, February 24, 1934.

Kahn's campaign; grand jury influenced: High, "St. Paul Wins a War."

Gehan's reform campaign: SPDN, February 5, 1934.

McCord family sympathy stories: SPDN, February 19, 1934.

McMullen beatings, Dahill orders probe: SPDN, March 7, 1934.

Clubs protected from raids, jury hears: PP, March 2, 1934.

Police round up seventeen, release thirteen: SPDN, March 19, 1934.

Bess Green on McMullen: H. H. Clegg to Hoover, June 22, 1934.

Gladys Sawyer identifies McMullen as a corrupt cop: Teletype from St. Paul to Hoover, May 15, 1936, HKF Sec. 8 #726.

Grand jury witnesses, including Kalmen, disappear: SPDN, March 4, 1934.

Casinos protected: SPDN, February 28, 1934.

Crumley on Kinkead-Brown link: Teletype to Hoover, May 18, 1936, HKF Sec. 8 #710.

Kinkead closes Hollyhocks: Noonan, May 14, 1936, HKF Sec. 9 #761, 10.

Grand jury whitewash: SPDN, March 31, 1934.

29. "ONE TOUGH SWEDE"

Dillinger flashes wooden gun, escapes: SPDN, March 3, 1934.

Army of 20,000 hunts Dillinger: PP, March 4, 1934.

Baby Face Nelson, Van Meter rejoined Dillinger for the Sioux Falls robbery: summarized from Steven Nickel and William J. Helmer, *Baby Face Nelson: Portrait of a Public Enemy* (Nashville, TN: Cumberland House, 2002), ch. 8.

South Dakota bandits kidnap four girls: SPDN, March 6, 1934.

Sioux Falls bank held up: DISP, March 6, 1934.

Reilly, Dillinger, Dr. Mortensen: H. H. Clegg, April 21, 1934, DF 670, 3.

Frechette's story in *Startling Detective Adventures* cited in FBI DF 3771x.

"'One tough Swede': Memories of John Dillinger," *Chicago Reader,* July 20, 1984, 33–34.

Bess Green's description of Frechette: memo for Hoover, April 15, 1934, DF Sec. 12 #565, 4.

Identification of Dillinger, Van Meter at shootout: E. G. Peterson memo, April 7, 1934, HKF Sec. 4 #313.

Green, Dillinger friction: Peterson memo, April 7, 1934, HKF Sec. 4 #313; also, Cowley, April 11, 1934, DF Sec. 10 #514; and memo, April 7, 1934, DF Sec. 9 #407.

News of Lincoln Court shootout: PP, SPDN, April 1, 1934; also SPDN, March 31, 1934.

Coulter's account of the Lexington Avenue shootout: DF Sec. 9 #382.

Billie Frechette's recollection of the shootout in St. Paul: SPDN, September 1 and 3, 1934.

Summary of Lincoln Court shootout: April 16, 1934, DF Sec. 32 #1580.

"Usual protection": SPDN, April 5, 1934.

Background on Eddie Green and Beth Green's first interview regarding Dillinger gang: H. H. Clegg, April 7, 1934, DF Sec. 9 #407.

Background on Bess Green: Rorer, April 9, 1934, DF Sec. 10 #491.

Accounts of how the Greens and Dillinger met, the Lincoln Court shootout, and its aftermath, including the shooting of Eddie Green: FBI summary, DF Sec. 10 #491.

Mrs. Coffey's accounts and descriptions of Dillinger gang: Hanni memo for Rorer, March 30, 1934, DF Sec. 8 #299.

Coulter's account of Dillinger shootout: Hanni memo for Rorer, March 30, 1934, DF Sec. 8 #291.

Hoover castigates agent for seeking help from St. Paul police: memo of phone conversation between Hoover and agent Rorer, April 1, 1934, DF Sec. 8 #264.

Mrs. Coffey's bill, letter included in May 2, 1934, DF Sec. 14 #660.

30. The Cleanup Man

The Secret Six: Hoffman, *Scarface Al and the Crime Crusaders,* 142–57.

Background on Wallace Jamie: SPDN, June 27, 1935, 2.

Richard Lilly forms group of wealthy men, excluding the Bremers, for a secret probe of the St. Paul police department: FBI, author unknown, June 12, 1936, BKF Sec. obscure #12176 (PDF Part 249, doc. #9). Lilly originally told his story to agent R. T. Noonan, but since the memo's second page is missing, its authorship is uncertain.

Citizens group enlists Kahn: SPDN, June 24–26, 1935.

Kahn, Warren hire Jamie: testimony in the Raasch trial, June 1936, SAM 47, roll 18, case #15041, transcript p. 116, Minnesota Historical Society.

Kahn's campaign: High, "St. Paul Wins a War."

Filben interrogated, betrayal by his lawyer, and maneuvers by the FBI and Judge Joyce: Clegg, February 7, 1936, BKF Sec. 166 #9469x.

Tips lead FBI to Eddie Green: S. P. Cowley for Hoover, April 3, 1934, DF Sec. 3 #293.

Eddie Green shooting: Clegg to Hoover, April 4, 1934, DF #402.

Bess Green on Barkers: D. G. Peterson, April 7, 1934, HKF Sec. 4 #313.

"Mystery red-head detained": SPDN, April 5, 1934.

Bess Green held incommunicado: Clegg, April 21, 1934, DF Sec. 14 #664.

Federal agents raid Sawyer farm: R. E. Newby, September 12, 1934, BKF Sec. 35 #2853; also SPDN, September 11, 1934.

McMullen's tip-off about the Sawyer raid: Clegg, April 15, 1934, DF Sec. 12 #565.

Sawyer's journey to Las Vegas, Cleveland; also Gladys returns to St. Paul to consult Peifer and doctor: Gladys Sawyer statement to FBI, September 15, 1934, BKF Sec. 35 #2869.

Sawyer's testimony about his life after fleeing St. Paul: *Cassius McDonald vs. United States,* 343–60.

Letter from Karpis reaches Sawyer in Las Vegas: Dewey, March 13, 1935, BKF
 Sec. 83 #5078. This memo includes many other details of Harry and Gladys's
 odyssey.
Karpis "almost helpless": FBI, Barker-Karpis Gang summary.
"Toledo turned out to be an unhappy town": Karpis and Trent, *Public Enemy
 Number One,* 174.
John DeCourcy, St. Paul attorney for Doc Barker, told the FBI his client had
 killed Dr. Moran: May 14, 1935, BKF Sec. 106 #6023.
Argument between Fred Barker, Davis; also Harry Sawyer's intention to "check
 out": Edna Murray testimony, PP, January 10, 1936.
Jimmy Wilson's story about the clash between the two Docs, Moran and Barker:
 Purvis, May 31, 1935, BKF Sec. 108 #6142.
Doc Moran's drinking and boasting: BKF Sec. 124, serial number obscure (PDF
 Part 151, doc. #86).
Doc Barker's "fishes" quote: October 15, 1935, BKF Sec. 137 #7691.

31. Death of a Comedian

Bess Green on Van Meter: H. H. Clegg, April 15, 1934, DF Sec. 12 #560.
Maria Conforti's account of Van Meter's last day: Clegg, November 19, 1935,
 BKF Sec. 172 #8153.
Cullen's assertion that Van Meter was on his way to meet a girlfriend: *Minneapo-
 lis Journal,* August 24, 1934.
Arrest of Opal Milligan: August 28, 1934, DF #3676.
Brown's version of Van Meter setup: PP, August 24, 1934.
Harry Sawyer, "sea lion": Dolores Delaney statement from Ramsey County Jail,
 Stein, January 28, 1936, BKF Sec. 163 #9282x.
Maria Conforti's accounts: DF #3702. This FBI report details how Conforti
 and Van Meter met in Chicago and journeyed to St. Paul. It includes the report
 that gangster Tommy Gannon was offered money by the St. Paul police to set
 up Van Meter.
Brown consorting with Doc Barker, Baby Face Nelson: A. Rosen memo to
 Hoover, April 3, 1936, BKF Sec. 179 #10371x.
Photo of four ambush cops: SPDN, August 24, 1934, 4. Also on this page, a note
 that over his 22-year career, Brown had killed three other men, the first being
 an auto thief named Sam Roberta, in 1918.
Mrs. Stedje's story ran under her byline: PP, August 24, 1934.
Peterson's account: SPDN, August 24, 1934, 2.
Opal Milligan's version of the Van Meter setup: Melvin, April 22, 1935, BKF Sec.
 100 #5732.
Witness reports at Van Meter shooting: PP, August 26, 1934.
Brown, Culligan conference with FBI agents: August 28, 1934, DF 2676.

Anonymous witness account of Van Meter shooting: PP, August 26, 1934.

Van Meter's pre-ambush moves: SPDN, August 24, 1934.

"A genuine Irishman": PP, August 26, 1934.

"the best marksmen": SPDN, August 24, 1934.

Van Meter's tooth for sale: SPDN, August 31, 1934.

Suspicion that Brown stole Van Meter's money: E. A. Tamm, April 30, 1936, HKF Sec. 8 #671; also K. R. McIntire, May 11, 1936, HKF Sec. 8 #707.

FBI reports on Van Meter shooting, both written by D. M. Ladd: Hoover, August 24, 1934, DF Sec. 59 #3595; August 28, 1934, DF 61 #3676. Both reports note Brown's contradictions concerning how Van Meter came to the attention of St. Paul police.

Gehan's congratulations: PP, August 24, 1934.

"Sincerity of police reform": PP editorial, August 24, 1934.

32. THAT TROUBLE IN CLEVELAND

Harrison "used as a stooge": John Madala, May 15, 1936, HKF Sec. 9 #1738, 15.

Harrison, saloonkeeper and rapist: R. D. Brown, October 17, 1934, BKF Sec. 40 #3190.

Karpis, Fred Barker, and the wet ransom cash: summarized from Burrough, *Public Enemies,* 435.

Sawyer, McDonald launder ransom in Cuba: D. F. Sullivan, March 5, 1935, BKF Sec. 81 #5001.

Sawyer trip to Florida, Cuba: *Cassius McDonald vs. United States,* 282.

"A notorious drunk": Clegg to Hoover, May 8, 1934, attributed to Bess Green, DF Sec. 25 #1310.

Gang women's troubles: Edna Murray statement from Wyandotte County Jail, February 12, 1935, BKF Sec. 69 #4546; also Wynona Burdette statement to FBI, September 1, 1934, BKF Sec. 36 #2919.

Gladys, Paula, Wynona were quarreling among themselves at the Cleveland Hotel: July 10, 1935, BKF Sec. 118 #6666x.

Gladys, et al., arrested in Cleveland: Gladys Sawyer statement to FBI, September 15, 1934, BKF Sec. 35 #2869.

Burdette's version of Cleveland arrest: Wynona Burdette statement to FBI, September 1, 1934, BKF Sec. 36 #2919.

Report of first FBI agent to interview Francine: D. E. Hall, September 25, 1934, BKF Sec. 36 #2978.

Chatter of girl may solve Hamm, Bremer kidnapping: SPDN, September 9, 1934.

Paula Harmon cracks under FBI pressure: Tamm, September 28, 1934, BKF Sec. 37 #3031.

Paula Harmon sent back to Texas: R. D. Brown, October 27, 1934, BKF Sec. 41 #3246.

Raid on Sawyer farm follows Gladys's arrest: PP, SPDN, September 7, 1934.

"Gangland would turn over every stone": SPDN, September 17, 1934.

Karpis on the efforts to launder the Bremer cash: Karpis and Trent, *Public Enemy Number One,* 177–82.

Doc Barker, "that dirty bastard killed Van Meter": A. Rosen to Hoover, April 3, 1936, BKF Sec. 179 #10371x.

Karpis and Delaney's life in Cuba: Hoover, April 11, 1935, Sec. 94 #5483.

Delaney describes Cuba residency: McKee, May 13, 1935, BKF Sec. 104 #5999.

33. THE SHOOTOUTS

Karpis describes Lake Weir house: Karpis and Trent, *Public Enemy Number One,* 183; "Ma had mellowed out," 186.

Accounts of the Barker gang at Lake Weir before the shootout: Tamm, BKF Sec. 65 #4315.

Doc Barker's arrest, FBI's determination to keep it quiet: Tamm, January 11, 1935, BKF Sec. 51 #3750.

Doc Barker arrested: PP, January 18, 1935.

Doc Barker's arrest, discovery of machine gun: Minnesota BCA file 37343, Minnesota Historical Society, St. Paul.

Agents hot on trail of Karpis gang: PP, January 10, 1935. This story contains the first public reference to Byron Bolton.

Bolton arrested: PP, January 10, 1935.

Bolton suspects Barkers in Ziegler murder: PP, January 25, 1935.

Bolton on the Barkers' Lake Weir hideout and "Old Joe": Newby, February 8, 1935, BKF Sec. 83 #1682.

Background on Bolton: October 15, 1934, BKF Sec. 38 #3159.

Ziegler "felt morally responsible": John Madala, May 15, 1936, HKF #1738. The source of this quote was Mrs. Walter Marsh, widow of legendary Chicago gangster Gus Winkler.

FBI agents discover Barker hideout, prepare Lake Weir raid: Tamm, BKF Sec. 65 #4315.

The shootout between the Barkers and the FBI was described by many of the agents involved. Reports prepared by Tamm include statements from agents Madala, Sullivan, White, Jones, et al., BKF Sec. 65 #4315.

Shootout at Lake Weir: *New York Times,* January 17, 1935, also PP, January 17, 1935; recalled in the *Orlando Sentinel,* January 19, 1988.

FBI admits use of Willie Woodberry: Newby, February 8, 1935, BKF Sec. 83 #5072.

FBI, Willie Woodberry: *Ocala Evening Star,* January 16, 1935.

Karpis tells how he learned of the Lake Weir shootout: Karpis and Trent, *Public Enemy Number One,* 187.

Delaney's version of events in Florida, Atlantic City: statement from Ramsey
County Jail, Stein, January 28, 1936, BKF Sec. 163 #9282x.
Shootout in Atlantic City: PP, January 21 and 31, 1935; also BKF Sec. 64 #4296.
Karpis's version of Atlantic City shootout: Karpis and Trent, *Public Enemy Number One*, 190–95.
Delaney's letter: Stein, January 28, 1936, BKF Sec. 163 #9282x.

34. "BOLTON? WHO'S BOLTON?"

Feds fear Weaver, Karpis ambush: SPDN, April 28, 1935.
Second plot to kidnap Bremer: Noonan, February 7, 1935, BKF Sec. 71 #4652.
Clegg memo to Hoover regarding "strange alliance": June 22, 1934, BKF Sec. 28
#2266.
"Bolton, who's Bolton?": SPDN, April 15, 1935.
Bremer testifies on kidnapping: SPDN, April 16, 1935.
Bremer tells "second gang" story in court: SPDN, April 17, 1935.
Doc Barker "never took his eyes off the witness": SPDN, April 17, 1935.
"Weak heart" and other Ed Bremer testimony: SPDN, April 18, 1935.
Adolph Bremer sobs: SPDN, April 18, 1935.
Sawyer's name surfaces in Bremer trial: SPDN, April 19, 1935.
Wynona Burdette's testimony against Doc Barker: SPDN, May 3, 1935.
Doc Barker fingerprint evidence introduced: SPDN, April 20, 1935.
Sawyer's arrest: SPDN, May 4–6, 1935.
FBI details Sawyer arrest: Tamm, May 3, 1935, BKF 103 #5856.
"A trembling underworld": SPDN, May 5, 1935.
Harry Sawyer testifies about his club in Mississippi: *Cassius McDonald vs. United States,* 355–56.
FBI describes Harry's Mississippi venture and his living circumstances: Tamm,
May 3, 1935, BKF Sec. 103 #5840.
FBI publicly links Barkers with Bremer, Hamm kidnappings: SPDN, April 20,
1935.
Bolton's testimony: SPDN, May 6, 1935.
Murray's "as told to": SPDN, May 7, 1935.
Doc Barker guilty: SPDN, May 17, 1935.
Hamm's suspicions and interview with Bolton: R. T. Noonan, May 14, 1936,
HKF Sec. 9 #761.
"Bitter enemies"; Hamm, Brown, and Tierney's jailhouse visit to Bolton; Dahill's
belief that Brown was trying to embarrass him: A. Rosen, April 5, 1936, HKF
Sec. 6 #469x.
Dahill's pursuit of Brown: C. W. Stein, April 4, 1936, HKF Sec. 5 #414; also John
Brennan, February 15, 1936, HKF Sec. 5 #423.
Dahill asks to interview Bolton: H. H. Andersen, April 28, 1935, HKF Sec. 4
#350.

35. The Recording Artist

"He drew a bunch of diagrams": PP, August 20, 1935.

Crumley tips off other cops: PP, June 28, 1935.

Recorded conversations between gamblers and cops were revealed in all three St. Paul newspapers June 24–28, 1935.

Raasch, Crumley fired: SPDN, June 24, 1935.

Fired detectives to fight: PP, June 25, 1935.

"This thing must be sifted": PP, June 25, 1935.

Police chief "genial and unperturbed": SPDN, June 28, 1935.

"Every confidence in Kinkead": PP, June 28, 1935.

Raasch's defense: PP, September 5, 1935.

"Not on the morals squad": DISP, September 8, 1935.

Details and quotes concerning the Koops, the Empress Hotel, and the bribes they paid to police: testimony in the trial of James Crumley, June 1936, SAM 47, roll 18, case #15040, Minnesota Historical Society.

Raasch's status as "clerk or office boy"; Hoffman's statement and interaction of judge and jury; police officials appear as Raasch character witnesses: testimony in the trial of Fred Raasch, June 1936, SAM 47, roll 18, case #15141, Minnesota Historical Society.

"It was known at the time": C. W. Stein to Hoover, June 12, 1936, HKF Sec. 10 #824, 1–2.

Brown's name "conspicuously absent": John Brennan, February 15, 1936, HKF Sec. 5 #423.

Tierney's assertion that Brown had insider knowledge of the wiretap probe of St. Paul police: March 14, 1936, Stein, BKF Sec. 205 #9941x.

"People wonder where Tom Brown": *Union Advocate,* June 27, 1935, 2.

"Tom Brown following the beaten trail": *Union Advocate,* July 18, 1935, 2.

Brown & Bigelow president financed Warren's candidacy: *Union Advocate,* September 27, 1934, 2.

36. Harry Takes the Stand

Photos of Harry and Gladys Sawyer, William Weaver, and Cash McDonald on their way to the courtroom appeared in the SPDN January 5 and 6, 1936.

Harry Sawyer's defense presented in court: PP, SPDN, January 21 and 22, 1936.

Sawyer on the witness stand: *Cassius McDonald vs. United States,* 335–60.

Sawyer's connections to the Bremers, *Cassius McDonald vs. United States,* 336.

"I had nothing to do with it, either directly or indirectly": *Cassius McDonald vs. United States,* 339.

Ed Bremer's testimony, including court reporter's note that "witness is overcome by emotion": *Cassius McDonald vs. United States,* 66–81.

Sawyer denies guilt: PP, January 21, 1936.

Ed Bremer "perfectly willing" to do business with criminals: FBI summary, February 21, 1934, BKF Sec. 8 #711.

Father Deere's demise: SPDN, January 9, 1936.

Cold snap: DISP, January 22, 1936, reported 33 below zero in St. Paul, 55 below in International Falls.

Testimony of Cuban witnesses: SPDN, January 13 and 14, 1936; PP, January 14, 1936.

Testimony of Cuban witnesses Bolivar and Zalacain: *Cassius McDonald vs. United States,* 156 and 177, respectively.

FBI's efforts to bring Cuban money changers to St. Paul as witnesses: McIntire, December 14, 1935, BKF Sec. 150 #8463.

Karpis father travels to St. Paul to witness trial, see Dolores in prison: January 8, 1936, BKF Sec. 158 #9035; also in SPDN, January 14, 1936, under the headline "Karpis Dad Here, Not Proud of Son."

Raymond Karpis, son of Alvin, arrested: *Chicago Tribune,* November 1, 1961.

Edna Murray's testimony: SPDN, PP, January 10, 1936.

Edna Murray testimony quotes: *Cassius McDonald vs. United States,* 120–32.

Bolton's testimony: DISP, SPDN, January 17, 1936; PP, January 18, 1936.

Bolton's testimony: *Cassius McDonald vs. United States,* 277–305.

Bolton tells of meeting Sawyer, Fred Barker in Elmer Farmer's tavern: *Cassius McDonald vs. United States,* 282.

Eaton child and courthouse scene setting: DISP, September 3, 1935.

Toddler "adopted" by Eaton is brought to St. Paul during trial: BKF Sec. 132 #7376.

Details of Weaver, Eaton capture in Florida: BKF Sec. 131 #7287; PP, September 3, 1935.

Harry Sawyer guilty: PP, January 25, 1936.

Baerwold's testimony: DISP, January 17, 1936.

Sawyer, Weaver put on train for Leavenworth: PP, January 26, 1936.

"It's a bum rap," as Harry, Gladys embrace: SPDN, January 25, 1936.

"See Tom Brown go there also": FBI, May 27, 1936, HKF Sec. 9 #759.

37. "DID YOU TELL THEM YOU KNOW ME, DAD?"

"Go into taverns with your hand out," "He must be on the take," and FBI report quoting Brown's brother-in-law, George Rafferty: R. T. Noonan, June 18, 1936, HKF Sec. 10 #880, 46, 47.

Hoover's "personal interest" in case against Brown: October 23, 1935, BKF Sec. 140 #7885, 2.

Hamm talks to the FBI in Honolulu: S. K. McKee, March 30, 1936, HKF Sec. 6 #458.

"Bitter enemies"; Hamm, Brown, and Tierney's jailhouse visit to Bolton; Dahill's belief that Brown was trying to embarrass him: A. Rosen, April 5, 1936, HKF Sec. 6 #469x.

Tanaka's arrest: K. R. McIntire, April 21, 1936, HKF Sec. 9 #603.

Peifer jailed in Hamm kidnapping: SPDN, April 18, 1936.

Fitzgerald arrested: K. R. McIntire, April 21, 1936, HKF Sec. 9 #603.

Fitzgerald confession: McKee, July 8, 1936, HKF Sec. 10 #913.

FBI brings Fitzgerald to St. Paul: SPDN, April 20, 1936.

"Did you tell them you know me, Dad?" and other details of Peifer interrogation: S. K. McKee, April 27, 1936, HKF Sec. 8 #647, 63.

Saph McKenna's visit with William Hamm: Stein to Hoover, April 30, 1936, BKF Sec. 201 #11564.

Seven indicted in Hamm kidnapping: PP, April 20, 1936.

Attorney Archie Cary tries to reduce Peifer's bail: SPDN, April 23, 1936.

"Move heaven and earth," to save Peifer: K. R. McIntire to Hoover, June 3, 1936, HKF Sec. 9 #800.

Peifer pleads not guilty: SPDN, April 28, 1936.

Ed Bremer approached regarding Peifer's bond: HKF 647, 48.

38. "AT PEACE WITH THE WORLD"

Gambler testifies against Crumley: SPDN, April 15, 1936.

Testimony regarding Pearl Miller: SPDN, April 16, 1936.

Crumley's attorney admits he talked with Pearl Miller: PP, April 17, 1936.

Crumley shown peacemaker in St. Paul gamblers war: SPDN, April 20, 1936, 5. The placement of this story, deep inside the newspaper, and its apologist slant hint that it may have been suggested by Crumley's defenders.

Crumley says police chief aware of his actions: PP, April 22, 1936.

"Twenty years without a black mark": PP, April 23, 1936.

Crumley jury deadlocked: SPDN, April 24, 1936.

"See my attorney": SPDN, PP, April 25, 1936.

Background on "Stuttering Bill" Hildebrandt: trial of Fred Raasch, June 1936, SAM 47, roll 18, case #15041, Minnesota Historical Society.

Crumley's arrest on charge of bribing a federal agent: PP, November 27, 1937.

Crumley pleads guilty in federal agent bribery: PP, December 7, 1937.

Bribery charges against Crumley detailed including wiretap conversations: PP, December 8, 1937.

Crumley sentenced in federal bribe case: PP, June 16, 1938.

39. "SIT HERE, ALVIN"

"Give up, son": Associated Press wire story, January 19, 1935, printed in PP, January 20, 1935.

FBI seeks Karpis in Hot Springs: October 17, 1935, BKF Sec. 138 #7721.

Karpis, Hot Springs police chief, and prostitute: May 21, 1936, BKF Sec. 204 #11741.

FBI surveillance of Karpavicz apartment: October 23, 1935, BKF Sec. 140 #7826.

Uncle Sam offers $5,000 reward for Karpis: SPDN, April 22, 1936.

Karpis arrest and neighbor's comment: *New York Times,* May 1, 1936.

"A yellow rat" and other details of the Karpis arrest: Kessler, *Bureau,* 51–52.

Hoover's threat to "kick his teeth in": Karpis and Trent, *Public Enemy Number One,* 242.

"I'd be a sucker": Karpis and Trent, *Public Enemy Number One,* 243. Also rendered as "I'd be a chump," Brennan, May 27, 1936, BKF Sec. 204 #11766.

"Particularly if the thieving copper is the head of the kidnap squad": Brennan, May 27, 1936, BKF Sec. 204 #11766.

Karpis on his time in custody in St. Paul: Karpis and Trent, *Public Enemy Number One,* 241–43; also FBI memo, C. W. Stein, HKF Sec. 10, 7.

Karpis in custody: S. K. McKee, May 8, 1936, BKF Sec. 200 #11529.

Karpis bail: PP, May 7, 1936.

40. HEAT WAVE

Heat wave: PP, SPDN, July 7 and 8, 1936; also heat wave kills 100 Twin Citians: SPDN, July 13, 1936.

People sleeping in parks: SPDN, July 16, 1936.

Dahill's café: SPDN, July 2, 1936.

Dr. Nippert drowns: PP, July 6, 1936.

DeVol's last days and obituary: DISP, July 9, 1936; PP, July 9 and 10, 1936; SPDN, July 9, 1936. Also: Robert Ernst, "The Last Days of Lawrence DeVol," *Oklahombres* (winter 1991): 10.

"Timid, dapper little man": SPDN, July 16, 1936.

Karpis plea: PP, July 15 and 28, 1936; SPDN, July 16, 1936.

Barthelmy a "respected citizen": SPDN, April 20, 1936.

Gladys Sawyer testifies: SPDN, July 16 and 17, 1936; testimony reintroduced, SPDN, July 20, 1936.

Barthelmy pleads guilty: SPDN, July 15, 1936.

Barthelmy's sentencing: SPDN, August 15, 1936.

Bolton quotes: statement to FBI, January 27, 1936, HKF Sec. 4 #365x.

Sullivan's accusations regarding ransom: SPDN, July 15, 1936.

Gladys Sawyer's confession to FBI: September 15, 1934, BKF Sec. 35 #2869.

Bolton's testimony: SPDN, July 24, 1936.

Brown suspended: DISP, July 17, 1936; SPDN, July 17 and 27, 1936.

John Doe indictments prepared: SPDN, July 18, 1936.

"The most unperturbed": SPDN, July 20, 1936.
Brown's "I love everybody" quote: SPDN, July 18, 1936.
Hamm's testimony: SPDN, July 31, 1936.
Dahill's testimony: SPDN, July 20, 1936.

41. "OH! I WANTED TO SEE HIM"

Peifer background: S. K. McKee, July 30, 1936, HKF Sec. 11 #1002.
FBI interview with Peifer: S. K. McKee, July 30, 1936, HKF Sec. 11 #1002.
Peifer "would talk if held long enough": C. W. Stein to Hoover, June 13, 1936, HKF Sec. 10 #853.
Bolton's testimony: PP, July 18, 1936.
Criminals' fear of Peifer: R. T. Noonan, June 18, 1936, HKF Sec. 10 #880.
Richard Peifer, farmer and leader: DISP, March 9, 1934.
Peifer trial scene: SPDN, July 23, 1936.
"Ordinary citizen . . . What's the odds?": PP, July 23, 1936.
"Nothing to worry about"; photo of Jack and Violet Peifer: PP, July 22, 1936.
Photo of Karpis, Fitzgerald manacled on way to prison: PP, July 29, 1936.
Karpis, Fitzgerald sentenced: SPDN, July 27, 1936.
Karpis newspaper ruse: PP, July 27, 1936.
Karpis declares Peifer innocent: SPDN, July 27, 1936.
Peifer convicted: SPDN, PP, July 26, 1936.
Vi Peifer's reaction to conviction: PP, July 26, 1936.
Karpis scheme to get his money from Peifer: C. W. Stein to Hoover, June 13, 1936, HKF Sec. 10 #853.
Justice Wilson's summation and quote on Tom Brown: PP, July 25, 1936, 1–2.
Peifer's sentencing, suicide: SPDN, July 31 and August 1, 1936.
Vi Peifer, "Oh! I wanted to see him": DISP, July 31, 1936.
Vi Peifer, "This is what you get for being good to people": SPDN, July 31, 1936.
Peifer's last moments told: Ed Barthelmy, SPDN, August 1, 1936.
Judge's fears: E. A. Tamm, July 31, 1936, HKF Sec. 11 #1001; also C. W. Stein to Hoover, August 5, 1936, HKF Sec. 11 #1032.
Peifer funeral: *Minneapolis Journal,* August 3, 1936.

42. "WILL YOU PLEASE TALK TO MR. MCKEE?"

Filben "very old friend" of Brown's: R. T. Noonan, May 27, 1936, HKF Sec. 9 #759, 3–10.
Dunn's interrogation, Filben interview; Dunn says the Hamms were "the best friends he had in the world": April 30, 1934, BKF #11564, 29.
Brown's fingerprint refusal, payoffs: R. T. Noonan, May 27, 1936, HKF Sec. 9 #759, 5.

St. Paul officials visit J. Edgar Hoover: letter, John L. Connolly, St. Paul Corporation Counsel, July 25, 1936, HKF Sec. 10 #972.

"Quite a rumor" about Brown: T. D. Quinn to Clyde Tolson, April 30, 1936, HKF Sec. 8 #664.

Cops might talk if Brown fired; suspicion that Brown stole Van Meter's money: E. A. Tamm, April 30, 1936, HKF Sec. 8 #671; also K. R. McIntire, May 11, 1936, HKF Sec. 8 #707.

Dunn's role; Barkers' pressure on Hamm: E. J. Connelley telegram to Hoover, May 1, 1936, HKF Sec. 8 #629.

Dunn said to have shared in the Hamm ransom; FBI's determination to "develop further information implicating Tom Brown": K. R. McIntire to Hoover, May 11, 1936, BKF Sec. 201 #11586.

Crumley willing to help convict Brown: Hoover, May 16, 1936, BKF Sec. 201 #11575.

McKee's trip to Leavenworth to interview Pat Reilly: C. W. Stein to Hoover, June 5, 1936, McKee, June 5, 1936, both HKF Sec. 4. #776.

Pat Reilly as potential informant: DF #1010. In this memo, Clegg was being quoted by FBI agent Sam Cowley.

Pat Reilly sentenced, story and photo: PP, September 18, 1934, 8.

"Chump" Pat Reilly talks to the press: SPDN, September 25, 1934.

"Crumley appears bitter": Teletype to Hoover, May 18, 1936, HKF Sec. 8 #710.

Crumley: "Anything in his power": K. R. McIntire to Hoover, June 3, 1936, HKF Sec. 9 #800, 2.

Crumley "no angel": C. W. Stein, May 27, 1936, HKF Sec. 9 #759, 17.

Dunn's connections in bribery schemes: April 30, 1934, BKF Sec. 201 #11564, 2–3.

Sandlovich "deep family pride": Social Welfare Society of Lincoln memo, March 31, 1936, Harry Sawyer file, GHRC.

"Gossiping around Lincoln": letter from Edmond T. Dolan, Chief, U.S. Probation Office, district of Nebraska, March 15, 1951, Harry Sawyer file, GHRC.

Gladys Sawyer's accusations against Bremers; letter to Harry at Alcatraz: S. K. McKee, May 20, 1936, HKF Sec. 8 #732, 9–13; also K. R. McIntire, May 26, 1936, HKF Sec. 9 #769.

Gladys Sawyer quotes and details: Teletype from St. Paul to Hoover, May 15, 1936, HKF Sec. 8 #726, 2.

First FBI interview with Gladys; she describes Brown's role in the Hamm kidnapping: R. A. Alt, May 12, 1936, HKF Sec. 9 #773.

"Your threats" letter from Clara McMullen: S. K. McKee, May 20, 1936, HKF Sec. 8 #732.

FBI pursuing leads on Dunn, Brown: K. R. McIntire, May 11, 1936, HKF Sec. 8 #707.

The FBI summarizes its case against Brown in an unsigned memo: November 10, 1936, HKF Sec. 11 #1082.

43. "SHE MUST BE CRAZY"

Prison officials' description of Harry in Alcatraz and Harry's plea for letters from his family: Harry Sawyer prison file, GHRC.

Description of Sam McKee: Karpis and Trent, *Public Enemy Number One*, 243.

"Double-crossed by his friends" and other details of McKee's visit to Sawyer at Alcatraz: S. K. McKee, May 20, 1936, HKF Sec. 8 #732.

Harry Sawyer's rejection of Gladys's advice: R. A. Alt, June 4, 1936, HKF Sec. 9 #762; also D. P. Sullivan, May 28, 1936, HKF Sec. 9 #772.

Revolt in Alcatraz: Kobler, *Capone*, 370.

Letter from Alcatraz, Harry Sawyer to Gladys Sawyer, May 18, 1936: S. K. McKee, May 20, 1936, HKF Sec. 8 #732.

Reilly prison interview: A. Rosen to Hoover, April 5, 1936, HKF Sec. 6 #469x.

Crumley's talk with Reilly; Crumley's "strong personal appeal" to Reilly; Gleckman's ambition to be mayor: C. W. Stein and S. K. McKee, June 5, 1936, HKF Sec. 9 #776.

Gleckman's talk with FBI at Leavenworth: Pearce: K. R. McIntire, June 15, 1936, HKF Sec. 10 #834; also S. K. McKee, June 5, 1936, HKF Sec. 9 #776, 2–4.

44. "I AIN'T BEEN SO FAR WRONG"

"The public will be completely convinced of my innocence": SPDN, August 5, 1936.

Bolton's testimony against Brown: SPDN, August 21 and 22, 1936.

Bolton's testimony regarding Brown, ransoms: SPDN, August 22, 1936.

"Brown's share": Bolton statement to FBI, January 27, 1936, HKF Sec. 4 #365x.

Bolton's weight loss, ill health: February 24, 1936, BKF Sec. 171 #9802.

Bolton: "I am very glad it is over": SPDN, August 25, 1936.

Brown takes exam to be chief: SPDN, August 24, 1936.

Crumley's testimony: SPDN, PP, September 5, 1936.

Summary of hearing: FBI, author uncertain, November 10, 1936, HKF Sec. 11 #1082.

45. A STRANGER COMES TO OMAHA

Gladys Sawyer deposition expected: SPDN, August 28 and September 3, 1936.

Crumley's testimony: SPDN, September 5, 1936.

Detective Tierney, attorneys find that Brown had beaten them to Omaha: Alt to Hoover, September 10, 1936, BKF Sec. 224 #12838.

"Friend" visits Gladys Sawyer: SPDN, DISP, September 16, 1936.

Brown attempt to prevent Gladys Sawyer testimony: SPDN, September 16, 1936.

"Keep quiet": DISP, September 16, 1936.

"$36,000 to split" and other testimony by Gladys Sawyer: DISP, September 16, 1936.

McLaren describes his return to his home, casual attitude of St. Paul cops: coverage of the Brown Civil Service hearings, PP, August 28, 1936.

Dahill links Brown to Vernon Street tipoff: SPDN, September 1, 1936.

Dahill testifies regarding Brown, leaked information: SPDN, September 2, 1936.

Dahill's milk bottle trap: S. K. McKee, April 27, 1934, HKF #647.

Crumley's accusation that Brown cased Bremer before the kidnapping: K. R. McIntire to Hoover, HKF Sec. 9 #759.

Magee testimony and Murray deposition read: SPDN, September 15, 1936.

"Go ahead and badger me": SPDN, September 24, 1936.

Brown's testimony: DISP, September 22 and 23, 1936.

Brown's financial transactions: DISP, SPDN, PP, September 23, 1936.

Eruption in hearing room: SPDN, September 24, 1936.

DeVol's fellow inmate talks: T. G. Melvin, June 16, 1936, HKF Sec. 10 #864.

"Nobody's going to push me around": SPDN, September 24, 1936.

Summary of hearing and Brown's background: FBI, author uncertain, November 10, 1936, HKF Sec. 11 #1082.

46. THE DISAPPEARING ACT

City of St. Paul Civil Service Board of Appeals findings of fact against Brown: HKF Sec. 11 #1071.

Brown guilty: C. W. Stein to Hoover, October 9, 1936, HKF Sec. 11 #1070.

Brown judgment reported to Hoover, along with a note that the statute of limitations had not expired in the Bremer case: E. A. Tamm, November 2, 1936, HKF Sec. 11 #1076.

Crane Lake properties described: Maccabee, *John Dillinger Slept Here*, 74–75.

"Certain he saw" and gangster activity at Crane Lake: O. G. Hall, July 27, 1933, Kansas City Massacre File #401, 28.

Brown's near drowning: PP, September 24, 1941.

Harry Sawyer's release: U.S. Parole Board Certificate, March 21, 1955, Harry Sawyer prison file, GHRC.

Sawyer's death: certificate from Chicago doctor A. M. Serby, June 23, 1955, Harry Sawyer prison file, GHRC.

Doc Barker and Alcatraz: FBI, Barker-Karpis Gang summary; also Doc Barker slain in Alcatraz break: *New York Times*, January 14, 1939.

Dahill obituary: PP, July 11, 1960, 17.

Crumley dies February 7, 1939: obituary, PP, February 8, 1939.

"Intense campaign" in Morris: *Morris Sun*, August 10, 1945.

Election results: *Morris Sun,* August 24, 1945.

Liquor licenses to expire: *Morris Sun,* December 26, 1945.

Brown's 1947 indictment: DISP, January 7, 1947.

"Statewide manhunt" for Brown: DISP, February 10, 1947.

Brown guilty of liquor violation: DISP, March 5, 1947.

"Sick man" Brown fined: DISP, April 30, 1947.

Brown's death reported: PP, January 6, 1959; also *Ely Miner,* January 8, 1959.

47. ONE PATH THROUGH THE WOODS

"Most damaging testimony" and the FBI's reasoning in the handling of Brown's
    case: November 10, 1936, HKF #1082, 18. This document contains the FBI's
    full summary of the case against Brown as presented at the Civil Service
    hearing.

Visit of St. Paul's mayor, corporation counsel to Hoover: FBI, July 25, 1936,
    HKF #972.

Hoover quotes on harboring law: FBI, May 16, 1936, HKF #715x.

INDEX

Page numbers in *italic* denote photos.

railroading, 3, 244
Randall, Duke, 170
Reed, Harry, 181–83
Reilly, Frank, 27, 36, 158, 249
Reilly, Pat, 24, 67, 97, 153; arrest and
 imprisonment of, 219, 224; and
 Brown, 219, 247; and Dillinger, 140,
 152, 247; photo, *23*
Reno, NV, 67, 95, 108, 151
Rerat, Eugene, 239
Rest Lake, 28, 33
Riverview Commercial Club, 183,
 186
Robbins, Albert, 32, 36, 37
Rodgers, Earl, 59
Roisner, Morris, 28, 29, 31, 33, 36
Roosevelt, Franklin D., 56, 66, 86,
 101, 109, 118
Rorer, William, 125, 130, 143, 144
Rosedale Pharmacy, 84, 103
Rothmeyer, Andy, 172
Rothstein, Andy, 88
Royal Cigar Store, 182, 186
Rust, Edwin, 9–10
Ryan Hotel, 21, 46, 47, 117, 182

St. Paul, MN: Barker gang arrival
 in, 41, 43; Barker-Karpis gang
 departure from, 55, 67–68; city hall
 building, 218; Dillinger arrival in,
 139–40; Dillinger escape from, 143–
 48; early history of, 66; economy
 of, 102, 239; expansion of, 5–6; Fort
 Road in, 127–28; gangster-era tours
 of, 243; Gleckman as de facto
 mayor of, 10, 35, 53–54, 123, 225;
 Grand Avenue in, 63; Great
 Depression in, 8; heat wave of 1936
 in, 206, 207, 209; Irish in, 17;
 mayoral elections in, 53, 55, 135,
 136; nightlife in, 7; as "poison spot"
 of American crime, 7, 8, 134, 136;

politics in, 11, 35, 55, 95; Seven
 Corners in, *5;* size of, 8
St. Paul Auto Company, 154, 159, 161
St. Paul Daily News, 10, 109, 146, 156,
 176, 188; on Bremer kidnapping,
 122, 123, 126; Brown ties to, 133–34,
 135, 187–88; crusade about police
 by, 133–34, 135–36, 137, 149; on
 Gleckman kidnapping, 30–31, 33;
 on Hamm kidnapping, 71, 92; on
 McCord shooting, 112, 113
St. Paul Dispatch, 13, 49, 103, 183, 233,
 235
St. Paul Pioneer Press, 10, 146, 162; on
 Dillinger, 139, 146; photos from, *55,
 173, 212;* on Touhy trial, 101, 104, 105
St. Paul police: anti-kidnapping
 squad of, 109–10, 210; and bootlegging, 12, 45, 54, 66, 247; bribes
 and payoffs to, 4, 9, 79–80, 96–
 97, 123, 184–86, 201, 203, 217–18,
 232, 244–45; Civil Service Board
 hearings on, 183–84; cleaning up
 of, 243; confession-beating out of
 suspects by, 3, 34, 37, 244; cynicism
 of, 134–35; Dahill efforts to reform,
 56–57, 82, 230–31; fear of Brown
 within, 62, 160–61, 187, 197, 219,
 220; gambling links of, 136, 181–83,
 186, 207, 217–18, 220; grand jury
 investigations of, 135–36, 138–39;
 indictments of cops, 181, 183–84;
 Nightclub Protective Association
 of, 138; and O'Connor System, 5, 7,
 8, 14, 17, 179, 242; press on, 133–34,
 135–36, 137, 149; protection racket
 of, 6, 41, 133, 161, 202, 239; public
 distrust of, 111, 180; Purity Squad
 of, 9, 11, 12, 13, 27; railroading to
 prison by, 3, 244; shakedowns by, 13,
 183, 185, 202, 204; traffic cops, 13.
 See also Brown, Tom